ESSENTIAL GUIDE TO

PERENNIAL GARDENING

Quarto.com

© 2025 Quarto Publishing Group USA Inc.
Text and photography © 2025 Quarto Publishing Group USA Inc., unless otherwise noted

First Published in 2025 by Cool Springs Press, an imprint of The Quarto Group,
100 Cummings Center, Suite 265-D, Beverly, MA 01915, USA.
T (978) 282-9590 F (978) 283-2742

Cool Springs Press titles are also available at discount for retail, wholesale, promotional, and bulk
purchase. For details, contact the Special Sales Manager by email at specialsales@quarto.com or
by mail at The Quarto Group, Attn: Special Sales Manager, 100 Cummings Center, Suite 265-D,
Beverly, MA 01915, USA.

29 28 27 26 25   1 2 3 4 5

ISBN: 978-0-7603-9283-6

Digital edition published in 2025
eISBN: 978-0-7603-9284-3

Library of Congress Cataloging-in-Publication Data available

Design and Page Layout: Samantha J. Bednarek, samanthabednarek.com
Cover Images: JLY Gardens (front background), Shutterstock (front left and right insets),
JLY Gardens (front center inset), JLY Gardens (back top), and
Tracy Walsh Photography (back bottom)
Illustration: Holly Neel on pages 84, 108, 152–153, and icons on pages 178–221

Printed in China

AMERICAN HORTICULTURAL SOCIETY

ESSENTIAL GUIDE TO

PERENNIAL GARDENING

Techniques and Know-How for Planning, Planting,
and Tending Low-Maintenance Perennial Plantings

COOL
SPRINGS
PRESS

CONTENTS

MEET *the* AMERICAN HORTICULTURAL SOCIETY

FOUNDED IN 1922, the nonprofit American Horticultural Society (AHS) is one of the most respected and longstanding member-based national gardening organizations in North America. The society's membership includes more than 22,000 aspiring, new, and experienced gardeners, plant enthusiasts, and horticultural professionals, as well as numerous regional and national partner organizations. Through its educational programs, awards, and publications, the AHS inspires a culture of gardening and horticultural practices that creates and sustains healthy, beautiful communities and a livable planet. AHS is headquartered at River Farm, a 25-acre (1 ha) site overlooking the Potomac River that is part of George Washington's original farmlands in Alexandria, Virginia. The AHS website is www.ahsgardening.org.

Twenty-five-acre River Farm is the home of the American Horticultural Society. It's located on part of George Washington's original farmlands overlooking the Potomac River.

AMERICAN HORTICULTURAL SOCIETY

INTRODUCTION:
WHAT PERENNIALS ARE *and* WHY YOU'LL LOVE THEM

Perennial plants are at home in every climate, from desert to bog.

WHEN MOST PEOPLE THINK of a flower garden, they think of perennials. From cottage-garden classics like peonies to beloved flower-laden natives like rudbeckia and phlox, perennial gardens are wonderful ways to fill your landscape with beauty, attract and support pollinators and other native wildlife, improve curb appeal, or just make a peaceful spot to relax and enjoy your outdoor space. If you are new to gardening, or gardening with perennials, don't worry. The techniques and information needed to create a healthy, thriving perennial garden are not complex or difficult, and there is a lot of basic know-how that will make the gardening journey easier and more fulfilling.

In this book, the aim is to give not only the details of *what* needs to be done in the perennial garden, but also some of the *why* behind those techniques, presenting information needed to make informed choices—to create the best garden for your needs and situation.

WHAT IS A PERENNIAL?

The simplest, most common description of a perennial is a plant that "comes back every year." While that definition isn't the most technically precise, it may be the most practically useful one.

When we're talking about perennials in this book, we're talking primarily about herbaceous perennials. *Herbaceous* means the above-ground parts of the plant are soft, not woody. Depending on the climate and the species, most perennials die back to the ground each winter, unlike woody plants (trees and shrubs), which produce stems that last from year to year. And they are *perennial*, meaning that the plants live for multiple years. More precisely, we call them *polycarpic* (Latin for multi-flowered) because perennials are plants that continue to live on after they have flowered, unlike monocarpic plants—like annuals—which, once they have successfully flowered and produced seeds, will die.

But all these definitions are messy. Plants don't always fit into neat, tidy categories. The line between herbaceous and woody is fuzzy, with a whole world of semi-woody subshrubs, including common plants like lavender and thyme, that do make woody stems that sometimes persist from year to year, but are frequently replaced by new stems coming from the roots. And being called a perennial, or living on after flowering for multiple years, well, that is messy indeed. Many plants familiar to most American gardeners as annuals—from petunias to impatiens—are, in fact, perennials in their native tropical or subtropical climates. We just grow them as annuals here in North America.

In practical gardening terms, the most useful definition of perennial is "A plant that comes back year after year in your conditions and climate." That means a perennial for you might be an annual in a different climate and perhaps even a biennial somewhere else.

Perennials are excellent additions to landscapes for so many reasons. When chosen wisely, they are long-lived and do not require replanting each season.

WHY PERENNIALS?

Perennials are the backbone of nearly every ornamental garden and for very good reasons. These long-lived plants are at once durable workhorses and flashy drama queens, combining reliability and ease of maintenance with beautiful flare in a way that makes them hard to replace.

One of the biggest reasons gardeners choose perennials over annuals in the garden is to reduce the time and effort required to create a beautiful display. Annuals, which have to be replaced each year, can be a huge amount of work. A bed of perennials is about as much work to plant as a bed of annuals, but that one planting can then give many years of flowers, foliage, and joy without the back break of annual replanting. This is not to say that perennials don't require maintenance, but reading on, you will learn that a well-designed perennial garden can require very little input from the gardener to keep it thriving and looking good.

That lack of annual replanting can also make a perennial garden a cost-saving option in the long term when compared to annuals. To be sure, a well-grown perennial at the garden center will cost more than an annual, so do expect to invest more in the initial planting (though if you are on a budget, check out the propagation section in chapter 4 for ways to make more plants), though it's a one-time cost, not an ongoing one. Well, maybe it is not entirely a one-time cost—any gardener will want to replace plants with new ones now and then, change their design, or splurge on a fun, new variety from the nursery. Ultimately, unlike an annual garden, a perennial garden doesn't require a big outlay of cash to replace everything every year.

Those cost savings have environmental impacts as well. The money you spend buying annuals goes toward the disposable plastic in their pots, the fossil fuels used to heat the greenhouses where they are grown, and fuel for the trucks that bring them from growers to retailers. Getting away from disposable annuals to longer-lived perennials can reduce the negative impact on the environment, especially when choosing locally grown varieties or taking the time to propagate your own plants.

In addition, the act of annual planting itself can be harmful to the environment. All the digging required to plant annuals in the spring disrupts the soil in a way rarely found in nature—degrading its structure and making it more vulnerable to erosion. Preparing annual beds encourages the decomposition of organic matter, which releases stored carbon in the soil in the form of carbon dioxide. Pulling annual plants in the fall further disrupts the soil and leaves it bare during the winter—which makes it even more likely to erode in the wind and rain. Perennial plantings allow soil to stay undisturbed, held in place by sturdy root systems.

The perennial plants, through photosynthesis, also help the environment by sequestering carbon in the soil from the air.

Beyond reducing environmental harm, perennials can also do a lot of good for the local ecosystem. The typical American front yard is a lot of lawn, a few shrubs, and maybe some petunias tucked in the ground every spring. But go to wild areas, and there will be perennials, whether they be the complex matrices of grasses and other perennials that make up a prairie, or a carpet of native wildflowers that thrive under the canopy of a forest. Filling your yard with perennials makes it more like what is found in natural areas, and wildlife—especially pollinators and other insects—will move in and thrive. That is not to say annuals and lawns are ecologically sterile—there are a few insects that make use of them—but the habitat and richness of life in a garden space filled with perennials will be greatly multiplied.

But for all the practical reasons to garden with perennials, the real payoff is their beauty. Across the wild diversity of perennial plants, there are forms with flowers and foliage in every color and texture that you can dream of, whether the huge, silky, sinfully fragrant blooms of a peony; the delicate lavender stars of an aster; the bold, broad foliage of a hosta; or the delicate filagree of a fern; the wide palette of perennial plants allows for the creation of a magical, beautiful space to enjoy. And perennials, more so than annuals or shrubs, are dynamic and exciting in the garden. Though, trees and shrubs do bring solidity and stability to the garden with their woody stems—backbones that stay the same every day of the year. Most common annual plants are sold for their ability to flower nonstop through the growing season, but let's be honest, after month three of petunias that just keep flowering away, they get a bit boring. After a while when walking out the front door, the petunias are hardly even noticed—no matter how spectacularly beautiful they were when first planted.

A well-designed perennial planting is continually changing and dynamic throughout the growing season—from the early-blooming bulbs and spring ephemerals that start the season to a parade of summer blooms and foliage that follows, right up to the last of the asters and chrysanthemums that signal the end of the fall with their cushions of flowers. In your perennial garden, every few weeks is a whole new display, a whole new view, all fresh and exciting.

If you want more beauty, more life, more connection to local ecology, more fun, and more dynamism in your garden, keep reading. Perennials are here to make it happen!

CHAPTER 1

YOUR PIECE
of the
PLANET

Understanding the climate, soil,
and conditions that make your garden unique

IMAGINE, FOR A MOMENT, being in Florida with lush tropical foliage and tall palm trees. Now, whisk your mind's eye off to the Arizona desert, full of low scrub, cacti, and grasses. Next, imagine the plains of Iowa, and then the woodlands of Maine.

Each of these places is wildly different, but in each of them perennials abound, thriving and growing vigorously without any help from anyone. Even seemingly barren spots in deserts are full of dormant perennials waiting to burst into growth and bloom after a rainfall—just as the quiet understory of an eastern forest explodes with early blooming ephemerals each spring.

The perennials that grow in each of these landscapes are perfectly adapted to the conditions where they live, but move them to a new location, and they will likely fail. The desert plants will quickly rot in the Florida humidity and the sun-loving plants of the Great Plains will fade away under the shade of a New England forest.

The simple reality that different plants are adapted to different climates is at the very heart of successful gardening with perennials. Choosing plants that are well adapted to the conditions of the garden means they will thrive and perform beautifully. Mismatch the plant and the garden and you'll spend hours in frustration, trying to keep struggling plants alive in a place where they just aren't suited to live. This means the very first step to a successful garden is really understanding the conditions in the garden. In this chapter, we'll go through every aspect of what makes the garden unique and how to choose perennials that will thrive in those conditions.

But before diving into the details, there is one very important thing to keep in mind: There is no such thing as a bad gardening climate or bad gardening conditions.

Wherever you live and whatever combination of sun, shade, and soil you have, there are countless plants that will absolutely thrive in your garden. There are so many perennial plants in the world that, no matter where you garden, there are more plants well-suited to your conditions than you will have time to try in a lifetime of gardening.

Often, however, gardeners focus on what *can't* grow rather than what *can* grow. It hurts when a desired plant fails to thrive. This focus can be exacerbated by spending time looking at gardens in other climates. Every time we travel or scroll through beautiful garden photos on social media, we see all these plants we can't grow, and it can make us feel a bit dejected—like our home climate is not as good, too limiting, or no fun. And at the same time, it's easy to forget to notice the plants that are thriving in our climate that other gardeners long for. For every northern gardener lusting after bold tropical gingers there is a southern

gardener pining for peonies. You can think of your garden conditions as problems and limitations, or you can think of them as opportunities. If your garden won't grow plants that seem common and easy to other gardeners, it might mean it *will* grow some very unusual or rare plants that no one else in the area can grow.

There are things, of course, that can be done to change garden conditions. Irrigation can be added, drainage increased, cooling shade added, or a warm microclimate created, but sometimes making modifications takes away the aspect that makes a garden space unique and special. Leaning into what is already existing will almost always make for a more satisfying and exciting garden, and one that is less work and less expensive to maintain. But, before you can embrace your garden's conditions, you have to know what they are. So let's dive in.

CLIMATE

Choosing perennials suitable for your climate is a key to success. Look for plants that evolved in climates similar to your own or those that are native to your region.

THE CLIMATE IS A COMPLEX topic made up of many interacting factors and, increasingly, factors that are changing and unstable. But in gardening terms, climate can be broken down into three main aspects: how cold it gets in the winter, how hot it gets in the summer, and how much—and when—it rains. Understanding these three variables gives a good sense of what types of plants will thrive in your climate.

WINTER COLD

How cold your winter gets is one of the biggest factors in determining what types of perennials can grow in the temperate zones in most of North America. It is also the one particular aspect of climate that gardeners in the United States talk about the most. Post a picture of a perennial on social media and the first comment is almost always, "How hardy is it?" Talk with a gardener from a different region and they'll be quick to ask, "What zone are you?"

Both these terms, *hardiness* and *hardiness zones*, are a little confusing to newcomers, and sometimes poorly understood even by long-time gardeners, so let's dive into the details a little more.

USDA Plant Hardiness Zone Map

When a gardener says a plant is "hardy," they mean it is able to reliably survive their winters. Plants that can't survive a winter are called "tender." So northern gardeners may talk about hardy hibiscus, the species that can handle colder temperatures instead of the tender hibiscus, the tropical species that turn up their toes the moment the thermometer dips below freezing. But, of course, these terms are relative. In South Florida, they're all hardy hibiscus.

To help gardeners (and farmers) understand just how cold their winters are and figure out if a plant will be hardy for them, the U.S. Department of Agriculture developed the USDA Plant Hardiness Zone Map. This map is what gardeners use when they talk about their "zone." The current version of the map is based on an average taken from data collected by weather centers of the lowest temperature each part of the United States experienced each winter for a recent thirty-year span. With the average low temperatures applied to the map, the country is divided up into sections zones) of common temperature readings in 10-degree Fahrenheit intervals. The zones are labeled

Average Annual Extreme Minimum Temperature 1991–2020

Temp (F)	Zone	Temp (C)	Temp (F)	Zone	Temp (C)
-60 to -55	1a	-51.1 to -48.3	0 to 5	7a	-17.8 to -15
-55 to -50	1b	-48.3 to -45.6	5 to 10	7b	-15 to -12.2
-50 to -45	2a	-45.6 to -42.8	10 to 15	8a	-12.2 to -9.4
-45 to -40	2b	-42.8 to -40	15 to 20	8b	-9.4 to -6.7
-40 to -35	3a	-40 to -37.2	20 to 25	9a	-6.7 to -3.9
-35 to -30	3b	-37.2 to -34.4	25 to 30	9b	-3.9 to -1.1
-30 to -25	4a	-34.4 to -31.7	30 to 35	10a	-1.1 to 1.7
-25 to -20	4b	-31.7 to -28.9	35 to 40	10b	1.7 to 4.4
-20 to -15	5a	-28.9 to -26.1	40 to 45	11a	4.4 to 7.2
-15 to -10	5b	-26.1 to -23.3	45 to 50	11b	7.2 to 10
-10 to -5	6a	-23.3 to -20.6	50 to 55	12a	10 to 12.8
-5 to 0	6b	-20.6 to -17.8	55 to 60	12b	12.8 to 15.6
			60 to 65	13a	15.6 to 18.3
			65 to 70	13b	18.3 to 21.1

from 1 (coldest) to 13 (warmest). So, for example, on average in Zone 5, the coldest temperature you can expect to see in your garden each winter will be between -10°F and -20°F (-23.3°C and -28.9°C), while Zone 4 is colder, averaging -20°F to -30°F (-28.9°C to -34.4°C) and Zone 6 is warmer, from 0°F to -10°F (-17.8°C to -23.3°C). To give further precision, each zone is divided into an "a" and a "b" section, with the "a" being the cooler half, and "b" the slightly warmer section.

The zone system is incredibly useful because it offers a quick way to compare different climates. Saying "I have very cold winters in my garden" doesn't really mean anything without a context. It will soon be apparent when spending time talking to other gardeners, that they all complain about cold winters, even though to some, cold means it hit freezing and to others that means it went down to -20°F (-28.9°C). The zone system gives a quick and easy way to actually compare cold temperatures. Nurseries and garden writers use this system extensively, gathering information from where plants have grown and thrived, and translating that into a zone rating for a plant. So, once you

look up what your zone is (easily done with your zip code on https://planthardiness.ars.usda.gov or see the map on page 15), you can then just look at a plant label or catalog description and see if a plant should be hardy and survive winters in your garden.

However, as powerful and useful as the zone system is, there are exceptions to it. Nonetheless, you should know your zone and use it as a starting point to tell if a plant will be hardy, but there are many other factors to consider as well.

Climate Change
Hardiness zones are based on thirty-year averages, but the unavoidable reality is that our climates are changing. The USDA periodically updates the zone maps based on new data, and during the last update, many locations got a half or full zone warmer simply because our winters have been getting milder. Because climate change isn't quite predictable, the data the zone rankings are based upon may be getting less useful. In general, temperatures are getting warmer, but the changing climate is also becoming less predictable and producing some unexpected cold snaps. So get used to things changing, and take zone rankings with a grain of salt.

Microclimates
The low temperature recorded at the official weather station nearest your house may or may not be the actual temperature seen in your garden. Many factors influence actual temperatures. Low-lying areas will often be cooler as cold air—which is heavier than warm air—flows down and collects in them. South- and west-facing walls will absorb heat from the sun during the day and release it at night, making for warmer conditions. If a house is poorly insulated, heat leaking out of the walls will keep the areas right next to the house warmer. The volume of walls and concrete and amount of artificial heat used in cities makes urban areas consistently warmer than rural areas nearby. These temperature differences may seem small, but they can add up to a lot because of the volume. The best way to understand temperature differences is to buy a good min-max thermometer and compare the readings with those reported by the nearest official weather station. The zone rating for your area is based on the official weather station, so if you are consistently warmer or colder than what's reported on the map, adjust your zone accordingly.

Microclimates, like the one created by this heat-absorbing stone wall, can allow you to push your zone a bit and grow perennials that may not otherwise be reliably hardy in your zone.

Snow Cover

Snow, for all our cursing when it clogs up roadways, can be beneficial for the garden. Snow is an insulator and offers protection against drying winds. If air temperatures drop to -20°F (-28.9°C) when there is a foot (30 cm) of snow on the ground at the time, the actual temperatures at the soil level will be significantly warmer. This effect is particularly relevant for perennials. Trees and shrubs stick up above the insulating blanket of snow and have to be hardy enough to survive. If herbaceous perennials, which die down to ground level each fall, are given a good, consistent, deep snow cover during the coldest parts of winter, the extra protection will allow plants that are more tender to grow.

Winter Wet

Absolute cold temperatures aren't the only reason a plant might not survive the winter. One of the biggest killers is cold, soggy soil—either during the winter or in early spring as the ground thaws. Some northern gardeners call the spring thaw the mud season, as melting snow prolongs soil saturation and can cause root systems to rot out, particularly for hardy succulents, cacti, and other perennials native to cold but dry climates.

Prolonged Cold

Zone rankings are based on the lowest temperature an area is likely to reach each winter. But they do not take into account how long those low temperatures persist. Some areas have cold temperatures that arrive in a sudden cold snap and then vanish. Others have more consistent temperatures, with long deep freezes. In general, prolonged periods of cold are more damaging to perennials. Because most perennials retreat to the ground each winter, they are insulated by the soil from sudden changes in air temperature. But when it gets cold and stays cold, the ground freezes solid and deep—which can do real damage to plants.

Limits of Data

One of the deeper issues of the zone rankings is to look at what temperature data is used. Looking at the data used to determine the temperatures of each region, each new version of the USDA Hardiness Zone Map uses more weather stations and more data to make sure those numbers are as good as possible. And it is easy to check the specific conditions in a garden with a thermometer to get an even more precise measurement. However, when looking at a plant tag that says hardy to Zone 5, take that with a grain of salt. In the best case, the hardiness numbers were determined from looking at the native range of a given plant and combining that with the experiences of a range of gardeners actually growing it in their Zone 5

Snow cover not only looks lovely on a perennial planting, it also provides an insulating blanket.

climate. In reality, those numbers are often little more than educated guesses. Sometimes a plant is listed as Zone 7 when it can actually grow in much colder conditions simply because an investigation wasn't done to see how it performs in more northern areas. Other times, a plant might be labeled as Zone 5 because closely related plants are that hardy and people assume this one will be the same. For common, widely grown plants, hardiness numbers end up being very accurate. It's the rarer, more infrequently grown plants that are more likely to have zone rankings that are less accurate.

When they are hardy in your growing zone, perennials, like this ornamental grass, shrug off snow and ice and return to the garden the following spring.

A layer of shredded leaf mulch, fabric row cover, or boughs from a discarded Christmas tree add a layer of winter insulation for plants that are only marginally hardy.

For those really curious about the hardiness of an unusual plant, track down people growing it in similar climates and ask for their feedback. Social media, local gardening groups, public gardens, Extension Service offices (see page 259), and good local garden centers or nurseries can be great places to get feedback from actual gardeners on how a plant performs. And, sometimes, it is best to just try it. Not everything will survive, but there is a lot of satisfaction in discovering a plant that thrives when all the books say it shouldn't live.

Mitigating Cold

Though it is recommended that the bulk of your perennials embrace your natural climatic conditions, there are things that can be done to make your local microclimate warmer so gardeners can get away with growing plants that normally aren't hardy for them. The simplest of these is using mulch. Piling fall leaves, wood chips, branches from your discarded Christmas tree, or other materials over your plants for the winter will add an additional layer of insulation and protect them from the most extreme cold. This can be very effective and is not a lot of work. There are two things to keep in mind. First, wait until there has been some real cold weather and plants are totally dormant before piling extra insulation over them. This ensures plants don't get too warm and try to start growing through their protection. And second, pull that extra insulating protection off early in the spring, well before the perennials push out new growth to make sure they don't get smothered and die.

Understanding the microclimates in the garden will let gardeners put plants in spots where they will experience less extreme temperatures. A house, especially if there's a sunny side to it, is usually the biggest warming influence in the garden. Tucking plants up against a south-facing wall is a classic way to get a borderline hardy plant through the winter.

But remember, winter cold isn't necessarily bad. Though cold winters are often panned for killing off plants, they also are necessary for some plants to survive and thrive. Many classic spring-blooming perennials in northern gardens like tulips and peonies require a cold dormancy in winter. Like every other aspect of the climate, cold winters can be seen as a problem, but they are also an opportunity.

SUMMER HEAT

Summer heat is another huge factor in how plants perform. Winter is often given more focus, but summer temperatures are just as big of a factor in determining which plants will do well in the garden. Some perennials, such as many ornamental grasses and the showy gingers, really need a long, hot summer to thrive and do their best. Other plants, like delphiniums and lupines, simply shrink and fade away if summer days—and particularly summer nights—turn too warm.

Determining just how hot summers get can be a challenge. The Hardiness Zone Map is only based on low temperatures during the winter. The zone map indicates nothing about summer heat, though sometimes it is used that way. Often plants will have a zone range. For example, a plant will be listed as hardy from Zone 5 to 8. But Portland, Oregon and Atlanta, Georgia are *both* in Zone 8. These two cities have pretty similar average winter low temperatures. Their summers, however, could hardly be more different.

Unfortunately, there is no widely used standard for gardeners to evaluate summer heat, which means heat can be harder to talk about and communicate its effects on plants clearly. Often the best stand-in for assessing your summer heat is looking at how many days a year an area gets over 90°F (32.2°C). A quick search online will turn up those numbers, and they can be a great way to compare one area to other regions.

Unlike cold temperatures, it is very difficult to mitigate heat in the summer. Shade helps, to an extent, but while it is cooler in the shade, plants also need light to photosynthesize. There's only so much cooling shade that can be added before the shade starts impacting plant growth. The best way to use shade to enhance cooling is to make sure it is afternoon shade. Shade in the afternoon protects plants during the very hottest parts of the day. Also, the north or east side of the house, fence, or tree is the best location to try plants that are better suited to a cooler climate.

Consider heat tolerance in addition to cold tolerance when selecting perennials for your landscape, particularly if you live in a hot, dry climate.

Water is the other tool we can use to cool plants. Hot and dry conditions are a killing combination for many plants. Making sure plants get ample irrigation during the hottest time of the day, week, month, or year can help to some extent. The impact watering has depends greatly on the climate. In a very dry climate, extra water evaporates to help cool plants. In places like the hot and humid Southeast, more water during the hottest months may promote other problems like root rot and fungal diseases. The simple fact is that, more than almost any other climatic factor, hot summer temperatures are hard to change. High summer temperatures are a very important factor to understand when it comes to plant choice and site conditions.

RAINFALL

After temperature, the amount of rain a region receives is the next biggest factor in determining what types of plants will thrive in garden conditions.

The amount of rain that falls—easily measured as average annual precipitation—is quick to look up online, and the rainfall numbers are a great first look at how moisture impacts the garden.

Plants adapted to low-rainfall areas tend to have succulent leaves, deep root systems, and other adaptations to minimize water loss and maximize water uptake. What plants don't have, however, is much resistance to various soil rots and diseases because those problems aren't prevalent in dry soil. These low-water plants are often quite slow growing as well, to make the most of lean conditions. Plants adapted to high-rainfall areas, on the other hand, transpire water faster and collapse under drought conditions. These plants grow fast and lush in moist conditions and they won't rot out when it has been raining for weeks on end and the soil is like soup.

The average annual rainfall in a region doesn't tell the whole picture, however, as patterns of rainfall also matter. The West Coast of North America, for example, has a dry summer climate, with most of the rain falling in the winter months and the summers being nearly without rain. Even the famously rainy Pacific Northwest gets almost no rain at all in the summer months. In response to those conditions, plants have evolved to go dormant during the summer, and, in fact, too much moisture during their normal dry season can kill those plants. In much of the rest of North America, even in quite dry areas, summer precipitation is more common, meaning plants have developed entirely different adaptations to thrive.

Conserving Water

Rainfall is one of the aspects of climate that gardeners are most likely to artificially adjust. Irrigation in its various forms is standard practice for many gardeners to make a dry climate wetter.

Take into account how much natural rainfall occurs in an average year in your climate. Select plants adapted to that expected rainfall amount to reduce the need for irrigation.

Dry-climate perennial gardens should be filled with plants adapted to low-water conditions. Working with nature is always easier than working against it. *Denver Botanic Gardens Chatfield Farms.*

There are many beautiful perennials beyond cacti and succulents to select from for dry regions.

If you garden in a dry climate, however, making conditions wetter should not start with irrigation, but should start with conserving the rainwater you receive. Begin by looking at what happens when rain does fall on the garden and make sure as much rain as possible is soaking into the soil rather than running off into drains or down the street. This means looking at slopes in the garden to be sure the landscape is guiding water into low-lying areas where it can soak into the ground. Replacing surfaces such as traditional concrete that simply lets water run away with pervious surfaces like gravel or specialty pervious concretes will conserve water by allowing it to soak in and hydrate the soil.

Next, be sure to lose as little soil moisture to the air as possible. Mulch is a simple and easy-to-use tool for this (see page 129). Spread 1 to 2 inches (2.5–5 cm) of shredded leaves, wood chips, or other organic material over the soil to make a protective barrier, keeping the soil moist below. Bare ground is the enemy when it comes to water conservation.

Then you can irrigate. While regular irrigation allows gardeners in dry climates to grow many more plants than they would be able to otherwise, irrigation is not without its risks. Water supplies are limited, water can be expensive, and the sad reality is that when your plants want water the most—during intense drought—this is the time when your water supplies are most likely to be cut off or reduced.

Embracing the Dry

Highly efficient irrigation systems—like drip systems—can mitigate the cost and amount of water used somewhat. The bottom line though, is that the most cost-effective, environmentally sound, and reliably healthy garden is going to be one planted with species that are well adapted to thrive with the amount of water your garden naturally receives. And, for those living in very dry climates, this does not mean the only things in the garden have to be cacti and rocks. There are countless beautiful perennials native to very dry climates to use to create a stunning garden—many of which gardeners in wetter areas wish they could grow. The practice of using dry climate-adapted plants in arid growing conditions is known as *xeriscaping*, and the plants that thrive in these low-water conditions are known as *xerophytes*. When effectively done, xeriscaping reduces or even eliminates the need for irrigation.

If you live in a dry climate and have your heart set on growing special, water-hungry plants, develop a small, irrigated area for them. Keep the high water-use plants in an irrigated zone by themselves to minimize the amount of water needed to be applied to the garden. This practice still allows for growing sentimental favorites from other climates.

In wet climates, slopes can help channel water away from plant roots.

Embracing the Wet

In rainy climates, the opposite can be done by limiting the amount of water plants receive. The simplest and usually most effective way to do this is by building raised beds and filling them with a very well-drained soil mix. Even in the rainiest climate, a bed filled with coarse sand and gravel will quickly let the extra water flow away and keep plants adapted to dry climates happy. These plants can also find a home in a well-drained sloped or rocky area, particularly one with a western exposure. But like supplemental irrigation, these methods are best practiced on a small scale. Transforming an entire garden into a well-drained desert in rainy Georgia is going to be prohibitively expensive. Alternatively, it is quite easy to make a little raised bed or use a west-facing slope and impress the neighbors by growing cacti outside in a rainy climate.

It is possible to go a step further and not just increase drainage, but actually limit rainfall, by building roofs over plants. These structures need to be transparent, of course. Essentially they are little greenhouses without walls that keep rain off the plants but let the light through. The structures are expensive and more work than most gardeners will want to take on, but it is possible.

Finding the Right Plants

The quickest way to find plants that are well adapted to the amount of rain the garden gets is to focus on local natives and plants native to similar climates (see page 14), but it is also possible to learn to recognize the adaptations that plants have developed to thrive in different climates. With experience, gardeners will be able to look at a plant and make a pretty good guess if it is going to be drought-tolerant or a lover of wet conditions—though sometimes these adaptations play out in unexpected ways.

Many plants adapted to dry conditions have thick, waxy leaves, sometimes thickened to the point that they can store water in them, and are called *succulents*. These leaves also often have layers of hair or silvery-looking wax to reflect excess heat from the sun, protecting the plants. Plants with grey and silver foliage are often drought-tolerant due to the presence of numerous fine hairs that prevent the leaf from drying out. Plants adapted to wet conditions, on the other hand, often have larger, thinner, more delicate leaves that lose water easily and rarely have the thick, waxy leaf coatings of dry-adapted plants.

Plants with gray or silver foliage are often noted as being drought-tolerant due to the fine hairs present on the leaves. These hairs prevent moisture loss through the leaf pores.

Many fungal diseases, such as the powdery mildew on this peony foliage, are exacerbated in wet and humid conditions.

Dry conditions can arrive in various ways and there are exceptions to these adaptations, of course. For example, evergreen conifers, like pines and junipers, have leaves that look very dry-adapted because they are small, tough, and waxy. These serve to conserve water, but often it's because they are native to very cold climates where they can't draw water from frozen soils during the winter. Similarly, tropical orchids, like the ones in bloom at the grocery store, have very thick, waxy leaves, despite being native to some of the rainiest places on the planet. These plants live perched on the branches of trees, with no soil to hold on to moisture. So despite the constant rain, orchids deal with a lack of water all the time. All of this is to say that looking at leaves can give you a clue as to how much the plant is adapted to dryness, but it is always important to pair that with more information about the plant and the region where it is native.

Humidity

One aspect of water in the garden that is the hardest to change or control is humidity—the amount of water in the air. No matter how much you irrigate your desert garden, the air blowing through it is still going to be quite dry, and even the best drained soil under the best rain cover is going to be humid on a South Carolina summer day. Humidity impacts plants a few different ways. Some plants—those adapted to high humidity climates—have delicate leaves that readily dry out and get crispy on the edges in very dry air. Conversely, many plants native to dry climates are prone to fungal diseases on their foliage in very humid climates. Humidity can be raised by irrigating, misting, planting densely, and adding walls or hedges to restrict air flow. Lowering humidity can be accomplished by limiting water and making sure air can move freely through the garden and between plants. But, at some point, it is time to face the fact that begonias that thrive in Florida will get brown leaf edges in Southern California and most peonies are very likely to get mildew on their leaves in rainy climates.

PUTTING IT ALL TOGETHER

The combination of winter cold, summer heat, and rainfall is what makes a particular climate unique. For the easiest, most sustainable gardening experience, focus on growing plants native to your region or plants from similar climates. For example, the summer-dry climate of the West Coast is very similar to areas around the Mediterranean and to parts of Australia. The hot, humid, rainy Southeast provides perfect conditions for a lot of plants from the similar climates of East Asia. Of course, the ultimate source of plants adapted to your climate are those native to your local area, which have the added bonus of supporting local native wildlife.

The challenge of growing plants native to very different climates can be a lot of fun for some gardeners. Often the easiest and best way to do this is to keep plants not suited to your climate in pots or other containers. Containers can be easily moved to a shed or garage to shelter plants from the coldest temperatures of winter, moved under grow lights in a basement to get plants out of a summer heat wave, or moved under a sheltering eve or porch during a prolonged rainstorm. It's also easy to quickly water them during a drought.

And remember, there is no such thing as a bad gardening climate. No matter where a garden is located, there is someone making a spectacular garden in a place hotter, colder, drier, wetter, or more extreme. The secret to a great garden is not finding the perfect climate but fully understanding and embracing the natural climate.

SOIL

IT IS HARD TO OVERSTATE how critical soil is to a healthy, thriving garden. It is awe-inspiring to realize that all the beautiful, interesting plant parts above ground are often mirrored by an even larger mass of roots growing below the ground. How those roots interact with the soil plays an enormous factor in determining if a plant thrives—perhaps just as important as the climatic factors of temperature and rainfall. But unlike temperature, most soil traits are hidden away and can easily be overlooked. Soil pH? Cation exchange capacity? These matter a lot to plants but are alien to our human experience. Luckily, they're easy to understand, and getting a handle on what is going on in the soil will give you gardening superpowers.

SOIL COMPONENTS

Soil is made up of three main parts. First is the mineral component. This part of the soil started as bedrock, and over time—thanks to erosion, freezing and thawing, the action of plant roots, rain, and everything else—has been ground down into tiny particles. Depending on their size, these particles are broken up into three groups. The largest are the sand particles, next are the smaller silt particles, and the smallest of all are the clay particles.

In addition to this mineral portion of the soil made up of pulverized rock, there is organic matter. This is the decomposing remains of all the things that have lived in and on the soil. This includes old plant roots, leaves, stems, living creatures, animal wastes, decomposing branches, and so on. When that original organic matter has decomposed to the point where gardeners can no longer tell what the parent material was, it is called *humus*. Humus holds a lot of nutrients and water and gives soil a dark brown color.

And finally, arguably the most important part of the soil: the pore space. This means, simply, the spaces between the mineral and organic portions of the soil—the areas that can be filled with water or air.

Pores are where all the action happens. Plant roots grow through the pore spaces. They take up oxygen from the air in the pores, they take up water from the pores, and they absorb the nutrients dissolved in the water. Plant roots interact with all the other things—invertebrates, fungi, bacteria—living in those pores. All the other parts of the soil only really matter to the extent that they impact the ratio of air and water in the pores.

Understanding how plants interact with the soil they live in is an important way to influence plant health.

Sand

Large particles of sand fit together loosely, and so there are large, wide-open pore spaces between them. Those big pore spaces mean everything—air, water, plant roots, nutrients—passes through sandy soils easily. So, after a rainstorm, sandy soils are great at absorbing water rather than letting it run off into storm drains. But, during a drought, since that water has drained out of the sandy soil so quickly, plants are left quite dry. Plant roots also grow very easily through sandy soils, quickly growing down, which can help them access water deep underground during dry spells. Gardeners also move easily in sand. Sand is easy to dig, and weeds are easy to pull in it. It can be a joy to garden on sandy soil, but these soils require the heavy use of drought-tolerant plants, and the realization that any fertilizers you add will easily leach out from the soil and into local waterways.

Clay

Clay is the opposite of sand. It packs tight and is sometimes slow to absorb moisture. On the positive side, it also stays wet long into dry spells. Clay holds nutrients in place, requiring less fertilization, and those nutrients are less likely to leach away. Clay can be a pain to work with as heavy clay soils are difficult to dig, and they easily become sticky and messy if worked when too wet. However, well-cared-for clay soils can have unparalleled fertility and impressive water-holding abilities.

Silt

Silt is in between clay and sand in size as well as all other attributes. Silty soils hold more water and nutrients than sand, but less than clay. Silt is easier to dig than clay, but more prone to compaction than sand. Silt-dominated soils are pretty rare, however.

All three of these soil samples are made of the same basic "ingredients": mineral particles, pore space, organic matter, and living organisms. The various ratios of all of these components determines a soil's composition and its traits.

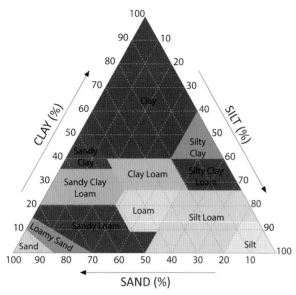

Use the soil pyramid to determine which type of soil you have based on the percentages of each particle size in your soil sample.

Soil Makeup

Virtually no soil is composed of 100 percent of any one type of particle. Almost always there is going to be some combination of clay, sand, and silt in soil. The performance of soil depends on what percentage of sand, silt, and clay particles are present. Soils with a fairly even mix of all three particle sizes are called *loams*, and many consider loam to be the best of all worlds, combining the water retention of clay with the looser structure of sand.

There are a few simple tests to help understand what kind of soil is in your garden. First, and simplest, is to just grab a shovel and turn over some soil. Sandy soils won't hold a clump shape, while those with more clay in them stay in the shape of the shovel head.

Next, grab some soil and rub it between your fingers. Sandy soils feel coarse between your fingers, while clay soils feel sticky and smooth.

To get a more accurate measure of soil components, put some soil in a glass jar with water and shake vigorously until the soil is completely broken up and suspended in the water. Then set it down and wait. The biggest particles— sand—will settle out of the water fastest, and the clay the slowest. After one minute, mark on the side of the jar where the soil has settled to the bottom. That is your sand. Wait another two hours and mark the second layer. The soil that has settled in those two hours is the silt component. Finally, after waiting 48 hours, mark the third layer. That last layer, the uppermost section, is the clay. Comparing the relative depth of the three different layers will provide a good estimate of the percentages of sand, silt, and clay in the soil sample. Then use the soil pyramid illustration on this page to determine which type of soil you have.

Organic Matter

Organic matter is often talked about as the magic solution to all soil problems—which it often is. Organic matter has an excellent ability to hold onto water like a sponge, so sandy soils with lots of organic matter won't dry out as fast as those without a high percentage of organic matter. Soils with high organic matter will also hold more nutrients than, for example, sandy soils without organic matter. But the real magic of organic matter is what it does with the smaller particles, especially clay, in creating good soil structure. Pure clay packs solid, with essentially no pore spaces at all. But as roots and worms and insects and fungi grow through clay soils, living, dying, and decomposing, they bind the clay particles together into little clusters called aggregates. These aggregates can clearly be seen in healthy soil.

Dig up a clump of soil high in organic matter and it should crumble apart into little chunks. These clumps are soft—rub a clump between two fingers and it will smear into nothing, but in the ground, the clumps hold their shape, fitting loosely together with lots of pore space between them. While a clay soil with little organic matter and therefore poor soil structure is a dense mass that is very hard for water or roots to penetrate, one with lots of organic matter and great structure can be almost as loose and open as a sandy soil, but instead of being made up of hard, impervious particles of sand, it is made up of aggregates that can actually hold moisture and nutrients like little sponges.

Most gardeners regularly add organic matter to their soil each season, typically in the form of some type of organic mulch or compost.

Poorly drained areas are a challenge for perennial gardeners. Avoid low-lying areas like this one, unless you plan to plant species that tolerate periodic flooding.

Soil with good structure is wonderful to work with and a great medium for plant roots to grow and thrive, but soil structure is a fragile thing. Those individual soil aggregates are delicate, and when digging or walking on the soil, especially when it is very wet, they can be crushed into a compaction problem.

DRAINAGE

Water runs downhill, so higher areas are drier than lower-lying ones. This is obvious, but often this simple fact is overlooked when trying to improve the drainage of a low, wet area in the garden. Adding sand or gravel to the soil will improve drainage, so it can be dug into the garden. But it simply doesn't matter how much is added if there is nowhere for that water to drain. With flat ground and a clay soil or a garden at the bottom of a slope, no amount of added drainage material will do anything unless you have somewhere for the water to go. For the home garden, the most practical way to increase drainage it to build up your soil. Rather than mixing something into the soil, building a raised garden with well-drained soil will allow extra moisture to easily drain away. These can be formal raised beds or just informal raised soil berms. Either way, raised beds or soil mounds can be marvelous places to grow plants because the well-drained soil prevents plants from drowning, and plants can easily send their roots through the loose soil to access the stored water and nutrients in the denser soil below.

One absolute rule when amending soil or building raised beds is to always put looser soil with bigger pore spaces on top of denser soils. Water moves easily from large pores into smaller ones, but not the other way around. Think of small pores as being like a sponge and large pores as being like a bowl of marbles. If you have marbles on top of a sponge, and pour water on them, the water will quickly flow through the marbles and settle in the sponge. But if you pour water onto a sponge sitting on top of marbles, most of the water will stay in the sponge. In soils, this is called a *perched water table*, and it is not good. With all the water held at the soil's surface, it can cause plants to suffer and drown because of the wet conditions. That same water can also quickly evaporate and vanish during droughts, leaving little stored water in the deeper, looser soils. So, if you have clay soil, feel free to pile loose sand or a soil with great structure on top of it to create a well-drained raised area, but if your soil is sandy, never add a heavier soil on top in an attempt to conserve water.

SOIL LIFE

In addition to the physical components of your soil, it is also home to life.
A **lot** of life.
So, so, so much life.
From earthworms, arthropods, and insects we can see with the naked eye, to tiny nematodes and microscopic fungi and bacteria, soil teams with life. It is estimated that fully half the species on the planet live in soil.

Healthy soil is full of living organisms, most of which live in harmony with plants.

Fungi are some of the most important soil organisms. There are countless species of fungi living in the soil, most of which do the important work of breaking down organic matter in the soil. But there is a group of fungi, called *mycorrhizae*, that form close connections to plant roots, sometimes even growing within the root tissue. These fungal connections serve as an extension of a plant's root system, taking up water and, most importantly, certain nutrients that plants are not as efficient at extracting from the soil. In return, the plants send some of the food they produce via photosynthesis down to the mycorrhizae in a beneficial exchange. In some cases, these beneficial fungi can also outcompete and protect against disease-causing pathogenic fungi. In healthy soils, especially in woodlands, mycorrhizae colonies are so large and extensive they functionally knit the root systems of all the plants in the area into one giant network, sharing water and nutrients and holding the soil together to resist erosion.

Keeping the complex networks of life in soil intact isn't hard; it usually just comes down to minimizing soil disruption, such as digging and tillage, and making sure to add organic matter to feed the soil life. It is not necessary to specifically add beneficial fungi and bacteria to garden soil. Those organisms are already there; just give them the conditions they need to thrive.

SOIL CHEMISTRY

Chemistry may feel like a strange word to use in this context, but what plant roots take from the soil are, in fact, chemicals. "Chemical" is sometimes thrown around in a vaguely scary way to mean synthetic compounds or even just "scary bad stuff you don't want," but water and all the nutrients plants need to thrive are perfectly natural, nonscary, and nondangerous (usually) things—they are, in fact, chemicals, and chemistry is the discipline needed to understand how they function and interact with soils and plants.

Nutrients

Nutrients are the chemicals plants need to take up in order to make new cells (and branches, leaves, flowers, and fruits). They're sometimes referred to as "plant food," which is a bit of a misnomer. Plants make their own food, in their leaves, via photosynthesis. The nutrients plants take up from the soil are more akin to the minerals humans require, such as iron and calcium—compounds necessary for life but needed in very small quantities. There are fourteen different elements essential for plants to thrive. Most of these are called *micronutrients* and are needed in such minuscule amounts that plants are rarely deficient in them. Then there are the big three, the macronutrients: nitrogen, phosphorus, and potassium. These are the three nutrients

These soil organisms interact with your plants in a lot of interesting ways. Some of them cause problems, like root rots and other diseases, but in truth, these kinds of problems in the garden are usually more a symptom of putting a plant in the wrong growing conditions. Root rots are generally the result of a plant that is sitting in wetter soil than it prefers. Some nurseries use fungicides to subdue root rot, which often returns as soon as these plants are put into wet soil in the garden. There are also insects and other organisms that live in the soil and can snack on your plants; more on these will be covered in chapter 6.

The vast majority of the living things in soil are either beneficial or harmless. A whole army of organisms are slowly breaking down the organic matter in the soil, and as they do so, they release the nutrients in that material into the soil pores where plant roots can take them up. Other microorganisms form mutually beneficial relationships with plants. Legumes, including perennials like baptisias and lupines, team up with bacteria in the soil to make nitrogen into a form that plants can uptake and use. These bacteria can't live in the presence of oxygen, so the leguminous plants make little homes, called nodules, for them on their roots, where the bacteria scrub the oxygen with a compound called *leghemoglobin*, which is actually very similar to the oxygen-absorbing hemoglobin in our blood.

Proper nutrition is important for plants, though thankfully, most perennials are not heavy feeders and require little to no fertilization.

that are found in virtually all fertilizers because they are needed by plants in larger amounts and they are more often deficient in soils.

On fertilizer labels, you will always see the quantities of these three nutrients listed in alphabetical order (nitrogen first, then phosphorus, then potassium), sometimes abbreviated as N-P-K (the symbol for each of these elements on the periodic table) or more often, just as three numbers, for example 10-5-15, meaning this particular fertilizer is 10 percent nitrogen, 5 percent phosphorus, and 15 percent potassium by weight.

Proper nutrition is important. If plants can't get the nutrients they need, they can grow slowly, show sickly yellowing leaves, and fail to flower or set fruit properly. But there are a lot of myths and bad assumptions around the uses of fertilizer.

Myth one: If some is good, more must be better. Almost all fertilizers are toxic to plants if used in too high concentrations. And, even more importantly, all fertilizers can cause significant damage to the environment if they leach out of the soil and contaminate groundwater, rivers, lakes, and other waterways. Excessive fertilizer causes

algal blooms in waterways that are capable of poisoning fish—and people—or creating dead zones by stripping the water of oxygen as the algae die and decompose. It is critical for the health of plants and the environment to use only the fertilizer plants actually need and no more.

Myth two: Organic is always safe. Organic fertilizers are made from things like compost, animal manure, mined minerals, or other naturally occurring compounds, while synthetic ones are made in chemical manufacturing facilities. However, at the end of the day, both of these types of fertilizers supply nitrogen, phosphorus, and potassium, and both will poison plants and contaminate waterways if used in excess. It is true that it is generally harder to over-fertilize with organic fertilizers as they tend to have lower concentrations of nutrients and release those nutrients more slowly than synthetic formulations, but don't think just because the bag says "organic" on it that it can be dumped on the garden without any negative consequences.

It is challenging to recognize possible nutrient deficiencies simply by looking at leaves. Visual symptoms can be misleading. A soil test is the only way to know for sure if your soil is lacking in a particular nutrient.

Understanding and testing your soil is important for understanding if and when a fertilizer is needed, how much to add, and the best time of year to do so.

Myth three: Looking at the leaves tells what nutrients a plant needs. This myth does have a kernel of truth to it. Plants with a significant nutrient deficiency will sometimes show specific visual symptoms, usually in the form of yellowing leaves. The yellowing does develop in slightly different patterns depending on the nutrient in question. However, the reality is that nearly anything wrong with a plant will cause yellowing leaves, and, unless you are a plant nutrition specialist, it is essentially impossible to diagnose what might be causing the problem just by looking at the leaf. Yellowing leaves on plants are usually (but not always!) a sign that something is wrong, but that's about all you can safely read into it.

Myth four: Bigger and faster is better. More fertilizer can (up to a point) make plants grow bigger, faster, and lusher. It's true, but that doesn't mean it's a good thing. In a vegetable garden, rapid, lush growth makes for tender crops and a bigger harvest. And at a nursery, faster growth means getting plants to sale quicker. But in a landscape or perennial garden, more is not always more. Over-fertilized plants grow taller and are more likely to need staking to keep them from collapsing onto other plants. They can also spread more aggressively, swamping out other plants, and they will need dividing, pruning, and other care more often. Gardeners may want to encourage rapid growth in a new planting to help plants fill in quickly, but once a garden is mature, slower growth can be a good thing. As long as the plants are flowering well and looking good, there is no need to try and push them to ever faster, lusher growth with excessive fertilizer use.

Myth five: One size fits all. No gardening book—including this one—can tell gardeners what fertilizer is needed because the type and quantity of fertilizer that will help plants grow best depends entirely on what nutrients are already in the soil. Many soils in the eastern half of North America have naturally high levels of phosphorus and there is no need to add more. In the western United States, soils often have low phosphorus but high potassium. And no matter where you live, the history of how your soil was used and fertilized *before you* started gardening there can radically change the nutrients available to your plants. All of this means that the right fertilizer for one garden may be a total waste—if not actually harmful—to another.

What all these myths point toward is: fertilize sparingly, thoughtfully, and *only* after getting a soil test. There are lots of places to get soil tests, including most land-grant university Extension Service offices (see the sidebar on the next page). A soil test usually costs less than a sandwich and fries at lunch, and the results give concrete information about what nutrients are in the soil and what fertilizers it may need. The soil test lab will have specific instructions on how to prepare soil for testing, but it usually requires taking a cup or so of soil, letting it dry, putting it in a bag, and mailing it to the soil testing lab. They'll send back extensive information about the soil, its makeup, the organic matter content, and recommendations for fertilization. Then take those soil test results and head to a good local garden center (with an educated staff) and have them help you find the fertilizer product that matches what the soil needs—if it needs any fertilizer at all! If your perennials are looking healthy and good, there is no need to add fertilizers.

Understanding pH

pH stands for "potential of hydrogen" and is a measure of the acidity or alkalinity of the water in your soil. The technical details of pH can seem abstract and confusing, but they translate to the perennial garden in a few important ways. pH is measured on a scale of 0 to 14, with the lower numbers being more acidic, 7 being neutral, and the high numbers being alkaline. As a reference point, acidic vinegar has a pH between 4 and 5 and bleach is extremely alkaline with a pH of 12.5. The acidity or alkalinity of soil matters to plants because it determines which elements and compounds will easily dissolve into soil water so plants can take them up, and which nutrients will remain tightly bound to the soil particles, making them inaccessible to plants.

You might be familiar with this dynamic when it comes to cleaning or getting stains out of clothes. A fabric stain might be stubborn—firmly bound to the fabric—but after treating it with vinegar (acidic) or bleach (alkali), many stains quickly and easily dissolve so they can be washed away. Similarly, different acidity levels in the soil make different elements more or less likely to dissolve into the soil water where roots can take them up. For example, in alkaline soils, iron tends to bind tightly to the soil, so even if there is lots of iron in the soil, plants may be deficient in it. And with acidic soils, sulphur tends to become unavailable, causing a deficiency in plants even though there is plenty of sulphur in the soil.

Sometimes an extremely high or low pH can be harmful to plants by making an element *too* available. Aluminum is a common element that is generally tightly bound to the soil except in very acidic soils. It isn't considered an essential nutrient for plants, but in highly acidic soils, aluminum can become so available that it can block magnesium absorption and cause aluminum toxicity in plants that aren't adapted to those conditions.

Some perennials, such as this *Filipendula*, prefer slightly acidic soils.

Two main factors determine the soil acidity in your area. The first is your type of parent bedrock (aka the source material for your soil). Most rock will break down into fairly neutral or acidic soils, but some, most notably limestone, produce very alkaline soils because of their high levels of calcium.

The Extension Service

Founded in the early 1900s, the Cooperative Extension Service is a government program whose mission is to communicate knowledge of agriculture and gardening from universities to farmers, home gardeners, and everyday citizens. Conduct an internet search for the name of your state and the word "extension" and you'll find online resources, fact sheets, and links to local Extension Service offices in your area. Many states even have helplines to call with gardening questions. Best of all, it is all science-based and funded by tax dollars, so there's quality information relevant to a specific regional growing zone.

Yellow lady's slipper orchids are native to regions with more alkaline soils and are a great choice for gardeners with high pH soils.

What does this mean for your plants? Perennials have adapted to the soil conditions in which they evolved. Most plants native to the rainy woodlands of eastern North America thrive in acidic soils, while most of the plants growing in the arid parts of the West will thrive in more alkaline soils. Most perennials grow just fine in soils close to the neutral part of the pH range, but there are plenty that really demand alkaline conditions and others that demand acidic soils. And, of course, the plants native to your local region will be adapted to the soil pH you naturally have. The good news is that gardeners don't need to change the soil pH in their garden; just choose plants that will thrive in their conditions. Like everything else, an unusual soil pH can seem like a challenge, but it is actually an opportunity. For example, eastern gardeners with limestone bedrock can lean into the often rare and very beautiful native plants that thrive in those conditions, changing out common, white trillium (*Trillium grandiflorum*) for the gorgeous and extremely early flowering, alkaline soil-adapted, snow trillium (*Trillium nivale*), or reveling in the gorgeous native yellow lady's slipper (*Cypripedium parviflorum*), which is adapted to more alkaline soils.

If you have your heart set on growing plants that don't thrive in existing soil pH, it is possible to adjust the soil acidity level. Adding agricultural lime or some other version of crushed limestone to an acidic soil will raise the pH, making it more alkaline, and the effect will last a couple of years. As with all soil adjustments, it is best to do this on a small scale, devoting maybe a bed or section of the garden to plants that like alkaline soil, rather than attempting to remake the soil chemistry of the entire garden. Also, there's the issue of dealing with adjustments that previous gardeners made to the soil's pH, intentionally or not. Limestone gravel, often used in driveways and paths, raises the pH of soil around it, and freshly poured concrete creates alkaline conditions around it, although the effect decreases with time.

The second main factor is rainfall. Water moving through soil, over time, tends to leach away the elements that make the soil alkaline. This results in more and more acidic soils. In general, the rainy climates of eastern North America and the rainy parts of the West Coast have acidic soils—sometimes extremely acidic—with soil conditions getting more and more alkaline moving westward into lower and lower rainfall regions. That is unless, of course, the parent bedrock prevents this from happening. For example, there is a band of limestone bedrock that runs through Ohio, producing a wide swath of alkaline soils in a climate that would otherwise have acidic soil conditions.

If the garden has alkaline soil, it is much more difficult to acidify it, than to make acidic soil more alkaline. Aluminum sulfate can be added to make a soil more acidic, but the effect is fairly short-lived and adding too much can be harmful to plants. If the garden has naturally alkaline soils, gardeners are really better off embracing the existing pH, and if they choose to grow a few prized acid-loving plants, growing them in containers where there's full control of the soil conditions through the use of soil-acidifying fertilizers and amendments.

Sea-side gardens or sidewalk-adjacent plantings regularly treated with salt-based ice-melting products should include salt-tolerant perennials such as (L to R) *Amsonia* and asters, milkweeds, and blanket flowers.

Salinity

Soil salinity is a measure of the salt content of your soil. The most common salt that people think about is table salt, sodium chloride, but there are many different compounds, including most fertilizers, that are salts. Having some salts in the soil is not only fine, it is also necessary for plants to thrive. But too much salt—of any kind, including fertilizers— is harmful or even lethal to plants.

There are three main reasons your plants might be exposed to excessive levels of salt. First, in cold, snowy climates, significant amounts of salt are applied to roads and sidewalks to melt ice, but this is generally not very harmful to perennials; de-icing salt quickly is washed away with snowmelt and other precipitation. Generally, the impact is only harmful if very large amounts of salt are used, or if plants with evergreen foliage are planted close to roads where they are coated with salt spray kicked up by car tires. Gardeners should choose de-icing products made from calcium chloride to apply on icy sidewalks or driveways, as they are less damaging to plants.

Second, if you live by the ocean, there is the issue of salt spray from the waves. Choose plants native to beach-front conditions to avoid salt damage and plant hedges of salt-spray–tolerant plants to help shield the garden from the ocean spray.

The third reason for salt in the soil is a very dry climate. Salts, by definition, dissolve easily in water, so if there is plenty of rainfall, excess salts are washed away. Water that seeps through the soil into the local groundwater or flows overground into waterways carries salt away with it, but water that evaporates leaves all of its salt behind. Dry climates naturally develop salty soils, and plants native to these conditions have developed a tolerance to it. Irrigation can exacerbate the situation. Most irrigation water does evaporate, leaving all the salt behind. Over time, regularly irrigated soils in very dry climates can become very salty, requiring large amounts of water to flush the salt out of the soil. This is one of the many reasons why it is best to limit the amount of irrigation as much as possible, and instead choose plants naturally adapted to the amount of rainfall for the area. Save the use of supplemental irrigation for the occasional times when it is really needed to get through a rare dry spell or to allow a newly planted garden to get established.

New home sites are often stripped of topsoil and compacted by heavy machinery, making gardening a challenge.

With time and the addition of organic matter, disturbed soils can be improved and regenerated.

DISRUPTED SOIL

The soil in your garden has developed over millennia through natural processes such as the slow wearing down of rock, the build-up of organic matter, and the action of communities of fungi and other microorganisms. In most places, the arrival of human agriculture and development has made much more extreme changes that have radically altered the whole makeup of the soil and how plants grow on it.

For most of North America, native soils have been altered at least once by agriculture as saws and plows cleared away native forests and grasslands and replaced them with farm fields. As a result of regular plowing, agriculture can leave excess fertilizer in the soil as well as contribute to the destruction of soil structure and the depletion of organic matter.

More radically for gardeners, however, the process of home construction can have huge impacts on the soil. The heavy machinery used to build a house is particularly damaging to soil. The open spaces between soil particles and aggregates are where plant roots grow, and the weight of heavy machines driving over soil compresses it, reducing or eliminating those open spaces (known as compaction), so water, air, and roots all have difficulty moving through the soil.

House building also requires excavation for the foundation, and in doing this, often the subsoil (the lower layers of soil with minimal, if any, structure or organic matter) is dug out and spread out on top of the upper layer of soil—putting this very infertile, poor soil right at the surface. Even more disruptive still, in newer subdivision areas, all the topsoil from a site is stripped off and sold. The subsoil from digging out foundations is used to level the lawn area, and then a very small amount of topsoil is brought in, just enough to keep new turfgrass alive.

As if that wasn't enough, all the fresh concrete used in foundations, sidewalks, and driveways leaches lime out into the soil, raising its pH.

All of that is to say, though plants native to an area are well adapted to the soils in that area, it's likely the soil around a home is very different from the soil conditions known by those local native plants.

The older a home is, the less likely this will be a problem, both because some of the most destructive practices—like stripping and selling topsoil—have only started in the last couple of decades and because, over time, the soil recovers. The pH effects of new concrete fade within a year, and the other soil attributes will improve and change slowly over time as well. Plants growing and dying add organic matter to the soil, gradually feeding soil fungi, bacteria, and invertebrates—eventually creating a new layer of topsoil and good soil structure. But this process can take years, even decades. Luckily, there are ways to speed that process up and return damaged soil to its natural, healthy state.

The simple act of leaving the leaves on established perennial beds is a great way to naturally return organic matter to the soil. This annual practice is really all that's needed to maintain healthy soil.

IMPROVING YOUR SOIL

Improving soil for a perennial garden is quite different from what the process might look like for a vegetable garden or even for a garden focused on growing mainstream flowering annuals. In both of these cases, the plants have been bred extensively by humans to respond to very rich soil that is high in nutrients and the plants really need the rich soil to thrive. For perennial gardens, it is recommended to choose mostly native plants and those well adapted to the natural conditions—including the soil conditions. Embracing the slower growth of perennial plants is a way to make the garden easier to maintain. The goal is not to have the richest, most fertile soil possible, but to have a healthy soil mimicking what would have been there naturally, before the disruption from agriculture and home construction.

In nature, soil structure and soil health are created and maintained over time as fallen leaves, stems, and faded flowers drop to the ground, break down, and mix into the soil to feed the soil life. If soil is relatively intact and healthy, all that is really needed is to keep it that way by allowing plant material to fall to the ground and compost in place— plus perhaps adding mulch in areas where plants haven't yet filled in to cover the bare soil.

To jump-start the process of reclamation where soil has been degraded, the best move is to spread a layer of compost 1 to 2 inches (2.5–5 cm) deep over the soil surface, then add a thick layer of mulch on top of the compost. The mulch can be shredded leaves, wood chips, or another organic matter. The compost is mostly decomposed already and will be quickly integrated into the soil through the action of soil organisms. The mulch on the soil surface will slowly break down as well. Keep adding mulch to any exposed areas each year and let all the plant material from the perennials stay and decompose in place. This way the natural cycle of organic matter entering the soil will be established, creating healthy conditions for the plants.

If a soil test result shows soil that is extremely low in nutrients, some fertilizer can be added as well. Only do so following the recommendations of a soil test. Fertilization usually only is needed when establishing a new garden to help plants fill in quickly. Once a bed is established, the decomposing organic matter will naturally recycle nutrients back into the soil for use by plants.

Building up a good layer of slowly decomposing organic matter is key if you are gardening under shade trees. As discussed earlier, mycorrhizae form a symbiotic network with roots, and they are particularly important in woodland conditions. Many of the perennials that have evolved to thrive under trees have adapted to plug into that mycorrhizal network and share water and nutrients with the trees above them and other perennials growing around them. But that network depends on a thick layer of organic matter. If fallen leaves have been continually raked away from under your shade trees, you'll have minimal if any mycorrhizae, and woodland perennials may struggle because, instead of sharing water and nutrients with the trees, they're competing with them. Tree roots create very difficult dry shade conditions, but adding organic matter and letting fallen leaves decompose naturally in place, as much as possible, feeds the soil fungi and helps plants in a shade garden thrive.

SUN *Versus* SHADE

ONCE GARDENERS HAVE DETERMINED which plant types are best for their soil conditions, the other main factor that determines plant choices is how much sun the garden receives.

Understanding light levels is critical because plants depend on sunlight as their sole source of energy through the photosynthesis process. If plants don't get enough light, they will not be able to produce enough food to grow and thrive. But too much sunlight can be harmful as well. The heat of the sun speeds up evaporation, drying out plants and exacerbating the effects of drought. Excessive sunlight can also result in sunscald on the foliage.

Plants adapted to full sun conditions can resist and repair damage from high light levels, but those adapted to shade don't have these adaptations and can be seriously harmed by intense, direct sunlight. Plants adapted to live in full shade have leaves capable of harvesting every last bit of sunlight that hits them. They usually have a slower and leggier growth rate than their full-sun relatives because there simply isn't as much energy to be had in the shade as there is in full sun locations.

Plants that evolved to thrive in full sun typically have a more rapid growth rate than their shade-loving cousins.

If a shade-loving plant is growing in too much sun, the effects are usually dramatic and obvious. Upper leaves will burn, showing brown patches on the surface or along the leaf edges. Sometimes this will become most apparent during droughty conditions, or at the height of summer when the days are the longest and hottest.

It is often harder to diagnose a problem with a plant growing in too little light since it mimics fertility deficiencies. A plant in too low light conditions usually has reduced flowering. Since flowering is the prelude to seed production, which is quite energy intensive, and perennial plants have to store up enough energy to grow again the next year, if they aren't getting enough energy from sunlight, they will typically reduce or stop flowering. They will focus instead on growing leaves to harvest more energy from the sun. Perennials grown in less light than they require also tend to grow thin, elongated stems to reach more sunlight (known as *etiolation*), and generally look sparse and thin compared to the denser, more compact growth habit the same perennial would have if grown in more sun.

Some plants have adapted to live in full sun and others in full shade, but individual plants can also change and grow different types of leaves to adjust to the amount of sunlight they are receiving. These two types of leaves are called *sun leaves* and *shade leaves*, and they can be quite different. A plant grown in full sun will produce leaves that are smaller, thicker, tougher, and filled with compounds that help resist and repair damage from ultraviolet light. Move that very same plant into a shaded spot, and it will grow larger, thinner, more delicate leaves. This distinction is important to remember any time a plant is moved from one location to another. If a plant isn't performing well because it is in too much shade, try moving it to a sunnier location. But watch: There may be some burning on the leaves at first until it is able to grow new, sun-adapted leaves. Moving plants during cooler, rainier times of year will help them adapt with fewer transplant shock issues. On the other hand, nurseries usually grow shade plants in as much sun as they can tolerate without burning the foliage because more sun results in faster growth and allows them to get a salable plant faster. This practice also means that these plants will take some time to adjust to the lower-light conditions in a shady home garden.

Plants are sometimes hybridized to tolerate more or less sun than the species naturally requires. An example is coleus, which is typically thought of as a shade plant, but now there are varieties available that will do well in sunnier locations.

Shade gardens offer a diversity of textures and a wealth of interest to the landscape.

It is critically important to know how much light different parts of the garden receive in order to choose plants that will thrive there, but sun and shade can be one of the most frustrating things for beginning gardeners to determine. This is partly because it is difficult to tell how much light there is in a space. The pupils in our eyes automatically adjust to the amount of light coming in to allow us to see a scene clearly, so very different light levels can look similar to us. With time, gardeners get better at telling the differences between different light levels. Remember, struggling plants can always be moved to conditions that suit them better.

The dappled light levels beneath a deciduous tree are different than the solid shade found on the north side of a structure. Pick your plants according to the type of shade you have.

CATEGORIES OF LIGHT

Light levels can be defined according to plant growing conditions. The simplest category is for full sun conditions—a garden space without any shade. Practically, this means at least six hours of direct sun a day hitting that part of the garden. It is not shaded by a tree or house or anything else. Full shade, at the other extreme, is a location under a tree canopy or on the north side of a building where there is no direct sunlight at all.

Those two extremes of light are easy to understand. What is difficult, sometimes, are the fuzzy "part shade" and "part sun" places in between. And frankly, for the in-between light levels, it's a sliding scale, going from just shy of full sun to mostly shade, receiving just an hour or two of sun a day.

The impact of sunlight is also influenced by other factors. If you live in a very sunny climate with few cloudy days, more sunlight will be going to all parts of the garden than somewhere that is frequently cloudy. A spot that is sunny in the morning but shaded in the afternoon will get the same amount of light as a spot that is shaded in the morning and

sunny in the afternoon, but the afternoon sun is hotter and more likely to burn delicate plants than the cooler, morning sun. If your house is painted white, it will reflect a lot of light on the plants around it and produce slightly brighter conditions than if your house is painted a very dark color.

The best way to really understand how much light your garden gets is to look at the plants growing there. Lawn grasses are actually a great way to tell how much light your garden is getting, and for many American landscapes, lawn is the default covering for nongarden areas. In full sun, turfgrass will be very dense and full, growing easily and lushly (if given enough water). In full shade, even the most shade-tolerant turf options will fade out. And in a part shade area, the turf will grow, but it tends to be a bit patchy and thin. Landscapes currently planted with thick, healthy turf can confidently be changed to a full-sun perennial garden. Change turf areas that are thin and patchy to a garden with part-shade perennial plants. And where turfgrass is struggling or nonexistent, change this area to a full-shade garden.

Light levels often change throughout the year, based on the density of the tree canopy and the angle of the sunlight. Plants that evolved in woodland environments are accustomed to such changes.

Shade levels also change through the seasons when the angle of the sun changes. This happens slowly a little every day. Overall, though, most gardens get shadier over time as trees grow and mature, casting more and more shade on the plants below. Eventually trees will succumb and fall, then creating a suddenly sunny site. It is important to keep reevaluating how much sun your plants receive and how they are performing. Sunny plantings that thrived years ago may need to be replaced with shade lovers as trees mature and cast more shade.

Shade in a garden is sometimes seen as a challenge. Thanks to the lower light levels, a shaded garden will grow and mature more slowly than one in full sun, and shady spaces never quite match the flower power of a sunny garden. Generally, a shaded perennial garden focuses more on foliage and texture than a full-sun garden. On the plus side, however, shade gardens are generally far less work to maintain than gardens in the sun. Having an emphasis on slower-growing, foliage plants will result in the garden that will look good every day without any deadheading or pruning (see pages 150 and 154). And if weeding is not a favorite task, build a shade garden, as the weeds will grow much more slowly than in a sunny garden. Shade may be of a particular benefit in our warming climate too. Plants grown with some shade fare better during scorching, foliage-frying heat waves than those growing in full sun.

CHANGING SHADE

Shade levels aren't constant in the garden. The shade produced by deciduous trees is the most dramatic in this regard. The space under a big maple is deep shade in the summer but switches to basically full sun in the winter when there are no leaves on the tree. Many perennials native to deciduous woodlands have evolved to take advantage of this by emerging early in the spring before the tree canopy leafs out, and then going dormant in the summer once the deep shade sets in. These spring ephemerals can be the key to successful perennial gardening under deciduous trees. Evergreen perennials are also great choices for deciduous shade, as they can take advantage of the sunny, winter months.

THE SIZE *of Your* GARDEN

Whether your garden is large or small, a good plan is essential.

This desert garden in the American Southwest is a perfect example of choosing plants appropriate for your garden's size, your climate, and your growing conditions.

SO FAR, THE PHYSICAL conditions in the garden that influence how plants grow have been discussed, as have what general types of plants should be chosen to create a thriving garden. But the size of the space also has a huge impact on what sort of perennial garden should be created. Designing and maintaining a very large, multi-acre garden is very different from maintaining a small, urban plot or tucking a few perennials into the landscape wherever there is room for them.

SMALL GARDEN AREAS

Whether it's a dedicated primula garden, a landscaped area between two shrubs, or a few perennial plants around the house foundation, small garden spaces can be seen as a limitation. But remember, there are huge benefits to caring for a small garden. First, and most obviously, small gardens are easy to maintain, and they are affordable. Every chore, from planting to weeding to deadheading, takes less time when done on a small plot, and the smaller the area, the less it costs to mulch or buy plants to fill the space. That ease and affordability allows you to focus more attention and care on the design and the maintenance of the garden. Small gardens can be perfect little jewel boxes with every detail carefully considered and maintained. Perhaps best of all, the ease of maintenance means there is more time to enjoy a small garden instead of being continually reminded of all the necessary chores. More good news for gardeners working in small spaces—there has been a huge trend in plant breeding recently to select smaller, more compact versions of many plants. These new, smaller selections being developed have very few cons and can allow gardeners to fit more beautiful plants into small, urban gardens. The pros and cons of growing human-made selections of plants (particularly native ones) are discussed in chapter 2.

Large perennial plantings can be real show-stoppers. They are also more costly to install and more time-intensive to care for.

Large, naturalistic gardens like this one mimic natural plant communities. You'll learn more about this planting style in a future chapter.

LARGE GARDEN AREAS

Large gardens offer their own set of opportunities and drawbacks. The upsides to having lots of room to collect beautiful plants and make long, engaging paths through the garden are obvious, but large gardens can be expensive and labor-intensive to maintain. One strategy to use with a large garden space is to designate smaller areas within it to be designed intensively and maintained frequently, and then fill the rest of the area with large, fast-growing plants that cover the soil without requiring a lot of labor and input.

THE TRUTH
Will Set YOU FREE

WHETHER YOU GROW perennials in a large space or a small one, the biggest gardening disappointments are really seen by gardeners who are in denial about their growing conditions. It can be hard, sometimes, to let go of the desire to grow a plant that is not hardy or to give up on trying to recreate a stunning garden that was seen while on vacation—somewhere that gets half as much rain. But if you can clearly understand and accept the physical conditions of your garden, both as limitations and opportunities, you'll be on your way to creating a garden that is easy to look after, beautiful, and truly magical.

CHAPTER 2

YOUR GARDEN
Is an
ECOSYSTEM

Making space for living things, big and small, to thrive

GARDENING, LIKE MUSIC, painting, and dance, is creative, beautiful, and endlessly complex. But unlike all those other art forms, the art that is the garden is created out of—and with the cooperation of—other living things.

This collaboration with other life forms is what makes gardening so exciting and fun—and sometimes, let's be honest, frustrating. A painter never has to give up using a certain color because their winters are too cold, and a pianist doesn't have to try and find an instrument that will thrive in the deep shade of the studio. The occasional obstacles (and challenges) presented by plants are more than forgiven because, as living things, plants do surprise us. Plants grow bigger or smaller than we expect, they seed into a corner of the garden where we never would have thought to plant them, and they weave themselves together into combinations we could never have imagined, much less created. A garden is as much beauty discovered as it is beauty created.

Beyond the Butterflies

There is a concept in conservation known as "charismatic species." These are species like pandas, tigers, and whales—well-known, attractive animals that people are excited about protecting. In the gardening world, "charismatic species" include the likes of monarch butterflies and hummingbirds. But these glamorous, easy-to-love species are just the tip of the iceberg when it comes to the incredible diversity your garden is able to support.

Take, for example, flies. You may think of them as nothing more than pests, but the "annoying" fly species are just a tiny part of an enormously diverse group. Many species of flies are important pollinators, as well as being some of your most reliable helpers when it comes to controlling certain pest insects munching on your plants. Take a closer look at flies, and you'll find many of them are incredibly beautiful—brightly colored, sometimes metallic, and each with a unique and fascinating life cycle and valuable place in the ecosystem of the garden.

"Charismatic species" like butterflies are a great starting point for cultivating a more in-depth interest in the assortment of life in your garden, but stop there, and you'll miss out.

Feather-legged tachinid fly *Trichopoda pennipes* on *Chrysanthemum x rubellum* 'Hillside Sheffield Pink'.

Gardens are collaborative works of art, made in conjunction with creatures great and small. This eastern black swallowtail (*Papilio polyxenes*) caterpillar feeds exclusively on members of the carrot family *Apiaceae*, including this 'Golden Alexanders' plant.

Plants in the garden are just the first layer of life gardeners get to collaborate with. Plants are the basis of a whole ecosystem. Caterpillars feed on the leaves, and then songbirds catch those caterpillars and feed them to their babies. All of these living things work together to create the whole experience of the garden. There's nothing like the feeling of walking out the door, hearing bird song, and seeing butterflies, dragonflies, and bees going about their business—knowing the role the garden plays in supporting all of it. The garden is a whole ecosystem; one that the gardener can support, care for, and enrich through the types of plants chosen and the ways they are maintained.

There are a lot of ways to think about the insects and other animals living in the garden. The old view was to consider them problems to be eliminated. "Bugs" on your plants were to be sprayed with insecticides to ensure no leaves were nibbled. Gardeners today are not so quick to grab the spray bottle, as we know more about the damage that the reckless use of pesticides does to the environment. Still, sometimes gardening with a sensitivity to the environment is seen as an onerous responsibility. A chore. A tiresome list of plants we can't grow, chemicals we can't spray, and annoyances we have to tolerate.

The truth could hardly be more different. Only thinking about the *plants* in your garden means missing out on half of the beauty and joy a garden space brings. Few need to be convinced that having butterflies and songbirds in the garden is a wonderful thing, but these friends are just the beginning. The more you garden—and the more time

Think of the insects and other wild creatures living in your garden as partners in your efforts to create a harmonious, life-filled garden welcoming to all.

Whether they are charismatic butterflies or homely worms, all the creatures in your garden have an important role to play in its ecosystem.

you spend looking at *all* the things living in the little bit of paradise you've created, the more blown away you'll be by the beauty. Perhaps it's a tiny, brilliant metallic green, stingless wasp gathering nectar and pollen from a flower to feed its young. Or perhaps there's a hosta leaf with near-surgically precise circles cut out of it—the work of a female leaf-cutter bee lining a nesting chamber for her brood. Even aphids—annoying as they are—will, if you leave them be, shortly become food for glossy ladybugs or aptly named lacewings.

Another great part about gardening with thoughts focused on the larger environment is that this is a space where gardeners have some level of control and can make a real, significant difference. Every day we get up and see news reports on problems that are huge and terrifying, feeling wildly beyond our ability as individuals to do anything about them. We can all do our part, trying to reduce the pollution we put in the atmosphere and the trash we put in our landfills, but so many of the world's problems are simply beyond the ability of any one human to fix. It is easy to feel helpless about how to make the world a better place.

But gardeners can, today, quite simply and easily, transform a garden, a backyard, even an apartment balcony, into a vibrant, safe, healthy ecosystem full of interesting, beautiful, and often threatened species. Tigers and whales need huge swaths of land or water to be preserved, but insects are small, and a garden, no matter how tiny, is all they need to thrive.

And the impact made by one garden is huge. How many species do you think live in your garden? Probably way more than you think. In 2020, three researchers spent a year documenting every species they found on the small—one-tenth of an acre (0.04 ha)—lot around their home in Brisbane, Australia. By the end of the year, they had documented 1,168 different species of plants, animals, and fungi (not to mention all the species in the soil they were not able to assess). Most people do not have the expertise to successfully find and identify everything living in their garden, but there is a similar enormous diversity of living things around each of us. By taking some simple actions with the design of a garden, we can help these species thrive and allow more and more species to find refuge in the garden. These steps aren't hard or complex. In fact, most of what is needed involves the cessation of harmful things. Researchers in Michigan showed just how easy creating a good habitat for native insects can be in a study looking at bumblebee diversity across the state. Unexpectedly, they found that the city of Detroit—thanks to vacant lots which were infrequently mowed and weren't being sprayed with any pesticides—had bumblebee numbers that were nearly the same as a carefully protected nature preserve. Of course, the garden shouldn't look like an overgrown vacant lot, but luckily making a beautiful garden and making a thriving habitat can go hand in hand. Here are the steps to take to get nature preserve–level diversity in the garden, while still keeping it beautiful and welcoming for human visitors.

DON'T *Poison* THINGS

Aesthetic damage, such as this marred foliage created by a columbine leaf miner, does not disrupt plant health in an impactful way. It is very unusual for a pest insect to kill its host plant outright. In most cases the plant will bounce back the following season.

ONE OF THE MOST IMPORTANT—and easiest—ways to make the garden a great home for all sorts of life is to refuse to use pesticides. The instinct to reach for a spray bottle when something is munching on our plants can be hard to break, but using chemicals to kill off those thought-to-be pest insects collapses the whole ecosystem. Plants, via photosynthesis, are the only things in the garden that actually produce food. Everything else is either eating plants or eating things that eat plants. To create the most vibrant garden possible, insects must be seen using and feeding on plants, and they can't do that if they keep getting wiped out with insecticides.

A key point here is that, when it comes to perennial gardening, this applies to *any* insecticide. Organic insecticides—those made from natural products—and synthetic insecticides—those made in a lab—both kill insects. Organic pesticides are often (but not always) less toxic to humans, and have less chance of persisting in the environment, but any product designed to kill insects is undermining, not helping, the garden's ecosystem.

This doesn't, however, mean that gardeners have to accept hungry insects eating the garden down to shreds. Once there is a healthy ecosystem established in the garden, the problematic insects will almost always be kept in check by all the other insects and birds eating them. If gardeners are used to using pesticides in the garden, there may be an adjustment period as natural predators move in, but with patience, insect pest problems fade away. There'll be a little more in chapter 6 about how to deal with the rare cases where a pest population becomes a major problem—usually because they are a non-native species without natural predators to control them—but in general, all that's needed is to learn to accept those holes in a few leaves as a sign of a healthy, biodiverse garden and wait for nature to keep itself in check.

PROVIDE FOOD

PLANTS ARE THE BASIS of almost every food chain, so perennials added to the garden will be the ultimate source of food for everything that comes to make its home there. Insects and other organisms feed on plants in several ways.

HERBIVORES

Herbivores are the garden residents that can be the hardest to accept. These are the ones who eat holes in the leaves of your favorite rudbeckia or collect on the stems of your beautiful milkweeds while sucking sugars out of the plant sap. Herbivorous insects that eat our plants are the ones most likely to be labeled as pests. But these insects are arguably the most important to the ecosystem of the garden. Besides the fact that annoying leaf-munching caterpillars often mature into beautiful butterflies and moths, these hungry insects are the basis of a food chain, supporting other insects and our many threatened songbirds. Sometimes herbivorous species can get out of hand and cause problems (chapter 6 has information on how to stop this from happening), but most of the time the right course of action is to just let them be and accept that a few ragged leaves are the price to pay for a garden full of butterflies and songbirds.

DETRITIVORES

Living mostly in the soil, there are a whole host of organisms that feed on dead plant material—the fallen leaves, stems, and flowers that drop to the ground as plants go through their life cycle. There's more about this in chapter 6, but remembering that countless worms, beetles, nematodes, bacteria, and fungi all live on dead plant material means that leaving those materials in place to decompose naturally, whenever possible, is a great way to feed the life in your soil and garden. This is a win-win situation. These detritivores don't harm plants, and as they break down plant material, they release nutrients back into the soil for plants to use again. These little organisms are the unsung—and usually unseen—heroes of the garden, critically important to the creation of healthy soil and a well-functioning ecosystem. Because they usually operate out of sight and rarely have the bright colors enjoyed so much in butterflies, it is easy to overlook this group of organisms, but it's important to not forget about them. The larvae of many species of fireflies, for example, feed almost entirely on the detritus-eating creatures living in your garden and soil. So, losing these unseen soil organisms also means losing the magical glowing lights of a summer evening.

While this caterpillar might look scary, soon enough it will turn into a Gulf fritillary butterfly. Ignore the temporary damage to its host plant (passionvine) and the ecosystem will be for the better.

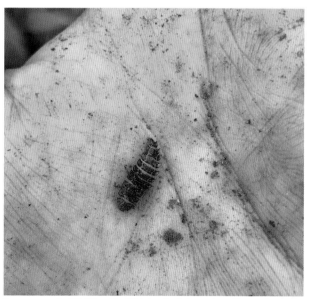

Do you recognize this little critter? This is a firefly larva whose diet consists almost exclusively of the tiny critters who feed on decaying organic matter in the soil (the detritivores).

There is room for pollinator-friendly perennial plantings just about anywhere!

POLLINATORS

Pollinators are the insects easiest to love. Everyone delights in the range of species that feed on the nectar or pollen produced by plant flowers. Pollinators help, rather than hurt, plants and are also critical to a large sector of agricultural systems that produce our food. Often we think of bees when talking about pollinators, but they are just the tip of the proverbial iceberg. Thousands of species of insects, from wasps to flies to beetles (along with a handful of bird and bat species), visit flowers to feed. It is also important to realize that very few pollinators live *only* on nectar or pollen through all stages of their lifecycle. Most of them rely on other sources of food while young and growing, and then just use nectar as a quick energy source as an adult. Many pollinating wasps feed on other insects early in their life cycle and butterflies and moths munch on leaves when in their caterpillar phase. Even hummingbirds, beloved pollinators and sippers of nectars, actually consume insects as a large part of their diet. This is why it isn't enough to just make a pollinator garden with some pretty flowers in it. Everything is interconnected. So it is important to keep all parts of the local ecosystem thriving to support pollinators, and, as a bonus, since so many pollinators also eat other insects at some stage in their life, supporting pollinators means supporting natural pest control as well.

The most famous pollinators of all are the honey bees. And while they are beautiful and fascinating insects (and very important to our agricultural system), honey bees are native to Africa, Asia, and Europe, and were introduced to North America by European settlers. So, while gardeners may want to keep a hive of honey bees in the garden to produce honey or aid in pollination, these bees are not part of our native ecosystem here in North America, and shouldn't take priority over supporting the many native bees and other pollinators.

Some gardeners fear painful stings when they hear about bees and wasps being attracted to their flowers, but stinging is very rarely a problem with native bee species. The vast majority of bees and wasps have no stingers, and the ones that do generally only sting when they are stepped on or otherwise threatened. The most aggressive members of the bee and wasp family are species like yellow jackets, which feed primarily on other insects, not nectar.

EMBRACE DIVERSITY

NUMEROUS STUDIES of insect populations in various gardens and landscapes have found that a diversity of plants is the *most* important factor in supporting a diversity of insects. Every different plant has a different relationship with the other things living in your garden. Monarch butterflies, famously, depend entirely on plants in the milkweed genus (*Asclepias*) to feed their caterpillars. This kind of close plant-to-insect relationship is not at all unusual. There are salvia bees that only feed on the flowers of *Salvia azurea*, a plant native to the Great Plains (shown on the book's front cover with a monarch butterfly). Endangered Karner blue butterflies have caterpillars that can only successfully develop on one species of lupine, and so on. And there are many other insects that need multiple types of plants to complete their life cycle: one to feed on when immature, another to provide nectar as an adult, and still a third with the right sort of hollow stems to hide in while hibernating through the winter. A diversity of plants creates a diversity of insects, which creates a robust, vibrant ecosystem. So rather than filling the whole garden with just a few types of plants, bring in a plethora of species.

For pollinators, maximize the diversity of shapes, colors, and bloom times of the flowers in the garden. Make sure there are flowers blooming from early spring right into late fall—and even through the winter in mild climates. This ensures pollinators always have enough to eat. The colors and shapes of flowers have evolved to cater to the preferences of different pollinators. Narrow-throated red flowers are generally pollinated by hummingbirds, wide-mouthed purple or pink flowers often cater to bees, wide-open umbels are beloved by pollinating wasps and flies, and large, white, nocturnal blooms are often the favored domain of moths. These long-evolved insect and plant relationships can be fascinating to learn about, but it isn't expected to have to know exactly what sort of pollinator visits which sort of flower in order to support a range of them. Simply fill the garden with as many different bloom shapes and colors as possible, and this will ensure a wide swath of insects have somewhere to feed.

Choose a diversity of flower colors, shapes, sizes, and structures to appeal to the broadest range of pollinators.

This little wool carder bee enjoys feeding on the hooded blooms of downy skullcap.

EMBRACE NATIVES

To create an ecologically sound and resilient garden, include as many regionally native plants as possible. Aim for a minimum of 70 percent native species.

Mixing perennial grasses in with forbs (flowering plants) is a great way to add more native species to your perennial garden.

BESIDES EMBRACING POLLINATORS, the other key concept in making the garden a good habitat is to grow primarily native plants. The reasoning behind this is pretty simple: The insects and other organisms in your area have evolved over centuries to live with the plants that are native to your area. So, when you grow native plants, they support native insects, which support native birds, and you recreate something like the ecosystem that would have existed in your area before it was disrupted to build roads and homes.

This does not mean, however, that to be an ecologically ethical gardener you have to recreate the exact mix of plants that were on the land before some point in history. In fact, this is often not going to be possible. As discussed in the last chapter, the act of building homes and communities has changed the local environment, altering the soil, creating new microclimates and new patterns of drainage. To garden successfully and create a thriving ecosystem, you have to adapt to the conditions that you have now, not what they were in the past. This is a reality that will only grow more intense as climate change progresses.

The other reality is that just because a plant is not native to an area doesn't necessarily mean it is harmful. As long as plants aren't invasive (a concept coming up shortly), species that originate in other parts of the world can be great components of a garden's ecosystem, and many of them will, in fact, provide food and shelter for a range of native insects. Research into the types of landscapes and gardens that support the most vibrant ecosystems has found that having about 70 percent native plants is the key threshold to reach to ensure the creation of a vibrant ecosystem. This figure is 70 percent of the plant mass in the garden, not 70 percent of the number of species. One large tree over a shaded perennial garden may be counted as half of the plant mass in the garden. It's difficult to measure the total plant mass in the garden in a precise way anyway, but the 70 percent threshold is a good rule of thumb and starting point. Using the 70 percent native plant rule also leaves plenty of room to keep some beloved plants originating from Europe or Asia in the garden too. Just make sure the priority is for beautiful plants that are native to your part of the world.

If you are looking at your landscape and wanting to move to a more native-centered garden, remember that any plant is a better habitat than no plants at all. So it is far better to start by adding natives, or slowly replacing non-native species with native plants, rather than ripping everything out and starting fresh.

WHAT IS NATIVE?

Native may seem like a simple word, but it is actually a bit hard to pin down an exact definition of it. This book is written for North American gardeners, so in the plant profiles, plants are marked as native if they originate in North America. But those gardening on the East Coast are in a radically different climate and ecosystem then those on the West Coast. As we get more precise looking at where plants grow and breaking habitats down by region or state, it can be harder to draw clear lines. Plants don't respect the artificial boundaries and categories that have been put on the world, and as climates change—and have changed in the past—plants migrate and move to new habitats. If gardeners are lucky, there may be a nursery in the area that specializes in growing plants that are local ecotypes—those propagated from seeds collected right in the local area. This is a fantastic option if you can find them, as these plants should be best adapted to your local soil and climate. However, just because a plant's historic range doesn't overlap with your precise location does not mean it won't be a wonderful addition to the garden and a great support to local pollinators and other wildlife. Any species native to your general region of the country can be counted as native in terms of its support for the local ecosystem, but species native to the opposite coast—while still beautiful and worth growing—should be limited to 30 percent or less of the plant mass in your garden.

The other question around natives involves those that are sometimes called *nativars*—selected varieties of native plants as opposed to what is called the "wild type" or "straight species." This can be confusing, involving a lot of grey areas and vague terminology, so let's walk through an example with one particular plant.

Don't Overlook Regional Natives

When creating a garden, it can be fun to collect the rarest, most unusual plants. There is real pleasure in having something blooming that no one else you know has even seen. And often it feels like all the rare and exciting plants come from some distant land, collected on the slopes of a Chinese mountain or native to the Australian outback. Certainly, these exotic plants can be fun to collect and, in moderation, can be great additions to the garden, but don't let the thrill of the exotic make you blind to the incredibly beautiful—and often under-appreciated—plants native to your own part of the world.

Take, for example, the genus *Trillium*. If you live in the eastern half of North America, trilliums are a pretty common wildflower in woodland areas. The name trillium refers to the fact that every part of this plant comes in threes. It has three leaves (technically leaf-like bracts) arranged around the stem, and above it there is a flower with three green sepals and three showy petals. The great white trillium (*Trillium grandiflorum*) is one of the most common, with huge white (or occasionally pink) blooms, but there are thirty-eight species of trilliums native to North America ranging from the tiny snow trillium (*Trillium nivale*), only about 3 inches (7.6 cm) or so tall, to species like little sweet Betsy (*Trillium cuneatum*), which has leaves beautifully patterned with silver.

In Europe, these American natives are treasured as rare, collectable exotics, but somehow, they rarely get that same attention in their homeland. If you have the urge to collect rare plants, don't forget the wonderful ones close to home—a woodland garden full of trillium would be a beautiful and very special garden indeed.

The difference in the ecological value of a straight species and a cultivated variety (cultivar) of that same species is much debated. Do your research and find what feels right to you. Coreopsis is one of many North American native plants with dozens of different cultivars available on the market.

Cultivars of North American native plants bred for a more compact growth habit are quite common these days. This gardener has opted to include compact varieties of coneflower and bee balm in their front garden.

The purple cone flower, *Echinacea purpurea*, is a wonderful perennial native to much of the eastern half of North America. As mentioned, people often use the terms "straight species" or "wild type" to refer to the sort of average appearance of this plant as found in the wild. But no plant comes in just one form. If you look at a wild field of purple coneflowers, you'll see some with darker pink flowers, some lighter pink or even white, some with bigger blooms, some with smaller blooms, taller plants, and shorter plants. And plants from the northern end of its native range up in Wisconsin have excellent tolerance for extreme cold, while those populations down in Louisiana will be the most heat-tolerant. Which is all to say that "straight species" is a bit of a myth. Every plant you buy labeled purple coneflower is a particular selection of unique genetics based on what population was the original source of the seeds. Remember, the best plants adapted to your local climate will be from populations originating closest to where you garden.

Gardeners and nursery people often look through the diversity they find in wild plant populations and pick out the forms they like best. These might be individuals with larger flowers, more compact growth habits, or brighter colors. Gardeners carefully propagate those individuals and give them names like 'Ruby Giant'. These plants are then called *cultivars*—short for cultivated varieties—but they may be very similar to plants you can find in wild populations.

The more popular a plant gets and the more nurseries grow them, the more plant propagators look for better selections, and plant breeding takes place. With echinaceas, nurseries discovered chance mutations that produced extra showy petals with double-flowered forms. They also hybridized a species with yellow flowers, *Echinacea paradoxa*, with the pink species, to produce forms that have bright red, orange, and yellow blooms. These selections are also cultivars, but are much farther removed from what you might find in a wild population.

So, do these new hybrids "count" as native plants? The latest bright-orange, double-flowered echinacea hybrid is derived exclusively from plants native to eastern North America, but the form and look of the plant has been radically altered by humans.

This bumblebee is enjoying nectar from a coneflower cultivar, oblivious to whether the variety is a natural mutation or one created by humans.

Luckily, there has been some research on this. Some of the traits that we humans like to select for in cultivated varieties do make them neutral or advantageous to insects, showing that they might use those plants as food. Generally, plant breeders select for rapid, vigorous growth and abundant flowering, which are win-win attributes for both humans and insects. Plants with shorter, more compact growth habits are very useful for smaller, urban gardens, and these are just as good for wildlife as the taller selections. However, when plant breeding done by humans radically changes the color or form of a flower, it can make the flowers less attractive to pollinators. Double forms of flowers—mutations that produce extra layers of petals—in particular can render a flower essentially useless for pollinators. Changes in flower color will also often make a bloom less attractive to pollinators, though not always. Similarly, changes to foliage color—be it variegated forms or varieties with darker purple foliage—may change both how attractive and nutritious the foliage is to feeding caterpillars.

The upshot of all this is that cultivated selections of native plants can be used in the perennial garden and this will still create an excellent habitat for the garden ecosystem. Try, though, to stick to varieties with blooms and leaves with a color and shape that is pretty similar to the forms found in the wild species. Gardeners can certainly still enjoy a bright, double-flowered hybrid in the garden—the foliage will still feed caterpillars just as well as the single-flowered forms—but these hybrids are best counted in the 30 percent or less group of non-native plants in the garden.

OUTSIDE *Your* GARDEN

The red lily beetle is a destructive invasive pest native to parts of Europe and Asia. It's impact here in North America is still unfolding.

SO FAR, THE DISCUSSION has been about how to make the space within a garden a better habitat and a more vibrant, healthy ecosystem. There are choices, though, that gardeners make in the garden that do spill out and impact the world around as well. Every ecosystem in the world is interconnected, and some simple choices can help make sure your little garden ecosystem is a positive force for the larger biosphere of our planet.

INVASIVE SPECIES

The word *invasive* can be confusing in its use sometimes, as some gardeners will use that word to describe a plant that spreads aggressively within their garden, whether it is native or exotic. The ecological concept of invasiveness refers to how species behave in wild areas, not within gardens. An exotic invasive species is one that is not native to a region and can readily move out into natural areas and begin reproducing there, out-competing or otherwise negatively impacting native species.

The most serious exotic invasive species for gardeners are insects and diseases, things like chestnut blight, emerald ash borer, and Dutch elm disease, which have driven native species of trees to near extinction and completely remade huge swaths of our native forests. Some of these exotic invasive pests and diseases were first imported into the country on infested nursery stock. Today, the USDA has a protocol of inspections for plant material entering the country to ensure it is not carrying any disruptive hitchhikers. As gardeners, be sure to respect that process and never bring home any kind of plant material from trips overseas without getting it properly inspected.

Sometimes plant species will jump the garden fence, spreading into natural areas. Luckily, these plants don't have nearly the same consequences as the invasive diseases and exotic insect pests, but garden-escaping plants can still outcompete native species and alter natural ecosystems. Our responsibility as gardeners is to avoid growing invasive plant species so that our gardens aren't the source of seeds that are spreading out into new areas. Remember that invasiveness is all about what a species does outside of the garden, not in it—so don't use how it performs in the garden as a gauge of how invasive it is. Some species may well seed around in your garden easily but never succeed in spreading beyond to a natural area, and there are many plants that appear to be perfectly well-behaved in the garden while popping up in natural areas from seeds carried by birds or the wind. Luckily, there are experts monitoring non-native species in each state, and creating lists of invasive species. A quick search online will turn up lists of species known to be invasive in your state. Don't plant anything on that invasive plant list in your garden and remember to eliminate any invasive exotic species that may have been planted by previous occupants too. The list of wonderful native, and noninvasive, non-native, plants is long, so there is really no need to indulge in any plants that might be harmful to the natural world around you.

LIGHT POLLUTION

Lighting in the landscape can be beautiful and of course practical. Lighting along walkways is a safety requirement if people are going to be out in the garden when the sun isn't up. Adding illumination to favorite plants or around seating areas extends the time everyone can enjoy the garden well into the evening, which is a huge boon for those who have to spend most of the daylight hours in an office working.

However, the artificial lights surrounding our home and gardens can have negative impacts on the other living things that share our space. Night-flying insects including fireflies, lacewings, and many moths, as well as migrating birds, use the light of the moon and stars to successfully navigate, and artificial lights can confuse them. Very bright lights can even confuse plants. Many fall-flowering perennials, like chrysanthemums, use the length of the night as a signal to know when to flower. Bright lights shining on plants can delay the flowering of these perennials and stop some deciduous trees from changing leaf color on time, putting them at risk of damage from early fall frosts.

There are a few ways you can get the benefits of lighting in your garden while minimizing the harm it does. All light should be shielded, meaning installed with reflective shades around the light source ensuring that all the light goes down to the ground—where it can help you walk safely—and minimizing the amount that shines up into the sky—where it can confuse birds and insects.

There is no reason to have a back path lit up all night while everyone is asleep, so use timers or motion sensors to ensure lights only turn on when they are needed. This simple addition to a lighting system will have the added bonus of saving money on your energy bill. Along the same lines, use the lowest brightness possible on outdoor lights. Even a dim light can safely mark a walkway.

Finally, try to choose bulbs with a "warm" (more yellowish) light rather than those with a "cool" (more blue) light. Light on the bluer end of the spectrum has more energy in it than light at the yellow and red end, and that higher energy level makes that bluer light more able to bounce off surfaces in the garden and reflect up into the sky.

If you are using light in the garden purely for aesthetic effect, focus again on using the lowest amount possible. Big floodlights shining up into trees can have a beautiful effect, but floodlights are far more disruptive to wildlife than a romantic string of tiny, twinkle lights.

CARBON FOOTPRINT

Healthy soils planted with perennials sequester carbon— this is a good thing, and gardeners can help soils sequester carbon even better by thinking about what is being added to the garden. Whenever possible, get compost and mulch from local sources rather than shipped long distances in plastic bags from a big box store. Better yet, if neighbors rake their leaves, go grab a few bags from the curb to shred and use as mulch rather than buying anything at all.

Shopping at local nurseries that grow their own plants on site (or locally) rather than having plants shipped in from large, out-of-state wholesale growers can also reduce the amount of fossil fuels involved in getting plants to your garden. Also, do ask your local nursery growers if they have a program to reuse old nursery pots. Plastic nursery pots—like most plastic items—are very difficult to recycle effectively, but some nurseries will wash and reuse them.

Learning to propagate your own plants (covered in chapter 4) is the ultimate way to get your plants locally. By learning the simple art of starting perennial seeds outdoors, you can get new plants with essentially no carbon footprint at all. Be sure to propagate some extras to share with friends so you can start improving the ecosystem of your whole neighborhood.

Limit light pollution by ensuring all outdoor lights have a downward-facing shade to target light onto walkways and seating areas rather than shining it upwards.

OTHER HUMANS

SOMETIMES THE BIGGEST barriers to transforming gardens into vibrant ecosystems are the other humans that live around us. In North America, the idea that a front yard has to be neatly mown grass is so deeply ingrained that sometimes cities or homeowners' associations (HOAs) have prohibited ripping out a lawn and putting in a native meadow.

Quite simply, the best way to avoid those problems is to make sure your perennial garden is both a great habitat for wildlife and beautiful to look at. And you can absolutely do both of those things at once. There's more about that in the next chapter. You can make any style of garden—even a very formal, tidy-looking one—into a great, vibrant ecosystem by choosing mostly native plants and avoiding pesticides. In fact, making a beautiful garden may be the best way to get other people in your community gardening

the same way. There is a misconception that an ecologically sensitive garden of native plants has to look wild or unkept, and that understandably turns many people off. Showing your neighbors how wrong that belief is with your beautiful landscape is doing great work for the natural world.

You can also win people over to your garden style and philosophy by sharing the wonderful things with them that are happening there. If your garden is where people will be walking past, small signs pointing out which butterflies use which plants as hosts can help others see the garden in a new light. Most neighborhoods also have community groups on social media where you can share pictures of the beautiful butterflies and other insects that visit the garden. Simply share the beauty, joy, and fun of living in a vibrant garden ecosystem, and others will want to enjoy it too.

Make your garden both ecologically vibrant and beautiful to look at and you're less likely to have problems with neighbors or HOAs. Keep the edges mown and post a "Pollinators Welcome" sign to artfully inform neighbors of your garden's purpose.

CELEBRATE THE LIFE
in Your GARDEN

THE LAST—AND MAYBE most important—thing you should be doing to make a garden a vibrant ecosystem is to spend time just observing all the insects and other organisms in your garden and learning as much as you can about them. The more we know about what lives in our gardens, the more beautiful, interesting, and precious they become. Get a field guide for insects native to your area. Go on a guided nature walk at a local park. Join groups on social media devoted to the love of native insects, share photos, and learn from the other members. Take pictures of every pollinator that visits your flowers and see how many of these species you can identify and put on your list. In doing this, the annoying "bugs" in your garden will become hover flies and parasitic wasps and butterfly caterpillars—each one with an amazing story and place in the world. The more you know about them, the more you'll enjoy them, and the more beautiful your garden will become.

Finding the joy and beauty in this process is key. Sometimes always trying to do the right thing in the garden can be paralyzing. Can we accept that a plant's wild range is close enough to our garden to really be native? Has a selected form of a perennial plant been modified too much to really serve pollinators? Will that last peony addition push the garden mass below the 70 percent native plant mark? In trying to create a vibrant ecosystem, don't let perfection stop you from doing good. It can be all too easy to feel like we're always making some mistake and falling short of some ideal. The truth is that gardening—even imperfect gardening—is good for the environment. A perennial bed full of beautiful flowers is a feast for pollinators and other insects even if it consists primarily of non-native species. Every bit of lawn transformed into a garden is doing good in the world. Every neighbor who sees your lovely garden and gets inspired to do some gardening themselves is spreading that good a little more. So, enjoy the garden and enjoy the beauty and life it supports. This chapter is not a list of ecological sins to avoid, but rather a guide to how you can make the good your garden does even better.

Visit public plantings and botanic gardens for inspiration, or maybe take a class and learn to identify not only the plants there, but also the insects you find visiting them.

Enjoy your garden not only for the beauty it provides, but also for the life it supports.

CHAPTER 3

FINDING *Your* GARDEN STYLE

Tools and tips for making a beautifully designed garden

DESIGNING A BEAUTIFUL garden seems like it should be pretty simple—put a bunch of beautiful plants together and it has to look good, right? Beautiful plants will never be ugly, but with careful and thoughtful design, a garden can be far more than the sum of its parts, the individual plants coming together to create a really breathtaking whole picture. There is no simple formula to making a great garden design, because, like any art form, garden design is very subjective and personal. Your favorite garden may be one that someone else may dislike. The goal of this chapter isn't to tell how to design your garden or give specific rules to follow, but rather to give some tools to think about what sort of garden you want to have, and the tools you'll need to create that garden space.

THE PRINCIPLES *of* GARDEN DESIGN

THE FIRST STEP to understanding what you want in a garden is to have the language to talk about what you are seeing when you look at a garden you love or hate. Understanding these principles can help you move from just "I like that" to "I like that *because* . . . " Once you know why you love a garden, you can start creating the garden you love of your own.

Color palettes can help unify a garden and create a cohesive design.

Harmonious color schemes, such as this one, often yield a calming, organized effect, even when the colors are bright.

CONTRAST AND HARMONY

The concept of balancing contrast and harmony in a garden is central to all the other principles discussed in this chapter. An overly harmonious garden is one that is boring. Just one or two plants used the same way over and over again makes a garden uninteresting. The quintessential overly harmonious garden is found around houses in a newly built subdivision. All the houses look pretty much the same, and they all have the same lawns, the same beds around the house, and are planted with the same few plant species. The landscaping is boring and sterile and needs something to liven it up, creating some interest to set each house apart from the neighbors. The other extreme, too much contrast, is a garden where every single plant is different, all blooming in different colors, accented by a collection of garden art in every possible style. Gardens like this can feel like a random mess with nothing to unify it or give it a calming sense of the whole.

The perfect middle road between the two extremes is different for every person, some liking the energy of a high-contrast design, and others preferring the calm intentionality of a strong harmony. Only you can decide where your personal tastes lie, and remember, your taste can change in different parts of the garden—a quiet reading and sitting nook might call for more harmony than a planting around the patio where you entertain your friends.

This principle plays out in all of the other design principles to follow, so there will be more discussion as the chapter moves forward. When evaluating your own garden to see what works, or visiting other gardens for ideas, keep asking yourself if what you are seeing seems boring, chaotic, or right in the sweet spot in between the two extremes.

COLOR

Some people have a natural eye for colors and how to combine them in an interesting and beautiful way. If you are someone who loves picking out paint and fabric colors to pull a living room together or gets a thrill out of putting together a great outfit, you'll probably dive into selecting the color palette of your garden with ease and pleasure. But if handling color doesn't come naturally, or if you always find yourself looking at your garden and wondering why it doesn't quite look right, here are some tips to help create beautiful and harmonious color schemes.

Color is the place where most gardeners inadvertently stray too far away from harmony. While it is possible to combine every color into a single garden bed and have it look good, it takes special skill and an excellent eye to make it happen. If you are unsure of using color, the easiest way to make

Color palette inspiration can come from anywhere. This piece of illustrated art translated into a great color scheme for the garden in the photo at right.

The warm oranges, peaches, and yellows of the illustration are accentuated by different shades of blues in the resulting garden.

your perennial bed look unified and appealing is to limit the colors you use. At the most extreme, limit a bed to just one flower color or perhaps just a couple. A garden of all-white flowers is serene and elegant. Add in some blue, and it will be harmonious but a little more dynamic. If you have trouble saying no, you might just eliminate one color from a planting—this bed will have no yellow!—and that step alone can bring unity and a sense of structure to a design. Creating a strongly harmonious color scheme can really allow gardeners to play with contrast elsewhere in the garden design without it ever feeling too chaotic.

Choosing a color scheme is often the easy part. The hard part is sticking to that color scheme when you go to the nursery and fall in love with a beautiful plant that's exactly the shade of yellow you just decided to avoid. Don't give in! One plant ill-fitted to an otherwise well-planned color scheme sticks out like a sore thumb. One trick to avoid this problem is to choose different color schemes for different parts of the garden and make sure every color has a place. Maybe the front garden is all hot colors—yellow, orange, and red—while the back garden gets the cool pinks, blues, purples, and whites. This way every impulse purchase has somewhere to go, no matter what color it is.

Choose color schemes made up of similar colors, like blues and purples, or contrasting colors, like blue and yellow. Either one can look beautiful, but contrasting colors tend to feel dynamic and energetic, while putting similar colors together creates a soothing, calm effect. Often the best results come from using mostly similar colors, but then choosing one contrasting color to sprinkle around. A bed of yellows and oranges looks all the brighter with a few purple flowers weaving through it.

Different colors have different effects on people as well. Red, yellow, and orange are called *hot colors*, and they tend to give us a feeling of more energy and excitement. They can appear to be closer to us than they actually are in the garden. There is a reason yellow and orange are used for safety vests—they are colors that catch the eye. Cool colors—blues and purples—have the opposite effect, seeming calmer, more relaxed, and sometimes appearing to fade into the distance. Which you prefer is all about personal taste, but you can also choose colors to achieve different effects. If there is a part of the garden with a hammock where you want to lay back, read, and relax, choosing cool, harmonious colors will amplify that restful, relaxing energy. A deck where you want to cook out and have fun gatherings with friends will feel even more energetic and fun when it is surrounded by hot colors.

Texture plays an important role in garden design. This garden combines the soft texture of grasses with the coarser texture of large-leaved plants and a broad diversity of flower shapes.

The upright, rigid leaves of this variegated yucca create an eye-catching form that contrasts with the mounded form of the coreopsis in front of it.

TEXTURE

Flower color catches our eyes and is often the first thing we notice in a garden, but there are other factors that go into making a combination of plants visually pleasing. Paying attention to these less obvious factors is often the secret magic to elevate an okay garden design to something spectacular.

Texture refers to the size of leaves and stems, and, to some degree, flowers. Very large leaves have a texture, while the small leaves of a fern or ornamental grass have a fine texture. With color, it is easy to get too chaotic and have too many different things going on. With texture, the biggest problem is usually the opposite. It is easy to buy plants based on their pretty flowers, and then end up with a garden where nearly everything has the same leaf size and shape. If the garden is looking flat and boring, step back and see if there are any big, bold leaves. Mixing in just a few bold textures can give the garden more energy and excitement. And positioning the boldest leaves right next to the finest, most delicate foliage can emphasize and pump up that contrast even more.

FORM

Much like texture, variation in form—the shape of plants—is a great way to keep a garden looking exciting and dynamic. Unfortunately, it is very easy to overlook the form of a garden. Form can vary from low groundcovers and more rounded plants to those with a narrow, upright columnar form or a vase shape. The easiest mistake when it comes to choosing plant forms is to get too many plants with a small, rounded shape. These tidy, compact mounds look very appealing and beautiful when growing in a pot by themselves, so they always look fantastic at the nursery. (When a plant looks good on a nursery bench, it tends to jump into our cart and come home with us!) However, if just rounded plant forms are used, the garden can turn into a sea of little bowling balls that all look the same. Taller, narrower growth habits and vase-shaped forms can look a little odd and top-heavy in a pot at the nursery, but remember, it isn't what a plant looks like at the nursery that matters—it is how the plant looks in the garden once it gets home. These taller, more upright plants are a beautiful contrast to rounded plants. Also, don't dismiss perennials with a very loose, open, spreading habit. Long, winding stems that sprawl every which way look messy and terrible in a pot at the nursery but are invaluable in a garden because they weave between other plants and can knit a collection of plants into a visually unified whole.

VALUE

Value may be the most overlooked aspect of great garden design. Value essentially means the brilliance of a color—how light or dark it is. A soft lavender has a much lighter value than a dark, intense purple, even though they are basically the same color. And value doesn't just apply to flowers, leaves also vary enormously in value. Variegated plants—those splashed or striped with yellow or white—give the lightest values, but even plain green leaves range from the deep, moody dark greens of a hellebore to the bright light green of lysimachia. Value influences how people experience a garden in a huge way, but often without us consciously noticing it. This makes a plant's color value easy to overlook. Deployed properly, a plant's color value is incredibly powerful. A shade perennial garden with no flowers in it will look beautiful and interesting if the leaves vary widely between shades of light and dark green. Gardeners can make a shady part of the garden feel brighter by filling it with light-colored plants, or make a cozy corner feel dark and mysterious by only deploying the darkest of plants. High contrasts in color value draw the eye. Show off a favorite plant by surrounding it with plants with a different value, such as using dark foliage all around a white lily or by using a dark bloom surrounded by bright, variegated foliage.

There's a wonderful tool to help gardeners think about color value in the garden right in your pocket—your cell phone camera. Just take a picture of a garden area and use a filter setting to shift it to a black-and-white view. With all the color stripped away, you'll just see the differences of the lightness and darkness of the plants. If everything ends up about the same shade of grey, you may need to go shopping for some lighter and darker plants to keep things interesting.

The many values of the color pink offered by the foliage and flowers in this garden create a stunning visual effect.

The sound of moving water in the garden introduces another sensual experience.

Scent has a role to play in the perennial garden as well. Nothing beats the fragrant exuberance of lilies.

THE OTHER SENSES

The design principles talked about so far are all focused on how a garden looks. Gardening is primarily a visual art form, but that is far from the only way people experience them. Sometimes gardens are described as "sensory gardens" because they focus on all the senses, not just sight. But really, all the senses should be a part of *every* successful garden design. To help evaluate how your other senses are being engaged by your garden, take a walk through it, stopping periodically to close your eyes. Just stand there and take in what you smell, hear, and feel.

Sound

Sound comes to the garden in the form of birdsong, trickling water, wind chimes, and the plants themselves—trees and grasses in particular make wonderful sounds while moving in a breeze. Sound can be a problem to be worked around as well. A noisy roadway or loud neighbor can have their sounds deadened with a strategically placed, thick hedge or masked by the sounds of a newly built waterfall.

Scent

Scent comes to the garden from the countless plants with fragrant flowers or foliage. When thinking about how to maximize the pleasant smells in the garden, remember that floral scents are easily diffused and blown away by the wind, so positioning the most fragrant plants in the most sheltered sections of the garden will allow for more enjoyment of the pleasing scents. Many plants have scented foliage as well but remember they need to be brushed against to release their aroma, so plan to position your favorites next to paths and seating areas where people can enjoy them.

Touch

Touch can be a tremendous part of enjoying the garden. Pleasing textures vary tremendously among perennials from the fuzzy leaves of lamb's ear (*Stachys byzantina*) to the glossy, smooth foliage of a wild ginger (*Asarum canadense*). If you are a person who loves to touch plants, position some touchables in raised beds or containers so they can be easily accessed. On the flip side, be careful where a spiny cactus is located to avoid an accidental touch of a less pleasant kind. Also, be aware that some plant foliage can cause allergic reactions or rashes on sensitive skin, so do some quick research before placing a plant in the touch zone. Remember also, just because you don't react to it doesn't mean you won't ever have a visitor sensitive to it in the garden.

Temperature is another touch-related factor to consider when planning an inviting garden. A chair in a sunny corner on a cold day will encourage people to sit down and take a moment to soak in the scene. But that same sunny corner may feel oppressively hot on a summer afternoon. Whenever you are in your garden, take note of how it feels. Is it comfortable? If not, consider adding or removing shade or wind blocks to either cool down or warm up the space.

Balance

Balance is a sense many don't think about too much, but it is another critical factor to consider when making a garden an inviting space—and one to spend more time in. Uneven paving stones are unpleasant to walk on when they shift under foot, and it is hard to relax in a chair that shifts or rocks when someone leans back. Your garden may be stunningly beautiful, but if it doesn't feel comfortable to walk through or sit down and relax, no one is going to be enjoying it.

Touch is another way to experience a garden. Soft grasses flanking a walkway beg to be touched, while spiky flowers and foliage, such as that of the *Eryngium* in this image, might not look inviting, but they do invite experimental touches.

Walkways and steppingstones should be solidly placed and pleasant to walk on.

Don't focus on blooms alone. Foliage has so much to offer to a garden's appeal.

SEASONALITY

One reality of gardening with perennials is that, unlike annuals, most of them bloom for relatively short periods during the year—and it can be easy to forget the specifics of blooming time when designing a garden bed. Two plants may grow in the same conditions and have flowers that would look great together, but if one blooms in the spring and the other in the fall, they'll never be seen blooming together.

A good way to take the seasonal blooming times of plants into account is to make a simple spreadsheet with each potential plant listed. Put the name of one plant in each row and label twelve columns, one for each month of the year. Then put an *X* in the month that each plant will be blooming. This will allow you to quickly look down the spreadsheet and see if there are any nonblooming times during the year.

A very easy mistake to make is to plan the garden so that the blooms are loaded too heavily in the spring. The vast majority of plant shopping gets done in the spring when nurseries are brimming with plants, and it is very tempting to just load your cart up with everything that is in flower and looking beautiful. But do that, and you will miss out on all the wonderful late summer- and fall-blooming perennials which, in the spring, may not look like much at all. So, take the time to make a plan and choose plants that will be blooming every month of the year.

Once your garden is planted and established, it is well worth taking stock of it throughout the season. Any time you walk into the garden and if nothing is really looking thrilling, it is time to take a trip to a local botanic garden to see what attracts your attention and is looking beautiful there. Then go buy those plants to add to your home landscape.

When arranging plants based on bloom time, there are two main strategies to take. Both work—they just give different effects. One strategy is to make sure each bed has things that will be blooming every season of the year (except for winter in cold climates) so that in spring, summer, and fall, every bed has something great going on. The other approach is to cluster plants that bloom at the same time together, so you may have one bed that explodes into beauty in the spring, another in the summer, and a third that peaks in the fall, with each fading into the background while another bed takes the limelight. Whichever style you choose is up to personal preference. If you *really* love drama, build your entire garden around one season and just enjoy that brief explosion of bloom to the hilt.

It can also be fun to plan special events and specific moments into your gardening year. If there is a particular plant you really love, turn the moment of its peak flowering into something really special by including lots of other plants that bloom at the same time in the garden design. It is incredibly fun to see a well-planned crescendo in the garden building and exploding into bloom—and a great excuse to invite friends over to see the garden and enjoy the display.

One of the best things about a perennial garden is that it is dynamic, always changing throughout the year. A perennial garden can look completely different in spring and fall, while a garden built around shrubs and annuals tends to be more static and predictable. This is a huge advantage for the home perennial garden because gardeners will be seeing it every single day, and keeping it changing throughout the seasons keeps it fresh and exciting.

We see this same dynamism in natural landscapes, which can be the inspirational starting point for our own garden design. Deciduous forests of eastern North America go through several phases. In early spring, countless ephemeral perennials burst into growth and bloom. Then the trees leaf out, bringing on deep shade and a cool restful time through most of the summer as the ephemerals retreat back underground. Then the understory is mostly quiet, punctuated here and there by plants that grow and bloom through the summer in sunnier spots. Finally, a symphony of autumn builds when color floods the landscape, thanks to changing leaves and ripening berries before the quiet dormancy of winter.

As we move west into the grass-dominated landscapes, we see a similar pattern. Early-blooming pasque flowers and other spring-blooming ephemerals take the stage at the start of spring, pushing through the faded stems and leaves of last year's perennials. Then there's a rotating cast of characters coming in and out of bloom through the summer as perennials expand and grasses get taller, ending once again in a burst of color in the fall as the iconic asters and goldenrods send the season off with a bang before the arrival of winter.

As we go further west, into the dry climates, and land on the West Coast, we enter a different dynamic—here the driving force behind the rhythm of the seasons is the rain. For most of the West Coast this is a summer-dry dynamic, with summer being a mostly dormant, quiet period, switching into a season of growth, greenery, and a sequence of blooms with the arrival of the rains in the winter.

Garden designs are the most energizing and entertaining when they embrace and emphasize natural seasonal rhythms.

One of the best ways to add more seasonal dynamism and dramatic change to your perennial garden is with the use of ephemeral plants. The most iconic of these are the classic spring bulbs—daffodils and tulips—that emerge early in the spring, flower, and then go dormant. These plants can be interplanted with other perennials that emerge later, and because they are growing at different times, they just add another layer of flowering beauty to the year without competing for sunlight or water.

Fall in the perennial garden brings seasonal colors and textures so different from those found in the spring.

Embrace the rhythms of nature as the garden progresses from spring to summer to autumn by including a range of plants with different bloom times and periods of interest.

Spring in a woodland garden is filled with ephemeral beauty, though the plants die back and shift into dormancy with the arrival of summer's heat.

Even though most of the classic spring bulbs are species that are native to Eurasia, there are many wonderful spring-blooming plants native to North America that give the same effect and produce plenty of spring beauty. Particularly if gardening in a shaded garden, the native woodland ephemerals will perform much better than the classic spring bulbs, which really grow best in nearly full sun. One thing to keep in mind when adding spring ephemerals is what the foliage will look like after the flowering is finished. Some of them have quite an ugly period as the foliage turns yellow and dies down. Remember that the foliage is critically important—it photosynthesizes to produce the energy the plant will store away underground to fuel next year's growth and flowering. So don't cut the foliage back until after it begins to yellow. Mixing spring

ephemerals in with summer-growing perennials is a great way to hide that fading foliage below the emerging growth of the summer plants. When it comes to foliage, some of our North American native ephemerals really shine. While daffodil foliage is very bulky and makes quite a mess as it fades, native trilliums and Virginia bluebells are far more graceful and even attractive as they go dormant, the leaves quickly going from green to yellow to brown and nearly becoming invisible without a lot of bulk or mess.

Include tall, "see-through" plants, like this *Verbena bonariensis*, in the garden—even toward the front—rather than always following the oft-given advice of planting tall plants in the back and short plants in the front. See-through plants add interest and depth to the planting.

PLANT HEIGHT

One of the most basic, often repeated pieces of advice on designing a perennial garden is to put taller plants in the back of a bed, and smaller ones in front. This can be good advice—you don't want to totally block your view of the rest of a planting by putting all the huge plants in the front—but don't be totally tied to this rule. In natural landscapes, you won't see this at all. Natural grasslands mix all the different heights together, and woodland landscapes have mostly low-growing perennials, dotted here and there with taller accents from understory shrubs and tree trunks.

In the garden, there are a few tricks you can use to mix up your plant heights to create a more naturalistic and interesting design.

First, make good use of "see-through" plants. Some perennials grow very thick and full. Plant a Joe-Pye weed (*Eutrochium purpureum*) in the front of your bed, and you won't be able to see a thing behind it. But prairie dock (*Silphium terebinthinaceum*) is quite different—the massive leaves stay mostly below 2 to 3 feet (61–91 cm), and though

the flower stems reach over to 6 feet (1.8-plus m), they are open, airy, and don't obscure the plants behind them. Many ornamental grasses can be used this way as well. Looking through a taller plant can make for exciting views of the plants behind.

Next, remember that anything below eye level won't block the plants behind it very much. A 1-foot (30 cm) plant will still be visible if a 3-foot (91 cm) plant is in front of it, because you will be looking at both of them from above.

And finally, you can use taller plants to break up the garden and add interest and excitement. A garden where you can see everything all at once isn't very interesting to explore. It is much more fun to walk down a path and keep discovering new treasures. So, using taller plants at the front of a bed will allow people to get up close and enjoy them, but it's also important to step past them, revealing hidden beauties behind.

Planting beds lined by boxwoods lend a more formal feel to a garden.

STYLE

Perennial gardens can be created in a range of styles. Some may find a particular style that perfectly matches their interests and tastes, or others may find they want to mix and match pieces from different styles. Most of the time, though, it is wise to choose and stick to one style for each part of the garden. Having one strictly formal bed right next to a bed that is inspired by a wildflower meadow will usually make the garden feel chaotic and unplanned. Take some time looking at the garden styles that you love and commit to the best style for your garden.

Formal Gardens

Formal gardens are defined by straight lines and square corners, with perennials that are often accented by neatly trimmed shrubs. In general, formal gardens are also perfectly symmetrical with matching plantings on either side of a path or walkway. With paths, walls, or hedges defining the geometric lines of a formal garden, the perennial plantings can be designed in two different ways. One plan is to keep your perennials very tidy and formal as well, choosing compact plants with tight growth habits and keeping them planted in straight lines. Or the perennials

There are so many styles to choose from when designing your perennial garden. Find one that suits your home and your personal preference.

Dreamy cottage gardens are known for their loose, relaxed vibe.

Naturalistic gardens mimic how plants grow in the wild. Typically a mixed matrix of species with plants placed closely together, these plantings often focus on native plants and include perennial grasses, as well as forbs.

can create contrast with the formal lines of the garden by using very wild, loose, informal perennial plantings within those tight, geometric beds. The contrast between formal and wild can be very effective and exciting. Strictly formal gardens were very popular in early American history, and they can be a great choice if you live in a historic home or older neighborhood.

Cottage Gardens

Cottage-style gardens emphasize flowers and fragrance over form and foliage. Usually, the beds are rounded and the paths are winding. Choose mown turfgrass or stepping stones for paths to keep the mood fun and relaxed. And definitely play with plant height here. A huge aster spilling out over the path is exactly the mood we're going for in a cottage garden, not tight, tidy growth habits. Cottage-style gardens can easily become too chaotic, with too many different plants and colors, so rein in the plants by choosing very harmonious color schemes or repeating a few key plants throughout the garden to give it more unity.

Naturalistic/Wildscaping

The naturalistic or wildscaping style is inspired by how plants grow in the wild. Mix plants of different heights together or keep changes in height subtle and gradual—taller plants can still be massed toward the back generally, but be sure to pull some forward to make it seem more like a happy accident than a plan. Be sure to plant in large numbers. In nature, if a plant is in a habitat where it is happy, it will always thrive and multiply. Finally, don't plant in defined blocks of just one variety. In nature, plants usually grow in what is called a *matrix*, with many plants of different species all growing together. In nature, there isn't a block of goldenrod here and a block of asters there and a block of grasses over there—they are found with all three of them growing mixed together. This matrix style of planting can be incredibly beautiful, very natural looking, and, if done well, very low maintenance. The plants growing close together make it almost impossible for weeds to take hold. It can also be tricky to pull off, as it is very important to match the vigor of plants planted together so that one doesn't smother and kill off the others. Sometimes naturalistic matrix plantings, which look the most effortless and wild, are actually the most technical and difficult to create effectively.

Also remember that design style doesn't define how good the ecosystem will be in a garden. Gardeners can certainly create great habitat and feed countless pollinators in a naturalistic landscape, but the exact same thing can be done with a very formal garden, simply by choosing mostly native plants and avoiding pesticides. Pollinators don't care if a plant is growing in straight lines or not!

Rock gardens offer an exciting way to display alpine plants and other low growers. If you love miniature plants, a rock garden is a perfect fit.

Rock Gardens

Rock gardens take inspiration from the natural landscapes found in mountains, with tiny, beautiful plants growing tucked into the cracks and crevices of a rocky terrain. A big part of the aesthetic of the rock garden is in the contrast between the harsh, inhospitable-looking rocks and the delicate beauty of the plants that thrive amongst them. Since many of the plants adapted to these conditions have very small, compact growth habits, rock gardens are often a celebration of great miniature plants. Rock gardens can be a perfect style for very small gardens, or if you have naturally rocky, sloped, and well-drained soils. Because rock garden beds are often raised to allow for perfect drainage, they are also a great style if you want to avoid having to bend over a lot in the garden.

Garden Styles from Other Parts of the World

The styles discussed so far, which come from Western Europe, have been the basis for a lot of our gardening culture here in the United States, but there are countless other garden design traditions from around the world to consider. Despite the United States being a country of immigrants, gardening traditions are sadly often left behind as new arrivals integrate into life in the United States. Researching and rediscovering the garden styles from your family background can be a wonderful way to find a garden style that you not only love but will speak to your personal history and ancestry. Of course, inspiration can be taken for a gardening style from cultures and parts of the world where there's no personal connection, just be sure to do it with respect. Many gardening traditions are strongly linked to religious or spiritual views and should be added to your garden only with the sincerest respect for the culture and worldview behind them.

The style you choose will depend on personal taste, personal history, and the context of your neighborhood and house. If you live in a historic Victorian house, you might choose a historically accurate, strictly formal style, while a charming bungalow might look most at home surrounded by an informal cottage garden style. But remember that this, again, is a chance to work with contrast and harmony. The incredibly popular High Line Garden in New York City is so effective because it uses a wild, naturalistic design style to contrast with the strict formality of the city streets and buildings around it.

The classic English border garden is a design style still coveted by many American gardeners.

If you take inspiration from the gardening styles of other cultures and parts of the world, be sure to do so with respect and reverence for the cultural, spiritual, or religious views behind them.

Whether ornate or organic, American gardeners have been drawing inspiration from other parts of the world, such as this Mediterranean landscape, for generations.

FIGURING OUT
WHAT *You* LIKE

NOW THAT SOME of the principles that go into successful garden design have been discussed, it is time to determine how you, personally, would like to see these principles applied. That means the next step is to look at lots and lots of gardens.

The very first places to go are gardens in your local area. This can be as simple as taking a walk through your neighborhood, but even better is connecting with local garden clubs and plant societies and going on garden tours. Viewing actual home gardens in the area is the very best source of inspiration for your own design because these gardens have the same climate and probably the same soil, so if you see a plant thriving on a garden tour, you'll know you can grow it at home as well. The ideas and designs you see will also be easy to translate to your space because these other home gardens will be on a scale similar to your own.

Local botanic gardens are also a fantastic source of inspiration. Most of them have well-labeled plants, so when you see something you love it is easy to write down the name—or photograph the tag—so you can add it to your wish list. Botanic gardens are great to visit throughout the year to get a sense of how the professional gardeners keep things beautiful and interesting throughout the seasons. There's a little more work translating what you see at a botanic garden to your home garden space because they will generally be much larger and have full-time staff to plant and care for them. A sweep of thousands and thousands of bulbs blooming in a botanic garden is incredible, but simply doesn't translate well to a small urban garden. And even if there's room for such a display, you may not have the budget to buy that many bulbs, or the time to plant them all. But you can certainly take note of the varieties and colors to recreate the same effect on a smaller scale.

When you visit other gardens, take lots of photos (with permission, of course) and really try to take note of everything you love—and don't love—about the garden. Don't just think, "Oh, that's beautiful!" Stop and reflect on the various topics covered in this chapter and take note of how they are being used in this garden. Is the style formal or informal? How does the garden use color, texture, form, and value to make a great design? Close your eyes and take in how the garden sounds and smells. Take note of what is and isn't blooming to get a sense of how the garden might change through the seasons. Notice the way the gardener uses plant heights to obscure or highlight views. The more you can say about why you loved or didn't love a garden, the more you'll be able to figure out what exactly you want your own space to look like.

Visit public and private gardens in your area to discover designs and plants that will easily translate to your space. *Greater Des Moines Botanical Gardens*

Traveling to places with climates different from your own is another way to be inspired. Perhaps your garden on the Eastern Seaboard is not suitable for a collection of cacti and succulents, but you can translate the effect into plants you can grow (such as hardy prickly pears and yuccas).

The goal is to find a style, color palette, and collection of plants *you* love that will thrive in your given growing conditions.

You can also look for garden inspiration when you travel. Gardens in other climates and other parts of the world may well be full of plants you cannot grow, but again, if you note *why* you love them, you can usually translate their effect into something you can grow, recreating color schemes or design ideas with different plants to achieve the same effect.

Finally, books, magazines, and social media are a great and nearly endless source of inspiration. But, let's be honest, sometimes this inspiration needs to be taken with a grain of salt. It is easy to shoot a photo that focuses on a beautiful mass of flowers and crop out the ugly, fading foliage below them. Also, following too many social media accounts in wildly different climates is likely to produce a case of "zonal envy," making gardeners wish for plants they cannot grow. Again, focusing on gardening principles rather than specific plants will help gardeners learn from these sources and apply the ideas to gardens in a productive way.

Once time has been spent looking at as many gardens as possible, sit down with all your notes and photos and start making a list of what you want and don't want in a garden. Work through each of the design principles discussed in this chapter and make note of your thoughts about them based on the gardens you have seen. You may not have a strong opinion about every single aspect of garden design, but try to think carefully about each one so you can understand your preferences and consider where you've seen them done well or poorly. It can be hard to choose between all the different ways to design a garden, but luckily there doesn't have to be just one preference. It might be possible to create different types of gardens in different parts of your property. Or another option is to be very selective and narrow down the design choices based on things like the color and style of your house.

CREATE *Your* DESIGN

WITH YOUR LIST of what you want in a garden in hand, it is time to start deciding where to put the garden beds, paths, and any other garden features you may want to add.

There are two main ways to approach figuring out the overall layout of your garden. The first method, used by professional garden designers, is to create a base plan. To do this, draw out the outlines of the garden space on a big sheet of paper, either by measuring everything, or by simply downloading an aerial view of the garden from an online mapping site or your local government's official records of the lot. With the outline of your property down on paper, then sketch where the existing features like trees, houses, garages, and driveways are located. With that base plan created, you can then sketch in possible places to put different beds and roughly make notes of the type of plantings you want to put in each area.

Creating a base plan and sketching out ideas on paper is a great exercise to think creatively about your space and quickly see which of the many ideas you've come up with will actually work in the space. However, it is a technique that doesn't work for everyone as it can be hard to look at a two-dimensional sketch and visualize what it will look like in the three-dimensional reality of a garden. Professional garden designers use this technique because they have years of experience mentally translating from a paper sketch to the real world, and because they need to be able to work on designing gardens from their studios after just one or two visits to the actual garden location. Designing your own garden at home means you have the luxury of getting out into the space every day and figuring out the design by looking at the garden, not just visualizing it on paper.

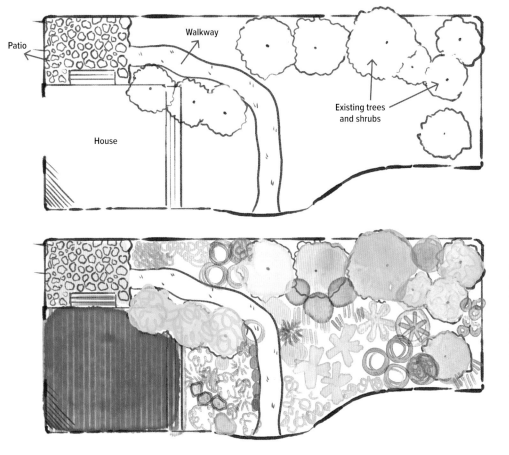

A basic base plan (shown at top) is a simple outline of your space, showing the structures, walkways, and large existing plants. A good base plan can then be transformed into a design for your perennial garden by adding outlines of various plant forms, colors, and textures to the original base plan (shown at bottom).

Mark off a new potential bed using a rope, hose, or marking paint to help you visualize the space.

To help visualize the garden design, go outside and physically lay out different possibilities. Lay out a garden hose to mark the potential outline of a bed. Place sticks, bamboo stakes, or even old cardboard boxes in the beds to get a sense of how tall and wide your plants will be. Set chairs outside on the proposed area to represent a patio and see if it feels big enough. Walk down the planned paths and see if they feel comfortable. Sit in all your favorite spots inside the house and see what parts of the design will be visible from the windows. And be sure to try multiple layouts and designs—even if you think they might not be your favorite. At this stage, trying a different design is easy, just a case of moving a few stakes, dragging the hose around, or sketching something new on paper. Once everything is planted, however, changing the design will mean hours of hard work. Take your time, try lots of options, and don't rush to a decision.

This can be a fun process to do with friends and family as well. Get everyone in the house involved, but invite others over to have input in the design as well. You can take some opinions with a grain of salt—it is your garden, not theirs—but more sets of eyes on the design can help bring in new ideas and point out potential issues.

One issue you might want to consider when designing your garden is accessibility. If no one in your family uses a wheelchair or a walker, you may not think this is something that needs to be taken into account, but there is great value in making sure the garden space is accessible to everyone. Making sure that paths are broad and smooth, and steps are kept to a minimum may not seem relevant now, but if the garden is accessible to everyone, you ensure that everyone can be welcomed into the garden without feeling like you have to make special accommodations for them (plus, wide, smooth paths make using garden carts and wheelbarrows a breeze). And remember, the person you are making the garden accessible for may very well be your future self. Unfortunate things, like sprained ankles, or joyous things, like pregnancies and babies in strollers, and the inevitable reality of growing older all mean that if the garden is designed with narrow, unstable paths or paths running straight down steep slopes—there most certainly will be regrets.

Garden accessibility can also be beautiful and well-integrated into the design. A perfect example of this is Chanticleer, the much-celebrated garden outside of Philadelphia, Pennsylvania. For years, one of the main sections of the garden could only be accessed by walking down a steep hill. They decided to make it accessible to

Consider the width of your paths and the type of surface—stone, mulch, gravel, etc.—when planning a garden.

all, and the result is a long, winding, serpentine path down the slope that is now an incredibly beautiful feature of the garden. Broad, smooth paths always feel luxurious and comfortable to everyone who is traversing it, regardless of their mobility level.

When you think you have a garden layout that you love, pick up some turf-marking spray paint and use it to mark out your design. This will last for a couple of weeks, giving you time to really evaluate your design. Try to always walk on the proposed paths and even sit at a potential patio site to see how it feels. Perhaps that winding walk being considered to the garage is actually an inconvenience when rushing to get to work in the morning. Maybe the patio is better closer to the house or in more shade. Work out the kinks and adjust the design accordingly.

WHEN TO HIRE A PROFESSIONAL

There are a few times when it is just the right choice to bring in a professional landscape designer to design your dream garden. The first reason is pretty simple—you just don't want to do it yourself. The design process can be a lot of fun, but it isn't for everyone. If after reading this chapter you think, "Ugh, that's a lot of work," then hiring someone else is the right option. Also, consider bringing in professionals for technically challenging situations. Steep slopes need careful management to prevent erosion, and building hardscapes like patios, retaining walls, and water features is easy to get wrong, sometimes with serious consequences. Be honest with yourself about your DIY skills and if in doubt, hire someone to do it instead.

When hiring help, shop around and do your research. Make sure they are properly licensed and insured for the work, and ask to see examples of previous projects they have done. If you don't love their work or have doubts about their qualifications or quality, keep looking.

BREAKING IT UP

You don't need to try and execute the entire garden design all in one season. Installing a new garden is hard work, can be expensive (though there's a discussion on ways to cut costs in chapter 4), and new garden beds are more work to maintain than established ones. For all these reasons, it is best to break up the garden design installation into stages, tackling one section at a time. If you've never created a perennial garden before, start with one small bed to get a sense of the time, money, and effort required to build it, and then you'll have a better sense to make decisions on when and how much more to tackle for future garden beds.

In some cases, it may be better to hire a professional to design or install your garden. Be honest with yourself about your capabilities.

The PLANTS

WITH YOUR GARDEN beds and paths laid out, it is time to start getting into the nitty-gritty details of choosing which plants to include in each part of the garden. This can be the most fun part of the process, but it also can be a little overwhelming.

There are a few ways to go about picking out the right combinations of plants to complete a garden design. One way is to start with the concept. Considering all the gardens visited and all your notes about color combinations and textures, forms, and styles that you enjoyed, you can quickly set a design theme for each part of the garden. For example, one bed will be shades of blue and yellow, mostly fine-textured leaves, with lots of ornamental grasses for a wild, prairie-like feel. Behind the house will be hot red and orange flowers with lots of big, bold foliage to give a high-energy, tropical effect, and so on.

Another approach is to build a design around a specific plant or combination of plants. If you just love echinacea, their flowers, all the pollinators they attract, and the way goldfinches love snacking on their seedheads, then start with that one plant, building the rest of the design around colors, textures, and growth habits that will complement your star plant.

Though you may know a few specific plants that you want in the design, you can also start making a plant list by simply describing the characteristics of plants that you are looking for. Perhaps you know in one bed you want some low-growing plants with flowers in shades of blue or purple, or in another bed you want tall, yellow, late-summer bloomers. Making a list of the attributes you are looking for can help when browsing reference books or visit nurseries. Good independent garden centers should have staff that can help find the perfect plant to match your needs. Just remember to make your list of desired attributes

Now that you have a basic plan in place, it's time to select your plants. Make a list of possibilities based on the attributes you are looking for and what plants thrive in your conditions.

reasonable. Few perennials will bloom nonstop all summer, and there are plenty of plants with flowers in yellow, pink, and white colors and very few plants with blooms in certain other colors. For example, true sky-blue flowers with no purple hues are rare in nature, so accept the fact that you may need to be flexible in your design wishes based on the reality of what is available. Similarly, don't get too hung up on a specific species or cultivar. Sometimes a plant seen in a picture or one you fall in love with at a botanic garden may not be available in the nursery trade, but well-trained nursery staff should be able to help find something similar that will give the same visual effect.

Another option for choosing plants is to largely pick out a plant palette at the nursery. Go in well-armed with notes on what you like and what you want from the garden space and see what strikes your fancy. This method can be a great way to avoid the heartache of falling in love with a plant in a book that you can't find for sale or isn't suited to your climate. Just remember not to ignore plants that aren't in flower yet to ensure there are blooms and interest throughout the seasons.

However you choose your plants, beware of the problem of falling in love with too many different things. There are so many great varieties to grow, it is easy to want to try everything and end up planting one of this and one of that. "One of everything" almost never looks good. In more formal gardens, plants should be repeated in drifts and blocks. In designs inspired by nature, plants almost always grow in big colonies that run through the garden. One tip to keep the garden from looking like a wild mix of too many different things is to choose a few signature plants. Pick three or four plants that you really love and you know really do great in your climate, and plant them by the dozens. Put them in drifts, or just use them as individual plants repeated here and there throughout the garden. Those repeated plants will tie your whole planting together and create a coherent structure in which to dot your one-off impulse purchases.

In well-designed gardens, there are typically patterns and repetitions. Choose a few plant species you love and repeat them here and there throughout the garden to tie it all together. *Chanticleer Garden*

Sentimental Plants

In addition to all the design principles discussed here, there is another factor that can drive plant choices and design decisions. And that is emotion. It could be a lily a friend gave you, a phlox your mother always loved, or a perennial planted in the memory of a beloved pet—all these plants can be a wonderful and significant part of the garden—and you should embrace that. Loving a plant is always reason enough to grow it. In fact, these deeply emotional plant decisions can be a great starting point for a garden design. If you must have peonies because they remind you of your mother, then build the rest of the garden with colors, textures, and bloom times that complement those sentimental peonies.

QUANTITIES

Figuring out exactly how many plants you need to fill garden beds requires a little bit of calculation, but the short answer is—probably more than you think. Skimping on plants and leaving lots and lots of space to be covered by mulch (or weeds) rarely results in a good garden aesthetic. Just look at the pictures of landscapes you love and gardens you've visited, and you'll see that the individual plants are positioned close enough together that they touch, or are growing into each other a little bit. Many lackluster home gardens fail because too few plants are dotted over too much space, giving a sparse, skimpy appearance. It is possible, though, to plant things *too* close together. It can be difficult to visualize just how big some perennials will grow. A small baptisia in a 1-gallon (3.8-L) pot looks petite, but in a few years it will mature into a very large plant indeed.

To calculate how close plants should be planted in the ground, look at the pot tag, the profiles in the back of this book, or a catalog to see how wide the mature plant will grow. If possible, check a few different sources. Plants sizes vary depending on climate and conditions, and comparing a couple of different resources can give you a better estimate of the actual mature size. The maximum space that should be between two perennials is half of their widths added together. So, if you have a 3-foot (91 cm)-wide plant next to a 1-foot (30 cm)-wide plant, they should be at most 2 feet (61 cm) apart. But you can plant them closer than that.

Shaving 6 inches (15 cm) or so off plant spacings will ensure they grow together nicely and cover the ground sooner. Famed garden designer Piet Oudolf spaces nearly all his perennials just 1 foot (30 cm) apart to give a very lush, dense planting effect. These very close plantings, however, require more care. If a tall, vigorous plant is close to a shorter, less-vigorous plant, the tall one will probably shade out and stifle the shorter neighbor. Two plants with similar heights and vigor, however, will usually coexist quite well.

Calculating the number of plants you need can be done two ways. Calculate the number of plants on paper by measuring the beds, multiplying the bed width by length to get a square footage, and then calculating the square footage covered by each plant. A 1-foot (30 cm)-wide plant covers 1 square foot (0.09 m²) maximum, and a 3-foot (91 cm) -wide plant covers a maximum of 3 square feet (0.27 m²), so an 18 square foot (1.6 m²) bed would need at least eighteen 1-foot (30 cm)-wide plants, six 3-foot (91 cm) -wide plants, or some combination of the two sizes. Tracing

Determining plant quantities for a given space can be a challenge. Careful calculations based on the mature size of each plant and its ideal spacing prevent over- or under-purchasing.

Most plants grow and spread with time, so even if a planting seems sparse at first, if you place plants based on their expected size at maturity, the planting will fill in soon enough.

out the bed dimensions on graph paper with each square representing 1 square foot (0.09 m²) and then drawing circles to represent the size of each plant can be another good way to get a plant count.

The other way to calculate the number of plants, if you are more of a visual than math person, is to go outside to the bed with stakes, flags, old pots, or another item to represent the plants and physically place them in the bed to get a visual sense of how many are needed to fill up the area. Don't stress the details here too much. You can always buy or propagate more plants to fill the space if the plant count is underestimated or transplant or give away extra plants if a bed is too full.

REVISE, *Revise*, REVISE

DESIGNING A GARDEN is not something that is just done once and then it is finished. Gardens are living, dynamic things, and plants mature, multiply, and sometimes die. Shade trees get bigger and limit the amount of sun, or the trees fall in a storm, turning a shade bed into an instant sunny garden. And, of course, you will be growing and maturing, too, as a gardener. Your tastes may change as you visit other gardens and get to know more plants. That big patch of lawn where the kids play may be used less and less as they get older. A dog joining the household may need more space to run. And the garden ultimately just turns out, in reality, different than it did in your imagination or on paper.

So when enjoying your garden, keep looking at it with a thoughtful eye. Do you love it or is it merely okay? Is that plant you thought you'd love just not living up to standards? Is the garden lagging in the middle of the summer, or finishing the end of the fall with a whimper rather than a bang? If so, run through the design principles in this chapter and see if playing with color, texture, value, and form might help add more energy and excitement to the space, or if you need to edit down your choices and bring in more harmony.

Garden historian Mac Griswold once said, "Gardening is the slowest of the performing arts," and that sums everything up nicely. Keep caring about and working with your garden's design and enjoy the performance as the garden grows and changes over the years.

Gardens are living things that change over time. Your garden this year will not be the same as next year's garden. Embrace change when it comes.

BE BOLD!

AS THE DISCUSSION of garden design wraps up, the best advice is to be bold. Go bigger and do more. The most common mistake home gardeners make is being too nervous to do enough, resulting in tiny, little beds that are overwhelmed by the size of the house, or sad little clumps of plants that don't fill out an area, or not making any kind of a statement. When in doubt, make the bed bigger and fill it with more plants. And remember, most of all, that your garden is for *you*, not anyone else. If you have an idea that just seems too weird or too nontraditional, do it! Let go of fear and design the garden you want, not the one you think other people will enjoy. Do you like it? Does it make you happy? Is it beautiful to you? If the answer to those questions is yes, then you have a successfully designed garden. If the answer is no, hopefully the design tips in this chapter can help you find ways to make it work better for you. And if your father-in-law or neighbor or anyone else doesn't like your garden, they can always make their own.

Whether you garden in Alaska, like this gardener, or in Florida, build the perennial garden you want, not the one you think will please others.

CHAPTER 4

POPULATING
Your
GARDEN

How to shop for and propagate beautiful plants

ONCE YOUR GARDEN design is completed, it is time to move on to the fun part—getting the plants.

Plant shopping can be a lot of fun, but it can also be a bit overwhelming if gardeners are new to the gardening hobby. Purchasing plants can also be dauntingly expensive, especially when there's a large property to fill or an ambitious design plan. Fortunately, there are ways to acquire or propagate the plants needed with very little expense. There are also a handful of simple tips to help find the best places to purchase plants. Ahead in this chapter, there are discussions on how to shop effectively for the highest quality plants and an outline of the simple skills that are needed to propagate your own plants from seeds or cuttings.

BUYING *Quality* PLANTS

YOUR FIRST NURSERY VISIT

On your first visit to a nursery or garden center, take some time to look around and see what they offer. Most nurseries divide plants into separate sections: one for annuals, one for perennials, and one for trees and shrubs. The perennial section will almost always be divided up into two additional groups for sun and shade. When looking in the sun and shade sections, remember that plants in the real world don't always fit neatly into one of those two categories, and some of the plants in the shade section may also thrive in full sun and vice versa. If you have a partially or lightly shaded garden, you'll probably do a lot of shopping in both the sun and shade sections.

Look plants over carefully before buying them. Check for pests, diseases, and weeds. If a plant looks questionable, save yourself the trouble and skip purchasing it.

Every nursery carries a different selection of plants. Be sure to visit several garden centers to see what's available.

Every nursery or garden center is different in terms of selection and quality. One good way to help figure out if a nursery is going to be your new favorite is to ask for help and see if you can get your questions answered clearly. Good garden centers have well-trained staff who know your local climate and can help find the right plant for a particular situation. Just be aware that sunny, spring weekends—especially around Mother's Day—are incredibly busy for garden centers, so if you have a lot of questions, try to go on a weekday or a weekend in the summer or fall when the staff will have time to give you their full attention.

Healthy Plants

Learning to recognize a healthy plant for sale is a good skill to have and will help you find the best places to go shopping. First, look for healthy green leaves mostly free of spots or blemishes. But don't turn away a plant because it has a few holes in the leaves—as discussed in chapter 2, plants are food for insects and other wildlife, so holes should be expected. However, a plant covered with aphids or chewed down to the soil is not a good sign. A few nibbles here and there are a good indication that the nursery you are buying from isn't using excessive amounts of pesticides.

After inspecting the foliage, check the pot for any weeds. A few small weeds in a pot aren't a huge problem in and of themselves, as they are easy to remove when planted, but lots of weeds are a red flag that the nursery isn't keeping up with maintaining their plants.

One of the most important factors in the health of a plant is the hardest to inspect: the roots. Roots are hard to see and easy to forget about. A plant with damaged leaves will recover if it has a healthy root system. Unhealthy roots, however, can be lethal. A perfect plant has roots that have filled out the soil in a pot but are not circling around inside (or outside) the container. If you buy a plant and most of the soil instantly falls away when it is taken out of the pot, it means the nursery just moved a small plant into a larger container, and, usually, marked up the price for the larger size, even though the plant is still small. On the other hand, if you have to strain to pull a plant out of its pot and see a solid wall of roots circling around the edge of the soil, that plant has been in the same pot for too long. Luckily, for perennials this is far less of a problem than it is for trees and shrubs, so if you get a very pot-bound perennial, simply cut off the roots from the edges and bottom of the pot, and plant it as usual.

One bonus to growing perennials is that, more than annuals, trees, or shrubs, you can get away with "clearance rack" plants that are looking a little rough around the edges. Annuals, of course, only have a short season of growth, so if they spend half the year recovering from mistreatment, you don't get much of a display from them. But perennials can live for years, so a couple months of recovery really doesn't matter much. On the other hand, shrubs—and especially trees—because they have a permanent, woody structure, may never recover from damaged or misshapen trunks and roots. But a slightly abused perennial can come back perfectly fine the next year. So, if gardeners are on a budget and want to shop the clearance rack, don't be afraid to do so. Just do check the status of the root system. Plants with mushy, rotting roots are unlikely to recover and should be avoided.

Healthy and well-grown plants are great criteria to indicate good places to shop. If you visit a nursery and see a lot of unhealthy, weedy, poorly grown plants, that's a sign to find somewhere else to spend your plant-shopping dollars.

Healthy roots are a must-have when purchasing plants. Do not purchase any with soft, dark brown, or mushy roots.

Plant Growth Regulators

Plant growth regulators are synthetic versions of plant hormones sometimes sprayed on plants during their production at nurseries to keep their growth habit shorter and more compact. Shorter plants are easier to ship from a wholesale nursery to a retail location, and they look better on the nursery bench. The effect of plant growth regulators is temporary, wearing off over the course of a growing season. That means you might buy a perennial in full bloom that's only 1 to 2 feet (30–61 cm) tall, but the next year, once the plant growth regulators have worn off, it might shoot up to 3 to 4 feet (91–120 cm). When shopping and planning, read tags and search online for information about a plant's height, and plant according to the listed mature heights, not the height it happens to be when you buy it. Growers that supply big box stores tend to use a lot of plant growth regulators to facilitate easy shipping, while small independent nurseries that grow their own plants rarely use them.

PLACES TO GET PLANTS

There are many places to buy plants, from generic big box stores to tiny—often quirky—specialty and rare plant nurseries. There are also lots of online stores that ship plants, as well as less traditional plant sources like getting plant gifts from friends and purchasing plants at sales held by nonprofits. Each of these places has its own pros and cons.

Big Box Stores

Wherever you are in North America, there is probably a big box store with a garden center section nearby. These stores can be very convenient and affordable places to get plants, but they do come with downsides. All the plants at a big box store are shipped in on trucks from wholesale growers, usually in full bloom. These logistics limit the range of plants they can offer. Because all the plants must fit on pre-made racks loaded onto semi-trucks, tall plants take up way too much room and add a lot to shipping costs. Similarly, plants with long, trailing stems are difficult to ship as they are easily damaged in transit. This logistic reality means that almost everything for sale at a big box store will have small, compact, rounded forms—either because they grow that way naturally or because they've been kept small through the use of plant growth regulators (see sidebar, page 97). Gardeners will need to look elsewhere to get other plant forms to fill out their garden design.

Another issue is that the decision about which plants to stock is usually made at a regional level and could be by people who don't know much about gardening in your area. This means you may find plants for sale at your local big box store that simply aren't well adapted to your local climate and conditions. This problem is exacerbated by the fact that the staff at a box store usually have little to no training in horticulture, so they may not have the knowledge to help you find the plants that will perform well in your garden.

The bottom line is that big box stores may be less expensive, but they can be difficult to use effectively, especially if you are a novice gardener.

A good local independent nursery is the perfect place to find plants and get all your questions answered by a pro.

Specialty nurseries often focus on a specific group of plants, such as these compact plants for rock gardens.

Independent Garden Centers

Independent garden centers are locally owned and operated, and they are almost always run by someone with a love of, and training in, gardening and horticulture. This means they generally have a more curated selection of plants. Gardeners can trust that everything for sale there will be well adapted to the local climate. Even better, good independent garden centers have well-trained staff who love gardening and can help answer questions or help find plants for a specific spot or use in the garden. Many independent garden centers also work with local growers, or they do their own growing so they can stock plants for sale that don't ship well.

A well-trained, helpful staff and a curated selection of plants will usually result in plants that cost a little more than the plants would be at a big box store, but the extra cost will be worth it because of the long-term success of your garden. One absolute rule though: Never go to the well-trained staff of an independent garden center to get advice but then buy the plants they recommend at a big box store. If you benefit from their advice, pay for it by shopping there.

Of course, not every single independent garden center is well-run. Some may have poor quality plants or staff that give out bad advice. Trust your judgement, and if possible, ask local gardeners that you respect—found on garden tours, or at garden club events or plant society meetings—where they shop to get ideas of the best places for plants in the area.

Specialty Nurseries

Specialty nurseries are often small and focused on growing very unusual groups of plants. Most of these nurseries propagate and grow all their plants themselves rather than purchasing them from big wholesale nurseries, so specialty nurseries can offer plants gardeners can't get anywhere else. If gardeners are lucky enough to have a specialty nursery in the area, be sure to visit often to find many beautiful and interesting plants for the garden. These nurseries are a plant-lover's passion project, and the staff and owners will be incredible resources for information and ideas about unusual plants well-suited to your climate. They may also be a bit rough around the edges, run by a tiny staff on a tiny budget, and tucked away at the end of some poorly marked dirt road. But that can be part of the fun and adventure of shopping there!

Local plant society sales are a great place to find unique plants.

Mail-Order/Online

In addition to shopping in person, there are a myriad of places to buy plants to be shipped home. The plus side to this is that gardeners get access to a much wider selection than they will be able to find locally. If gardeners are looking for specific, unusual plants, shopping online may be the only option. On the downside, of course, is that these sources will not be curated to your local conditions so gardeners will need to do more research to make sure they are buying plants that will thrive in the garden.

Shipping costs for online purchases can be high (and they keep getting higher). Shipping costs are particularly steep for large plants. Gardeners will almost always spend more money, and get smaller plants, when shopping online compared to buying in person from a brick-and-mortar store. Good mail-order nurseries take great care in packing plants, but plants may still get damaged in the mail. Shipping companies don't always handle plant boxes with care, and plants can get banged up, overheated, or frozen while on their way to your home. Save online shopping as the last resort if you really want something and can't find it locally. And before you give up, do ask your local independent garden center if they can get a plant for you. They may be able to get you a particular variety, saving you money, and letting you support a local business at the same time.

Plant Sales

Many garden clubs, botanic gardens, and plant societies have plant sales, usually in the spring, as a fundraiser for the organization. These sales can be fantastic places to pick up unusual plants at a great price while also supporting local organizations promoting beautiful gardens. These sales are also a huge amount of fun. Sometimes a plant sale is as much about seeing old friends and comparing plant purchases as it is about actually getting plants for the garden. So have fun, ask strangers about the plants in their carts, and make new gardening friends. Quantities of plants (especially the rare and unusual ones) at these events may be quite limited, so, if possible, try to get there right as the doors open on the first day of the sale.

Friends

Gardeners are generous people and if you connect with a local garden club or plant society, you are likely to end up having plants gifted to you. Tour someone's garden and gush about a particular variety, and you might just go home with a piece of it in a bag. The great thing about gift plants is that you absolutely know they're going to perform well in your local climate, and you can see just how they're going to look once they've matured in the ground. Even better, the back story and friendship they represent adds to the happiness they'll bring to your own garden.

There is an unspoken etiquette about sharing plants in most gardening circles. First, if you are visiting a garden and see a plant that you love, don't ask for a piece of it, and certainly never take cuttings or seeds without permission. If you love a plant, compliment the gardener on it, and ask where they got it so you can buy one for yourself. That way if they want to share the plant—which many gardeners enjoy doing—they know you are interested, but they don't have to awkwardly turn you down if they don't want to (or can't) share it with you.

The other rule is to share plants generously. The information on propagation later in this chapter will help you learn how to make more of your favorite plants. Giving plants away generously to anyone who admires them is one of the great pleasures of gardening and helps create a community of sharing.

WHERE TO SOURCE PERENNIALS

SOURCE	COST	SELECTION	NOTES
Big box store	Often inexpensive	Limited, may not be well-curated for your local climate and conditions	Staff can't help answer questions or pick out plants.
Independent garden center	Varies, often more expensive than box stores	Usually a wide selection of plants chosen to thrive in your climate	Trained staff can help you find just the right plant.
Specialty nursery	Varies, often more expensive than regular garden centers	Unusual, sometimes idiosyncratic, selection you won't find for sale elsewhere	Run by passionate plant lovers who will be a wealth of information.
Online nursery	Most expensive, especially with shipping charges	Very wide, but not targeted to your region	Plants are generally small and may be harmed during shipping.
Local plant sales	Varies, but often very good prices	Wide selection, often unusual varieties rarely available elsewhere	These events are like parties put on by local plant societies and botanic gardens, so go early and have fun!
Friends	Free!	Unpredictable, but always locally adapted	The best way to get great plant gifts is to give great plant gifts. Just watch out for invasive species or aggressive spreaders.
Propagate your own	Very inexpensive, often nearly free	Widest possible range of plants	It requires time and patience to grow plants up to a mature size.

Gallon pots are a common way to find perennials for sale. They are more costly than smaller pot sizes but result in a mature plant quickly.

PLANT SIZES

Wherever you shop, you'll have a range of sizes and stages of perennial plants to purchase, ranging from little starts in cell packs up to enormous pots holding big, mature perennials. Novice gardeners often assume that bigger is better, but that isn't always the case. There are pluses and minuses to each size of plants.

Gallons and Bigger Pots

These are the pot sizes that contain nearly full-grown plants. Gallon (3.8-L) pots (or larger) are generally the sizes gardeners find most often in the perennial section at local garden centers. The size and maturity of these plants is an obvious positive. If you plant a garden with these large pot sizes, it will look good its first season, quickly filling in the space. Larger plants are also pretty durable, and they don't need a lot of babying and care after planting. Because these large plants are mostly mature, they are easy to design with because they won't change a whole lot after they are planted. These large-size perennials are often sold in bloom, so gardeners can grab them at the nursery, put them next to each other, and get a good sense of what they will look like for years in the home garden. This is not true of every perennial, however. Some very large plants (like *Silphium*) or slow-growing perennials (like *Baptisia*) will expand and change dramatically in the garden, even if planted when at a large size.

The obvious downside to bigger plants is that they are more expensive. Big plants have been grown for more years at the nursery and all the labor and time spent caring for them adds up to a bigger price tag. The less obvious downside is that bigger pots are a lot more work to plant. The bigger the pot, the bigger the planting hole. If gardeners are just planting a few things, this difference doesn't matter much, but when putting in a large new garden, all the extra digging can really add up fast. This can be especially significant if planting in a shade garden under trees or adding plants to an existing garden. Big pots can be hard to fit in between tree roots or to get in the ground without disrupting the plants around them.

Quart pots are quick and easy to plant and less expensive than larger pot sizes.

Quarts and Smaller Pots

The quart (1-L) (or smaller) pot sizes are harder to find at the nursery, but they have a lot to offer. They are quite affordable, and the small size makes them quick and easy to plant. Often they are still large enough, with well-developed root systems, that they don't need a lot of babying and aftercare once they are in the ground. Gardeners may have trouble finding perennials in these smaller sizes, however. More and more nurseries offer only larger-sized perennials. One reason for this is that many perennials are less likely to bloom at these smaller sizes, so they simply don't look as pretty sitting on the bench at the nursery. But if you have done your research and know what plants you are looking for, don't hesitate to snatch up perennials in this more affordable, easy-to-plant size.

Plugs

Plugs are the smallest plants you can buy, growing in compartments just a few inches deep. These compartments are not individual pots but rather sections of what is called a *plug tray*—a connected sheet of small containers. Most plugs are sold at the wholesale level, purchased by other nurseries to be potted up into bigger containers, and grown for a year or two before being sold to the consumer in gallon (3.8-L) pots. You are unlikely to be able to find plugs for sale at a local nursery, but there are an increasing number of online sources for these small plants, and they have a lot of pluses.

The biggest benefit to buying plugs is the price. They are the cheapest way to buy plants if gardeners are buying larger quantities. For a drift of thirty plants, purchasing a plug tray will be dramatically more affordable than buying all those plants in gallon (3.8-L) pots. Most sources will not sell plugs in small quantities, so they're not an option if just one or two specimens are needed.

Plug-sized perennials are so easy to plant, but they take a longer time to establish and reach maturity, requiring more water and care than larger plants.

BARE-ROOT

Except for a few groups of plants like peonies and oriental poppies, bare-root perennials can be hard to find for sale, but they are an excellent value if gardeners can find a source. As the name implies, bare-root plants are sold with the roots washed clean of soil and bagged in sphagnum peat moss, wood shavings, or another damp, loose material. They are sold when the plant is completely dormant, so no leaves or above-ground stems are present, just roots and dormant buds ready to push out new growth. Bare-root perennials are usually grown in the field rather than in containers, and then dug up, washed, packaged, and sold. Growing in ground rather than in pots means they don't have circling roots and planting them when dormant means minimal transplant shock. Field growing is also a much simpler process than growing in pots in a greenhouse, so it makes bare-root perennials incredibly affordable. Much like plugs, most bare-root perennials are sold at the wholesale level to nurseries who pot them up, let them grow a little, and then sell them to the public as containerized plants.

Bare-root perennials are the most affordable way to get large, robust plants; they are cheap to ship, and they tend to transplant well. But sadly, they are hard to find for sale because they don't look pretty. It is much easier to sell a pot full of flowers and foliage than a clump of weird-looking roots. And even more unfortunately, they're most often seen packaged in boxes or bags at a big box store where they are left sitting out in warm temperatures for too long and start sprouting in their containers. All of which is to say that gardeners might not be able to find good quality bare-root perennials for sale, but if you do, they are an incredible value.

Plugs are also wonderfully easy and fast to plant—they are so small that gardeners can plant them quickly with just a small trowel or soil knife, and they are easy to slip in between the roots of trees or other plants. Thirty plugs can go in the ground faster and easier than just a couple of gallon (3.8-L) pots.

There are downsides, however, to buying plugs. Gardeners will have to be patient while the plants mature and develop into full-sized specimens. A garden newly planted with plugs looks like . . . well, kind of like nothing at all. And since the plants are so small, they need careful tending their first year. The small root system of newly planted plugs means they dry out quickly, so regular watering is necessary while they get established throughout the first year.

Plugs are often the best option if gardeners are planting in large numbers, both for their affordability and ease of planting. In chapter 3, choosing a few signature plants and repeating them throughout your garden was discussed to give unity to the design. Buying a few flats of plugs is a great, affordable way to achieve that.

Some perennials, such as this peony, are available for purchase as bare-root plants. They are very affordable, but they are also prone to dessication if not stored properly prior to planting.

PROPAGATION

GARDENERS DON'T NECESSARILY *need* to learn how to propagate their own perennial plants. Gardeners can, if they want, leave propagation up to the professionals and simply purchase all the plants for the garden. But knowing how to propagate plants is a very useful skill to have, especially when on a limited budget, if you love rare and unusual plants, or to enjoy the fun of sharing favorite plants with friends, family, and neighbors. And while the process of starting seeds or rooting cuttings may seem intimidating, it doesn't have to be all that complex, especially for the perennial gardener. Grafting trees is quite technical and can take years of practice to truly master, but the process of turning one perennial plant into a dozen is, in most cases, pretty straightforward and easy.

DIVISION

Division is the simplest method of multiplying your plants and can be an important part of maintaining a garden—find out why in chapter 6. Whether gardeners are doing it to keep a perennial healthy or to make more plants, dividing a perennial is simply a matter of taking a mature clump and cutting it into two or more smaller plants.

Perennials can be divided once they have matured enough that there are multiple growth points emerging from the soil. If there is just one stem coming up from the soil, wait to divide that plant. In theory, as long as there are two growing points coming out of the crown of a perennial, it can be successfully divided, but waiting for it to get bigger and more robust means you'll get more divisions from the plant and each division can be larger. Many perennials bulk up to a dividable size quite quickly. Plus, in many cases, if a perennial is purchased in a large pot at the nursery, it can be divided right away, even before initially planting it. Doing a quick division before planting a newly purchased perennial is an easy way to stretch your plant-shopping dollar.

Regularly dividing perennials is a great way to get more plants for free. Spring division is an easy task best done when the plants are emerging at the start of the growing season.

The best time to divide most perennials is in early spring when they are just about to push into active growth. This first burst of growth in the spring allows plants to recover from the damage done during the dividing process. It is also easier to handle a plant without damaging it when there are no leaves or stems to break. It is possible to divide plants during the summer, when they are in active growth, but it is harder to do this without causing damage, and the heat of summer can be hard on the foliage while the root system recovers from the shock. Fall or winter can also be good times to divide plants, and some perennials—notably peonies—prefer being divided at that time.

PLANT DIVISION

Dividing perennials like this phlox is an easy process.

Materials needed

- Perennial in need of dividing
- Shovel or garden fork
- A shady spot
- Pruning saw (for large or thick plant crowns)

Step 1: Dig it up

Lifting a perennial up out of the ground is the first step to dividing plants—and physically the hardest. Large perennials can be quite heavy, particularly if gardeners are digging them out of clay soil. It may be a two-person job. Your goal when digging up a plant for division is to minimize damage to the roots. The best way to do this is to stick your shovel or a garden fork into the ground 6 to 12 inches (15–30 cm) away from the crown of the plant and then pull the handle back like a lever to pry the plant up and out of the soil. Pull the shovel/fork out of the soil, move a quarter of the way around the clump,

and repeat. The idea here is to cut through as few roots as possible, using your shovel or fork to lift the root system out of the soil rather than slicing through it. Keep going around the plant, prying up with your shovel or fork until the entire plant lifts up out of the ground.

Step 2: Shake it off

Once the plant is out of the ground, knock off as much of the soil as possible. You don't need to wash the roots clean, just remove the bulk of the soil. Simply lifting the clump up a few inches and dropping it down against the ground a few times, or pulling at the soil with your hands, will allow a lot of the soil to fall away, making it lighter and easier to handle. It also allows you to see the structure of the plant crown for the next step.

Step 3: Find shade
Exposed roots can be killed very quickly if they dry out or are exposed to direct sunlight, so as soon as you get your plant out of the ground and most of the soil cleared away, move it to a cool, shaded location for the subsequent steps. If you need to take a break before you can get the divided plant back in the ground, throw a damp cloth or towel over the roots to make sure they don't dry out.

Step 4: Plan your division
With most of the soil cleared away, look closely at the crown of the plant. The crown is the point where the roots and shoots meet. If you are dividing a dormant plant, you should be able to see large dormant buds present where the new shoots will emerge when conditions are right. These buds are sometimes called *eyes*. In most cases, as long as each piece of plant you separate has a healthy piece of root and at least one eye, the division will grow onto a new plant. So, if you are trying to make the most plants possible, you might plan to create smaller divisions with just one or two eyes each. But bigger divisions with more eyes will form bigger, more mature-looking plants. If you'd prefer bigger divisions, cut the full mass of the plant in half or into quarters.

If you are dividing a plant in active growth instead of in dormancy, there will be stems and leaves, but the principle is the same. Any division with leaves and roots should be able to grow into a new mature plant, and bigger chunks will mature faster and recover more easily from the dividing process.

Step 5: Make the cuts
How hard it is to separate a plant really depends on the species. Some species, like hostas and daylilies, have crowns that can simply be pulled or cracked apart with your hands. If you can do this, it is ideal. The more you pull and the less you cut, the more roots stay intact in each of the divisions. But other plants, like some ornamental grasses, have very thick, woody crowns that need to be cut apart with a saw.

To make the division, take the uprooted plant, lay it on its side so the roots are toward you and the crown of the plant is facing away from you, and with your hands try and pull the clump in half. If it pulls apart easily, keep pulling chunks apart until you are happy with the number and size of plants you have created.

If the plant does not yield to pulling, take a small pruning saw (keyhole saws work well too, and for small plants, cheap steak knives are great) and cut into the mass of the crown. Don't cut it all the way though; start just going a quarter of the way, and then half, pausing to pull with your hands after each cut. Often the root ball will tear apart easily once you've made a small cut, but sometimes you may need to saw nearly all the way through.

Step 6: Replant
Now it's time to replant your new divisions. One piece can go back where the original plant was, and the other divisions can go wherever you'd like more of them. If you don't know where to plant them, or if you have extras, pop the divisions into leftover nursery pots with some soil to wait for their final location or give them to a friend or neighbor. Treat new divisions like you would new plantings by keeping them well-watered for their first year as they reestablish. Be particularly diligent about watering them if you are dividing plants in active growth in the summer. Put any divisions you have potted up somewhere where they will get a little shade in the afternoon for the first couple of weeks while their root system recovers.

Some plants can be divided while the plant is still in the ground, rather than having to dig up the entire crown. This is a judgement call on the part of the gardener.

STEM CUTTINGS

Some plants can be propagated by stem cuttings. The process is a bit more complex than division, but it is much simpler than many gardeners realize. Taking stem cuttings involves removing a piece of the plant stem and providing it with the right conditions to grow new roots. Unlike division, taking cuttings causes minimal disruption to the parent plant. You can take a few cuttings off a favorite perennial without it being noticed at all, while newly divided perennials may need a year to recover. The other plus to taking cuttings is that gardeners can usually get a lot more new plants. One healthy perennial can yield dozens of cuttings, while division usually produces just three or four new plants. This can be great if you have a rare or expensive plant and want to fill your garden with it. Plus, cuttings are the best way to share plants with friends. It is a lot to ask to dig up a whole perennial from the garden and divide it to give to someone else, but it's quick and easy to trim off a few branches and pop them in a bag for someone to take home and root.

The basic mechanics of rooting cuttings are simple. A stem removed from a plant is still alive and can almost always grow new roots and become its own plant. However, that little cutting needs to photosynthesize to produce the energy to grow those roots and without any roots to take up water, it is easy for cuttings to dry out and die. To get cuttings to root, you need to keep them in high—nearly 100 percent—humidity so they don't dry out, while also giving them bright light to allow them to photosynthesize. If you've taken cuttings from houseplants, you are probably familiar with sticking them in a vase of water on a sunny windowsill to root. This method is very simple, but unfortunately, it usually only works with plants that root from cuttings very quickly. For plants—including most garden perennials—that take longer to root, the stem submerged in the water tends to rot and die before roots grow. Because of this, rooting most garden perennials requires a different process. The exceptions to this are perennials with succulent leaves, like sedums and delosperma. Because succulents store a lot of water in their leaves and stems, they will usually root from cuttings simply stuck in soil.

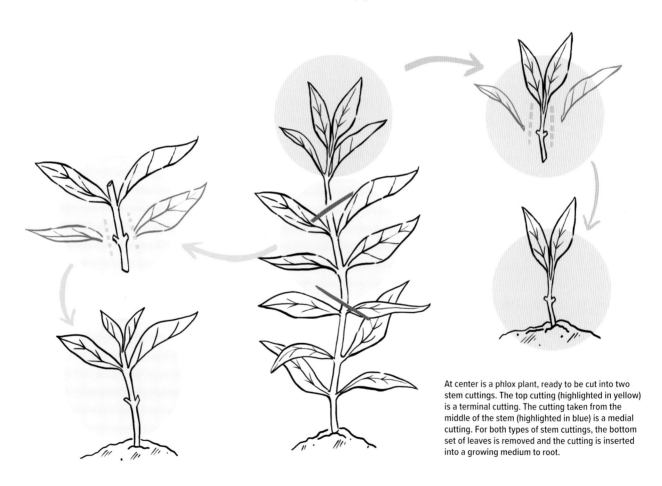

At center is a phlox plant, ready to be cut into two stem cuttings. The top cutting (highlighted in yellow) is a terminal cutting. The cutting taken from the middle of the stem (highlighted in blue) is a medial cutting. For both types of stem cuttings, the bottom set of leaves is removed and the cutting is inserted into a growing medium to root.

Before we get into the step-by-step process of rooting stem cuttings, there are a few concepts to keep in mind:

* **Some plants root easily, others are difficult.** The biology of a plant determines how easily it can create new roots. For first attempts at rooting cuttings, stick to plants described as rooting easily, but once you have the hang of it, don't be afraid to do a little trial and error on some harder plants. Taking cuttings doesn't require much time or effort, so there is no reason not to try rooting a cutting from a favorite perennial even if it is known to be slow to root.

* **Timing matters.** Some plants root best from cuttings taken in spring, others from cuttings taken later in the season. Plants that root easily can be cut just about any time, but fussier ones may have a narrow window when cuttings will root. If you can't find a reference telling you the best time to root a cutting, try it in spring with the first flush of growth, and then feel free to experiment with other times of the year.

* **Rooting hormone helps.** Hormones within a plant tell it where to focus its energies. Rooting hormone powders—usually available for sale at your local garden center—essentially tell the cutting to put all its energy into growing roots instead of trying to grow new leaves. Using rooting hormone isn't strictly necessary; you can root cuttings without it, but cuttings will almost always root faster, easier, and with higher success rates if you use a hormone.

* **Don't fall for gimmicks.** There are countless videos and posts online about weird ways to root cuttings. These range from the strange and very unlikely to work—like dipping them in honey—to ones that aren't terrible ideas but are more work and less reliable than simply using commercial rooting hormone—like making a DIY rooting hormone from willow twigs. The process of rooting cuttings is very well studied because it is big business. The majority of the plants gardeners buy from a nursery started their lives as cuttings and countless companies and professionals have spent their lives perfecting the process. Do yourself a favor and just grab a jar of rooting hormone and take advantage of all that professional experience rather than trying to reinvent the wheel with clickbait.

* **No flowers, please.** If possible, choose cuttings from plants that aren't about to flower. Flower bud development takes a lot of energy and will slow down or even prevent the rooting process. Plants that are in active growth but not near their flowering time are the best. If you can't find a stem without flower buds, simply pinch the buds off your cuttings prior to rooting them.

* **Keep the humidity up.** For propagating, use an enclosed container that lets light in and holds moist potting soil. The options are endless. Use recycled food containers with a clear plastic lid. Disposable aluminum casserole pans sold with matching clear plastic lids work great, too. Resealable plastic bags work as well, though they tend to fall over and can be annoying. Gardeners can also buy clear plastic humidity domes specifically designed for the job, but they are certainly not necessary.

* **Keep your rooting soil simple.** A few inches of standard potting soil in your container works great to support plants and give their roots somewhere to grow. If possible, avoid potting soils with added fertilizer. Gardeners can also use pure vermiculite or perlite. These are often added to potting soils to increase drainage, but they also work great for rooting cuttings as they are nearly sterile, which reduces the chances of cuttings rotting before they grow roots.

* **Get the lighting right.** Cuttings need light to photosynthesize, but direct sun will cause the little container to heat up and cook the cuttings. If rooting cuttings outside, the north side of a wall or fence where the direct sun never shines works great. Bright windowsills can work as well for indoor cuttings. But the best location is indoors under artificial lights. Modern LED lights produce virtually no heat but emit a great wavelength for photosynthesis, so they produce perfect conditions for rooting cuttings. If you have a grow light set up for starting seeds it will also work perfectly for rooting cuttings. If not, nearly any lamp with an LED bulb adjusted to shine directly on your cuttings for 12 to 14 hours a day works fantastically.

ROOTING *Stem* CUTTINGS

Stem cuttings are an easy way to propagate many perennials, including the lavender (*Lavandula* sp.) shown here.

Materials needed

- Sterile potting soil
- Clean pots or containers
- Clear plastic cover or dome
- Clean, sharp pruning shears or plant snips
- Rooting hormone powder
- Perennial plant you want to propagate
- Water

Step 1: Fill the container

Whatever container you are using to root the cutting, fill it with moist—but not soggy—potting soil. Add water until the soil is moistened. If you grab a handful of the potting soil and give it a light squeeze, it should feel wet, but no water should stream out. If it is too wet, add some additional dry soil. If it's too dry, add a little more water.

Step 2: Take the cutting

The perfect perennial cutting is taken from the tip of a stem in active growth. It should have three or four leaves and no flowers, seed pods, or flower buds. It's best to take cuttings on a cool morning when the plant is fully hydrated. But the reality is that you won't always get perfect cuttings, depending on the timing of your efforts and other factors. If your cutting has flower buds, just pinch them off. If you can't get enough tip cuttings, take a longer stem and cut it into sections, each with three or four leaves, and root those. If the weather has been hot and dry and the plant is a little wilted, soak the entire cutting in cool water until it plumps up. Don't expect 100 percent success, so always take extra cuttings to account for potential failures. If all the cuttings end up rooting, well, you'll just have extra plants to share with friends!

Step 3: Remove the lower leaves

Remove one or two leaves from the base of the cutting, either by pulling or snipping them off. Keep the top-most two or three leaves; more if they are very small or just one or two if they are very large. Very large leaves can be cut in half.

Step 4: Dip the base in rooting hormone

Take the now-leafless bottom end of the cutting and dip it in rooting hormone powder. Freshly cut stem surfaces absorb the hormones best, so dip the cutting in hormone promptly after taking it and removing the leaves. If you've had to store the cutting for a while—for example, if a friend gave you a cutting and you drove home with it in a plastic bag—re-trim the end to get a fresh cut surface before dipping it in the hormone powder. Knock off any excess hormone powder.

Step 5: Stick the cutting into the soil

Insert the hormone-covered base of the cutting into the pot of soil. Be sure

Remove the lower leaves from stem cuttings before adding the rooting hormone.

Insert the base of the hormone-covered stem into a pot of new, sterile potting soil.

at least one of the nodes at the base of the leaves you removed is below the soil and that any remaining leaves are above the soil.

Step 6: Cover and wait
Put the cover or dome on your container and move it into a bright location (but avoid direct sun). Wait for the cutting to put down roots. The timing here can vary a lot depending on the plant, the time of year, and temperature, but generally, it takes two to three weeks for roots to start forming.

Step 7: Check the cutting regularly
About once a week, open the lid and look at the cutting. Remove any brown leaves and check for soft and moldy spots. This happens sometimes (it isn't a big deal), but mold will spread to other nearby cuttings, so discard any cuttings that develop mold.

Step 8: Check for roots
After about two weeks, start checking to see if your cutting has rooted. Experienced propagators use the "tug test"—which means gently pulling up on a cutting. Cuttings without roots pull out of the soil easily, while those with roots cling to the soil, giving a little resistance when you pull on them. However, if you pull too hard, you run the risk of damaging newly developed roots. If you are unsure, gently slide a finger into the soil and lift the cutting up from below, so you can get a better look at what's going on beneath the soil. No roots? Stick it back in and wait. Just a few roots? Best to let the roots grow a little more. Cuttings are ready to be repotted when they have a nice crop of roots. As a rule of thumb, when the root mass is about the same size as the leaf mass growing above ground, the root system is big enough to support the plant.

Step 9: Pot up the cutting
Newly rooted cuttings are delicate. Give them a little extra care while they adjust to life outside of their little humidity bubble. Pot each one into a slightly larger container with good potting soil and place them in a shaded spot outdoors for a few days, gradually moving them into more sun over the next few weeks. If they wilt during the heat of the afternoon, move them back into the shade. Plant them out in the garden when they are fully adjusted.

Cover the pot of cuttings with a clear plastic bag or a rigid plastic dome and place the pot in a bright location.

ROOT CUTTINGS

Some plants are most easily propagated from root cuttings. Instead of taking a piece of stem and encouraging it to grow roots, you take a piece of root and encourage it to grow stems.

This technique will only work for a few perennials. Because roots, of course, do not photosynthesize, root cuttings can't produce any new energy during the propagation process, so they have to rely on stored energy already in the roots. Reference books and websites will list which species can be propagated by root cuttings, but gardeners can also use visual cues to make an educated guess. Perennials that can be propagated via root cuttings have thick, fleshy roots with more food stored in them. Those species with just thin, fibrous roots, generally cannot be propagated this way.

One downside to root cuttings is that you have to dig up a plant to get them, so often the best time to take root cuttings is when you'll be disrupting a plant anyway, for example if you're digging it up to move or divide it. Planting time can also be a good chance to take root cuttings. If a plant is very potbound and has nice thick roots circling around in the pot, those outer roots need to be removed anyway, so you might as well use them as root cuttings.

The upside to root cuttings is that they are very easy. Unlike stem cuttings, there's no need to worry about them drying out. You don't have to keep them in high humidity or protect them from hot sun, and there's no need for rooting hormones. Harvesting the cuttings is the hard part; after that it is as easy as can be.

Root cuttings are a great way to propagate species with thick, fleshy roots.

Common Perennials to Propagate from Root Cuttings

Tall phlox (*Phlox paniculata*)

Yucca (*Yucca* species)

Oriental poppy (*Papaver orientale*)

Drumstick primrose (*Primula denticulata*)

Bear's britches (*Acanthus* species)

Mullein (*Verbascum* species)

Fall-blooming anemones (*Anemone hupehensis* and related hybrids)

Globe thistle (*Echinops* species)

ROOT CUTTINGS

Use a clean, sharp knife to take root cuttings.

Materials needed

- Perennial with thick, fleshy roots
- Clean, sharp knife
- Damp towel
- Clean garden pot
- Potting soil
- Label

Step 1: Remove the roots

Gently dig or lift your plant out of the soil, or if it is in a pot, slide it out of the pot. Working in the shade and using a sharp pair of pruners or scissors, cut one or two sturdy roots from the plant. Look for firm, thick roots. Thin, fibrous feeder roots will not work, nor will any that feel soft or have rot on them. If the weather is hot and dry, have a damp towel nearby to place over the root cuttings to keep them from drying out while you work.

Step 2: Make multiple cuttings

Take your root pieces and cut them into multiple segments each 3 to 4 inches (7.6–10 cm) long, though longer cuttings will certainly work too, and somewhat shorter ones may be successful depending on the plant. When cutting the roots, it is critically important to remember which end of the root was facing up. If you plant your root cuttings upside down they will not produce shoots. The traditional way to keep this straight is to trim the top of the root with a flat cut, and trim the bottom with an angled cut, so even if you drop the cutting, you can tell which end is up. If a plant is very special and you want added insurance, dust the cut ends of the roots with a fungicide to ward off rot. But this is not necessary.

Trim the top of the root with a straight cut and the bottom of the root with an angled cut so you can always tell which end is up.

Step 3: Plant your cuttings

Get a pot large enough for the cuttings to sit inside when oriented vertically and fill it with potting soil. Insert the cuttings into the soil vertically so the top of the cutting is just at or very slightly below the soil surface. You can put multiple cuttings in one pot, and then separate them into individual pots once they've grown shoots, or just put one cutting per pot at the start.

All is not lost if somehow you weren't paying attention and don't know which end of the root is up. Simply place them horizontally toward the top of the pot and cover them very thinly with soil. Once shoots begin to develop, you can replant the root the right way vertically down into the soil, which will help it start a deep, healthy root system.

Step 4: Wait

Put the cuttings in a sunny spot, keeping them watered, and then just wait. During the growing season, you should see shoots in about three weeks. If you took cuttings in the fall, as the plant was going dormant, you will not see growth until the spring. Root cuttings need basically no special care. Just watch them grow and plant them out in the garden when they've gotten big enough.

STARTING FROM SEED

Growing a plant—any plant—from seed is often seen as advanced gardening, and many gardeners mistakenly think that growing perennials from seed is the hardest of all. Gardeners might venture to try some tomatoes for the vegetable garden, but usually don't think to grow echinaceas for the perennial bed.

The happy reality is that growing plants from seed isn't hard at all, and perennials are arguably the most forgiving group of plants to start this way. Seeds, after all, are how plants propagate themselves in nature. Germinating seeds is not about manipulating a plant to do something odd; it is simply giving the seeds the conditions to do what millennia of evolution has designed them to do.

Perennials are very forgiving to grow from seed because gardeners have multiple years to get things right. Edibles, like tomatoes, are many gardeners' first foray into seed starting, but they are actually quite fussy. Because they only live for one season, if you start them too late you won't get any harvest. But a perennial that germinates late in the season? Why, it will just overwinter and keep on growing next year.

If starting seeds instantly conjures up images of rows of grow lights in a basement, well, those aren't necessary for perennial seeds either. Starting seeds early indoors under lights is critical for annuals, to give them a head start for a good performance over the summer. You certainly can start perennials indoors under lights, and that can be a lot of fun, but it isn't needed at all. With years to grow in your garden, a few extra weeks at the beginning of their life will make no difference at all in the long-term.

Benefits of Growing from Seed

Mastering the skill of propagating perennials from seed has a lot of huge benefits for gardeners and the garden. Seeds are the cheapest way to get new plants for the garden. Seeds may even be free if collected from a friend's garden, but even a full-price packet of rare seeds is going to be a tiny fraction of the cost of even a small potted perennial. And the smallest of seed packets will contain enough seeds to grow dozens of plants. For gardeners wanting to fill a garden on a budget, seeds are the way to go.

Starting perennials from seed is a rewarding experience that yields lots of plants for very little cost.

Seeds are the only form of plants that are easy to manage as inventory. This may seem like a weird thing to say, but most plants are very delicate perishable items. They are hard to ship and hard to store. If they don't sell right away, they outgrow their pots or even die. This means that nurseries have to be very careful about choosing the most popular, durable plants if they want to stay in business. Nearly all seeds, on the other hand, can be stored for years in cool temperatures, are lightweight, easy to ship, and are very easy to manage. That means countless species of perennials that are never found for sale as plants are easily available as seeds. There are many small, specialty seed companies offering unique native plants for sale. Gardeners may even find local venders who collect—with the proper permits and permissions—seeds from local native plants in your area. Learning to grow from seed opens up a whole new world of plant material to enjoy.

There are many good environmental reasons to grow from seed. A few packets of seed arriving through the mail uses almost no energy to ship, especially compared to the amount of fossil fuels used to heat greenhouses and then ship heavy plants in wet pots of soil from wholesalers to big box stores. When gardeners grow from seed, they can skip the pesticides and easily reuse their plastic pots year after year.

Seeds are also just about the only form of a plant that can be sustainably taken from the wild. The poaching of whole plants from the wild is still, sadly, a serious problem, especially with cacti and other succulents, and when buying live plants, make sure they are nursery propagated and not wild-collected. But a single wild plant produces hundreds or even thousands of seeds each year, and a few of these can be collected—with proper permits and permissions—without harming wild populations. Because of this, seeds are simply the most responsible way to get native plants to grow in the home garden.

Propagation by cuttings and division produces genetically identical clones of the parent plant. This can be a good thing because it recreates any unusually good traits of the parent plant, but there are downsides as well. In nature, populations of plants are all genetically a little different, and this helps them deal with unexpected challenges, as some individuals will do better in a drought year, others thrive in a wet year. This diversity makes the population as a whole more resilient.

Gardeners can benefit from this diversity in the garden, too. When growing out a flat of seedlings, each one will be a little bit different genetically—especially if they came from wild-collected seeds. That diversity means you will have a better chance of finding individuals that are better adapted to the exact conditions in your garden. If a few die the first cold winter or dry summer, you are left with better adapted survivors.

If you plan to start perennial seeds indoors, a grow light is essential.

That diversity can be great visually as well, especially if you are going for an informal or naturalistic design. A mass of twenty identical clonal plants can look good, but that same mass grown from seed will have subtle variations in height and flower color that gives more interest and a much more natural look.

Why Seed Might Not Sprout

There are a few twists to realize when starting perennial seeds. One challenge is that many of them have a built-in genetically determined seed dormancy. Most perennials native to climates with cold winters have seeds that will not germinate until after they've experienced a period of cold temperatures. This is a simple adaptation that ensures their seeds sprout in the spring. This means you can't just sow these seeds in warm conditions like you would a marigold and have them sprout a week later. But you can use this built-in timer to ensure perennial seeds germinate at just the right time to thrive by sowing them outside in the fall and letting them experience the natural winter temperatures. Or, if you want, you can mimic the cold temperatures of winter by putting the seeds in your refrigerator—but starting them outdoors is far easier.

Seeds from wild perennial populations tend to not germinate all at once, even if conditions are perfect. This is nature's way of having insurance against a whole generation of seeds getting wiped out by a freak late freeze or a hungry rabbit. When seeds germinate a few at a time over a matter of weeks, it is harder for any one thing to harm them all. Gardeners tend to find this frustrating because when sowing seeds we can protect them against freak accidents and it is more convenient if they all germinate at the same time.

Because of this, many plants, like most vegetables and common annual flowers, have been bred by humans to germinate fast and uniformly. If you plant a packet of zinnia seeds, you'll get near 100 percent germination in just a week or two. Perennials, because they are less commonly grown from seed and usually have fewer generations of breeding behind them, will often have lower germination percentages, and may not all sprout at once. This is not much of a problem as most seed packets will have far more seeds than the average home gardener can use, so just sow a few extra.

Collecting seeds from local plants (with permission from the landowner) is a great way to raise plants that are better adapted to your local growing conditions.

Seed Starting Outside

Starting perennial seeds outside is the easiest method. No special equipment is needed, and you don't have to go through the hassle of slowly adapting young plants to outdoor conditions because they're already growing there. Basically, all gardeners need to do is give pots of seeds a little extra protection to make sure they aren't damaged by the weather and pests, and they are good to go.

The best time to start the process of germinating seeds outside is in early winter using a technique sometimes called winter sowing. Placed outside, the seeds will naturally receive any cold treatment they require, and then germinate in the spring as the weather warms. This method also means gardeners don't need to look up last frost dates in the spring or otherwise research much about the seeds and how they grow. Basically, just rely on their naturally evolved schedule for germination and growth.

OUTDOOR SEED STARTING

Plastic milk jugs are great for starting perennial seeds outdoors using a process known as winter sowing. Cut the jug tops almost all the way off, leaving a hinge where the bottom of the handle connects.

most of the top of the jug and then reattach it with tape so it serves as a sort of greenhouse cover over the seeds. This can be helpful to protect the seeds from hungry rodents but can also be problematic. The plastic cover will obscure some of the sunlight from getting to the seeds, and on sunny days, the cover can trap a lot of heat, potentially leading to scorched seedlings or causing some seeds to germinate too early. If you do put any kind of clear plastic cover over your seeds, be sure to remove it on sunny days to keep the temperatures moderated.

Gardeners can also sow perennial seeds in a dedicated seed bed, which is essentially a small, raised bed filled with good potting soil. Avoid regular garden soil or homemade compost as they will usually have weed seeds in them (which can be easily confused with your germinating perennials). Cover the seed bed with a wire screen to keep rodents and other pests out. Seed beds are great because they are more insulated from sudden temperature changes than containers and they don't dry out as easily.

Step 2: Sow your seeds

The visual appearance of seeds will often help you determine how to plant them. Very tiny seeds, the size of poppy seeds or smaller, should be sown directly on the soil surface, and not covered at all (or only covered with a tiny sprinkle of soil). These tiny seeds usually need light to germinate, and they don't have enough stored food to push up through a deep layer of soil. The rule of thumb with bigger seeds is to cover them with a layer of soil equal to the width of the seed. So, the bigger the seed, the deeper you plant it.

Materials needed

- Perennial seeds
- Plastic gallon jugs
- Potting soil
- Scissors
- Permanent marker
- Duct tape
- Watering can or hose with a mist nozzle

Step 1: Prep your containers

Gardeners can germinate perennial seeds in a variety of containers, and really, almost anything will work. Probably the easiest is to simply fill a regular nursery pot with good quality potting soil. To protect against hungry mice, squirrels, and other rodents, lay a sheet of wire hardware cloth or another fine, metal screening over the tops of the pots. You can also recycle old food containers and jugs to start seeds. Old gallon (3.8 L) plastic milk jugs are a popular option. Punch drainage holes in the bottom. Cut off

Use standard potting mix to fill the base of the jugs to just below the hinge.

After the seeds are planted, close the jug and use duct tape to secure it closed. Put the jug in a sheltered, sunny spot.

When conditions are right, the perennial seeds germinate. Pot them up into larger containers when they have a few sets of true leaves.

Step 3: Water

Gently water your sowing containers or seed bed. Be sure to use a watering can or hose with a fine spray of water to avoid disturbing the soil and seeds too much. With very tiny seeds, it can be easiest to set the pots or containers in a tray of water and let moisture soak up through the soil from the bottom.

Step 4: Put them in the right spot

A sheltered, sunny spot is best for your seed containers. Choose a place where the pots will be insulated from extreme temperature swings and where they will get some light but not be baked by the hot, direct sun. Against the east wall of a house or shed is often perfect, as the wall provides a little insulation and the seed pots will get morning sun, but shade during the heat of the afternoon.

Step 5: Wait

During the winter, you don't have to do much. Check the pots periodically during warm spells to make sure they are not drying out, but otherwise, just let them nestle under the snow and through the freezing weather.

Step 6: Check for germination

As spring arrives, start checking on the seeds a few times a week, watering if needed and looking for the first signs of green life. If using a container with a cover, remove it as soon as a few seeds germinate so the seedlings can adjust to the conditions out in the real world. The first visual cue of success is the appearance of special leaves called *cotyledons*—the leaves pre-formed inside the seeds (sometimes called the *seed leaves*). These look quite different than the mature leaves of the plant. The cotyledons will then be followed by the true leaves, which will look more like the mature leaves of a plant.

Step 7: Pot up the seedlings

Once the seedlings have grown a little—usually as soon they have a few sets of true leaves—move them into individual containers. This process is sometimes called *pricking out*. Ideally, do this when the seedlings are big enough to handle without breaking, but before the root system has gotten so large they are difficult to separate. Seedlings are generally pretty robust and tolerant, and the exact timing isn't critical.

To separate the seedlings, slide all the soil and root mass out of the container and onto a tray, and gently tease the seedlings apart. If they are growing in a seed bed, just gently scoop under the soil with a trowel and lift up the mass of soil with the seedlings. Next, gently squeeze the soil to help it crumble and separate, and then, holding by the leaves, gently pull each seedling apart from the others. Never handle baby seedlings by the base of the stem. Torn leaves can be replaced, but if you break the stem off at the base, the seedling is a goner.

Once your seedlings are separated, gently tuck the roots of each into their own pot full of potting soil, and water them thoroughly.

Step 8: Keep them growing

Once your individual seedlings have been potted up, keep them watered and fertilized as they grow. Most perennials will be ready to plant out in the garden that fall. If you decide to keep them in pots for another year so they can grow bigger and not be lost in the garden, be sure to give the pots some extra insulation during the winter to protect the roots from sudden temperature swings. Surrounding the outside of the pots with straw mulch or shredded leaves does a good insulating job.

Starting perennials indoors requires more specialized equipment and patience, but it is a fun process.

Starting Perennial Seeds Indoors

Most of the mechanics of starting seeds indoors is the same as outside, with the addition of just placing the seed pots under lights. But gardeners will have to look out for more potential problems and do a bit of planning to ensure perennial seeds germinate well, have enough light, avoid disease, and adjust smoothly to life outside in the real world.

Since many perennial seeds need cold to germinate but they won't receive that naturally indoors, start with some research. Usually putting the name of a plant and the word "germination" into your favorite online search engine will turn up information about germination requirements. If a species needs a cold treatment to initiate germination (called *stratification*), put the seeds in a resealable plastic bag with a little moist sand or sphagnum moss and place the bag in the refrigerator for two to three months. After that time, take the seeds out of the bag and sow them as you normally would. Alternatively, you can plant the seeds in pots and put the pots outside in the fall, just as you would for outdoor seed sowing, but then, once the seeds have been exposed to a few months of cold temperatures, move the pots inside to let them get a jumpstart on spring by spending time indoors under lights.

Instead of sunlight, gardeners will be relying on artificial lights for starting perennial seeds indoors. A variety of lights can be used, but cool white LED shop lights are cheap and available at any hardware or home improvement store. LED bulbs produce great light for plants to photosynthesize and are very cheap and ecofriendly to operate. If seedlings are growing long and lanky, they need more light. Add another shop light or, if you can, move the pots outside on warm sunny days when the temperature is above freezing.

The still air, high humidity, and lack of UV light found indoors makes for perfect conditions for *damping off*. This is a general name for a variety of fungal and bacterial diseases that thrive in moist conditions and can cause seedlings to rot off right where their stem meets the soil. Damping off can be devastating—one moment, your seedlings look healthy and perfect, and the next they are collapsed and dead. To limit the incidents of damping off, always use fresh, high-quality potting soil, wash and disinfect your pots with bleach and soapy water before reusing them, sprinkle a layer of grit (fine gravel—farm supply stores sell small bags of it as "Chick Grit" for feeding to young chickens) on the soil surface, and add a small fan to your growing area to gently keep the air moving. For very precious seedlings, a fungicidal spray can be added insurance. Or gardeners can just start the seeds outside where natural air movement and sunlight make damping off very rare.

The other place where starting perennial seeds indoors is different from other types of seeds is at the end of the process. Sometimes if you just take plants straight from the sheltered conditions of your indoor growing setup out to the rough and tumble of the outside world, they can get sunburned and damaged. Most of the time, this is because plants haven't adapted to the bright intense sunlight outside. Some of this is because grow lights generally produce less intense light than the actual sun, and some of it is because grow lights produce no ultraviolet light at all, and plants need UV light to produce their version of sunscreen to protect against sunburn.

The process of slowly acclimating seedings to outdoor growing conditions is known as *hardening off*. The traditional way to harden seedlings off is to start a week or two before planting your seedlings outside, and slowly give them more and more time outdoors each day. First just an hour, the next day two hours, and so on until they are staying outside full time, at which point they are ready for planting.

There are a few things you can do to make this process easier and limit the amount of stress the seedlings undergo during the transition.

First, while inside, keep light levels as high as possible. As was discussed in the section on sun and shade in chapter two, plants produce different types of leaves depending on the conditions where they are growing. Plants produce thin, delicate shade leaves in low light, and thicker, tougher sun leaves in high light. So, if your plants are burning from too much sun—developing bleached out or brown patches on the leaves—when you put them outside, you might need to add another grow light to your setup to increase the light levels.

Another trick is to take as much advantage of outside growing conditions as possible. If gardeners are growing indoors in the winter to get a jumpstart on the growing season, take your plants outside on warm, sunny days, even when they are still small. This regular exposure to natural sunlight gets them ready for outdoor conditions and basically eliminates the need to harden them off when spring arrives. Just be very sure to bring them inside again before temperatures drop near freezing again. Even plants that can take very cold temperatures in winter will suffer cold damage if they experience sudden changes from warm conditions to freezing ones without time to adjust.

Some perennials, like this lupine, are easier to start from seed than others. Don't be afraid to experiment.

CONCLUSION

WHETHER YOU GO plant shopping, germinate seeds, or grow from cuttings, acquiring new plants is a fun and ongoing part of managing a garden. Learning how to manage that process and get the very best plants will set your garden up for success. Mastering the art of propagation will allow you to fill your garden with unusual plants without breaking the bank. It is also a fun way to share your favorite plants with friends and neighbors.

Next, let's move on to investigate the process of preparing for and planting new plants in the garden.

CHAPTER 5

PUTTING PLANTS
in the
GROUND

How to prepare and plant your garden

UP TO THIS POINT, there has been much work and planning done in anticipation of a new perennial garden. So far, every detail of understanding your garden and its place in the world and larger ecosystem has been discussed. As well, all the concepts and principles needed to plan your garden and shop for plants are well versed. Finally, it is time to get outside and start turning all those plans and preparations into a reality.

PREPARING
the SOIL

BEFORE STARTING TO PUT plants in the ground, gardeners need to clear and prepare the space to receive them. For most North Americans, this means starting with a lawn, as that is the default groundcover on this continent, but you might also be starting with an overgrown meadow, a patch of brush and invasive weeds, or even an old or neglected garden. Regardless of what is there, it is critically important to completely remove any plants already growing there before you start planting. Anything you leave behind

will just keep rearing its ugly head as an annoying weed in the future. A little work to thoroughly eliminate those unwanted plants at the beginning of the process will make life much easier for years to come.

A weed is defined as a plant growing where you don't want it, so there might be a few plants in the area that aren't actually weeds and don't need to be killed off. Maybe a former homeowner plopped a few nice perennials at the edge of the boring lawn right where you want to transform it into a garden. Or maybe that overgrown meadow has a few nice native perennials in among the invasive weeds. It is possible to work around those plants, but often the easiest way to move forward is to just dig out the plants you want to keep and put them in pots while you prepare the rest of the space. Fundamentally, the process of clearing ground is killing off plants, so it is just easier to move anything you want to keep out of the way so you can work smoothly and directly to make space for the new garden.

CLEARING THE GROUND

There are lots of ways to clear the ground, and frankly, none of them are perfect. The process will always be somewhat disruptive and picking the right method is a matter of balancing the pros and cons of each and matching them up to what will work for you personally.

Tilling using a mechanical tiller is one way to start a new garden, but it disrupts soil structure and is a lot of work. It can also bring up a lot of dormant weed seeds from beneath the soil's surface, creating a lasting weed issue.

Double digging is a traditional way to create a new planting bed, but it is a lot of work for very little reward.

Tilling

Renting a tiller and using it to clear an area is a very traditional method, stretching back to the use of horse-drawn plows, but it has some serious drawbacks. Tillage harms soil structure, breaking up those precious soil aggregates. If you have light, sandy soil, this impact will be minimal, but if you have very heavy clay soil that really requires great soil structure for healthy drainage and plant growth, even one round of tillage when the soil is too wet can have lasting negative impacts on the soil health. Tilling is also physically a lot of work—again, especially on heavy clay soils—and doesn't always kill the plants living there. You may have to rake out the remaining clumps of grass to keep them from regrowing and you may have to dig out more pervasive weeds. Also, turning over the soil can expose dormant weed seeds to light, triggering a mass germination of weeds. It can also be difficult or even impossible to use this method if you are dealing with a very overgrown or weedy field, as most tillers will struggle with root systems more substantial than lawn grasses.

The plus side to tillage is that it is fast. While many of the other methods require waiting for plants to die, a newly tilled bed can be planted the same afternoon. It also mixes the soil, so it can, to some degree, break up surface compaction if a soil has been tramped down by foot traffic or heavy machinery. Tilling can also incorporate compost or other organic matter into the soil if it needs it, though this benefit is limited by the depth to which you can till.

Double Digging

This is a traditional, and backbreaking, method of preparing garden soil that is no longer recommended since it is also extremely disruptive to soil life. It involves digging a trench one shovel's depth deep and placing the soil to the side on a tarp or in a wheelbarrow. Take a shovel and work down in that trench to loosen the soil and mix in compost or other soil amendments. Next, you move down and dig another trench, filling in the first trench with that soil from the next, so you can reach the subsoil there, amend that, and so on to the end of the bed, until you fill the last trench with the soil you dug from the first one.

This method is a huge amount of work, and the thinking was it created very rich, deep soil, by mixing in compost and organic matter deep into the subsoil. The reality is that that extreme amount of work doesn't give an equally extreme payoff. Most plant roots stay close to the soil surface except in the lightest, sandiest of soils, and organic matter will move from the soil surface into the deeper soil naturally as roots and soil life grow, move, and die.

Sod stripping using a shovel or mechanical sod stripper is a great way to create a new planting bed in places where lawn exists. However, it does require a lot of effort, though it is only a one-time effort.

Solarization involves placing a sheet of clear plastic over the future garden site and waiting for the sun's heat to kill all the plants beneath it.

Sod Stripping

If you have a thick, healthy lawn right where you want your garden to go, you can use a special tool called a *sod cutter*—you'll probably want to rent one—to peel the lawn turf off the soil below like the skin off an orange. This can also be done by hand with a sharp shovel and a very strong back, though it is a lot of work if you are clearing a large area. Like tilling, sod stripping is fast, and you can plant immediately afterward. Unlike tilling, it doesn't disrupt soil structure, but you do end up removing a layer of vital topsoil with the sod. If you have deep, rich soil, this may be just fine. But if your soil is already low on organic matter or is thin, this process may be removing the only good soil there is in your garden.

A variation of the sod stripping method is to not remove the turf completely, but rather to flip it upside down to kill the grass but keep all the topsoil in place. In this case, you'd do best to follow up the sod stripping and flipping with a layer of deep mulch to keep the grass from coming back. You will have to wait a few weeks for the grass to die and begin to break down before you can plant.

Solarization

The solarization method requires taking a sheet of clear plastic, placing it over your future garden area, and holding down the edges so it doesn't blow away. On a warm, sunny day, the plastic will trap enough heat to kill all the plants under it. This method can be very effective if you live in a hot, sunny climate. It is less effective if you live in the North, in one of the cloudy parts of North America, or are trying to prepare a bed in the cool weather of spring or autumn. If the soil under the plastic doesn't get hot enough, it may just kill off the surface growth but leave viable roots below ground to resprout. It can be hard to know for sure how effective this has been, so, ideally, wait a couple of weeks after solarizing an area to be sure nothing is growing back before planting. On the plus side, this method doesn't disturb the soil structure at all, but on the negative side, the heat will also kill a lot of the soil life in the top few inches of soil. It is also very little work—no heavy digging or lifting required.

Smothering with Opaque Plastic

This method is similar to solarization but uses a dark sheet of plastic to cover the ground. In this case, instead of killing everything off with heat, you simply exclude all light and wait for the plants to die. It will generally take a week or two—faster in warm weather, slower in cooler temperatures. To check the progress, lift the plastic and check to see that everything under the plastic is brown and dead before removing it. If you have the time, it can be great to pull off the plastic and wait a week or two, which will encourage any weed seeds in the soil to germinate, then put the plastic back down for another week to kill them off. This can significantly reduce your weed problems long-term in the garden.

The biggest downside to this method is the time it takes, but it causes minimal disruption to the soil and is very little work.

Sheet Mulching

This is a simple and very popular method. First, cover your soon-to-be garden area with a layer of cardboard or newspaper. In these days of online shopping and online news reading, you will likely have more cardboard than newspaper, but both will work well. Just be sure to remove any plastic tape from the cardboard boxes, which will not break down. Then, cover all the cardboard with layers of organic matter (untreated grass clippings, fall leaves, straw, compost, etc.) or a thick layer of mulch. Just as with the previous method, the cardboard excludes light, killing off the plants below, but unlike plastic, over several months it will decompose and disappear, so you don't have to remove it.

If you are working with large plants—in gallon (3.8-L) or quart (1-L)-size pots—you can even plant and sheet mulch all at once. First, put your plants straight into the grass, and then put down the cardboard and mulch around them to smother out the weeds. This becomes quite tedious if you have a lot of plants to install or are using small plugs. In those cases, it is better to sheet mulch and then wait three weeks or so for the weeds to die and the cardboard to begin to break down before planting through it.

Sheet mulching is a simple way to create a new planting bed. Smother the existing grass or weeds with a layer of cardboard or multiple sheets of newspaper, then cover that with layers of organic matter, compost, or mulch.

The cardboard layer will block normal water and airflow into the soil, which isn't great for the various organisms living in the soil, but the effect is temporary, vanishing as the cardboard decomposes. Just be extra careful to hand-water newly installed plants until the cardboard has completely vanished as normal rainfall or water from sprinklers may just hit the cardboard and run off.

Landscape Fabric

Landscape fabric, popularly promoted in the past, is no longer recommended. It is a thin, usually woven, porous fabric sheet tthat is put down over the area and then covered with mulch. Gardeners then would cut holes in it to install plants. In theory, landscape fabric smothers weeds while allowing water and air to move through it into the soil. Landscape fabric often feels like a magical solution the first year or two, but then the mulch and fallen leaves on the surface break down to create enough soil for weeds to grow. These plant roots push their way through the fabric making holes for more weeds to grow. After a few years, there is a tangled, torn layer of fabric in the soil that has to be tediously removed.

Deep Mulching

This method of mulching is probably only feasible if gardeners have access to large quantities of free wood chips and have an area that you are planning to plant in a couple of years. Deep mulching is a variant on sheet mulching where, instead of putting down a layer of cardboard, you simply mow whatever grass or other plants are on the site down as low as possible and then pile wood chip mulch on the area to a depth of 1 foot (30 cm) or more. Wait at least three weeks, and then plant, being sure to push the wood chips away from the crowns of plants so they don't get smothered. This method is probably the best for the soil, but it is also more challenging for beginning gardeners. The deep mulch kills plants while allowing water and air to move through it, and the eventually decomposing wood chips add lots of organic matter. But the many downsides mean this method often just isn't practical. Most obviously, shoveling that amount of wood chips into place is a lot of work. It is also quite difficult to plant through the mulch layer, particularly if installing a large number of small plants. Cost can be an issue here as well. If you live in an urban area with a lot of trees, you may be able to get the wood chips for free from a local arborist, but if you have to purchase the mulch, it can eat up a lot of the gardening budget. Finally, this method will not work to smother all plants. Large, robust perennial weeds can push up through even very deep mulch, and some lawn grasses will as well. Do not attempt this method if you have Bermuda grass in your lawn—as is common in the southeastern United States—because the rhizomes are capable of growing up through 2 feet (61 cm) or more of mulch. After a long wait, the mulch will have broken down significantly, enriching the soil and making it much easier to plant through.

Herbicide

The American Horticultural Society does not advocate using synthetic pesticides, including herbicides, in the garden, but if gardeners feel the need to use an herbicide to clear unwanted plants before installing a garden, there are a few things of which to be aware. First, read the label thoroughly and follow all safety precautions—gloves, respirator, and so on—as recommended, even if it is an organic herbicide. Horticultural vinegar will kill (knock back) plants, but it is a very strong acid and can harm your skin, arms, or any wildlife you may have accidentally sprayed it on. Also be very wary of DIY herbicides. Periodically, there are social media posts recommending using things like salt, dish soap, or household chemicals to kill weeds. These are usually both ineffective and also can do lasting damage to your soil. If you feel you must use a spray to kill plants, use an herbicide properly labeled for the use and read and follow the label instructions thoroughly.

New planting beds can be amended with a few inches of compost prior to planting.

AMENDING YOUR SOIL

As discussed in the section on understanding your garden, local native plants are adapted to your local soil types, but your soil may be significantly damaged by the processes of development and may need some help recovering. What your soil needs most often is to rebuild the rich topsoil layer, which is high in organic matter, nutrients, and water-holding capacity. Gardeners can amend soil anytime, but it is always easier to do it before planting, as you can dump the soil amendments down and rake them out rather than having to laboriously spread them around each plant.

Compost

Compost is organic matter that has mostly decomposed, and a layer spread over the soil will quickly get mixed in by soil organisms and begin rebuilding the topsoil. If possible, avoid compost from plastic bags. Storing compost in plastic kills off the beneficial organisms living in it, and the less plastic that is used in our gardening efforts the better. Many cities have programs where they collect yard waste, turn it into compost, and then citizens can get it either for free or for a small charge. This is the ideal source of compost—unless you make your own—as it is local.

Be wary of composted manure from local farms as sometimes herbicides used on hay fields and in growing animal feeds persists in the manure and compost made from it.

If you have healthy, rich soil, compost will not be necessary. Otherwise, add 1 to 2 inches (2.5–5 cm) over your existing soil. No need to dig it in. That will only disrupt the natural soil structure. The organisms in soil will incorporate it into the ground.

Peat

Sphagnum moss growing in bogs slowly creates peat over time as layers and layers of the dead mosses build up, never fully decomposing due to the extremely acidic conditions in the bog. Peat bogs are a unique habitat home to many plants found nowhere else, and they are great carbon sinks. The moss takes carbon dioxide from the air and then stores it in those layers of peat. Peat takes a long time to accumulate, with a healthy bog only producing a millimeter or so of new peat each year. Because of that, harvesting peat to use for gardening is not sustainable, destroys valuable habitat, and potentially exacerbates global climate change by releasing carbon. Avoid peat as a soil amendment and rely on local compost instead.

Inorganic Amendments

In addition to organic matter like compost, gardeners can also add inorganic items. The most commonly used are coarse sand and special clay or heat-expanded stone products, such as Turface, PermaTill, and expanded shale. The idea behind these products is to lighten heavy clay soil and improve drainage, allow more air into the soil, and help roots penetrate the soil more easily. The use of these products is most likely to help if gardeners are trying to restore a soil that has been heavily compacted by machinery or cars driving over it, or if you want to create a special bed with different conditions than the rest of your garden to grow plants that require excellent drainage. Unlike organic matter, worms and microbes can't integrate these sorts of amendments into the soil, so you will have to dig them in yourself either by hand or with a tiller.

MULCH

Natural mulch is simply dead plant material. Most often we see wood chips or shredded bark used as mulch, but you can also use fall leaves or even grass clippings provided they are mixed 50/50 with another material so they don't pack down too tight. Mulch mimics what happens in nature as leaves, stems, and branches fall to the ground and slowly decompose. Almost never do we see bare soil in nature; it is almost always covered with a layer of slowly decomposing plant materials. Mimicking that cycle with a layer of mulch on a new garden will add organic matter to the soil, slow water evaporation from the ground, protect roots from sudden swings in temperature, and significantly reduce germination of weed seeds. Basically, mulch is the simplest and easiest way to make your garden grow better and reduce the amount of work it takes to maintain. One to two inches (2.5–5 cm) of natural mulch should be applied to every new garden bed unless you are specifically creating a bed to grow perennials like cacti, succulents, or alpine plants that are native to dry or rocky landscapes. In those cases, instead use a thin layer of gravel mulch.

Gardeners can mulch their new garden before or after planting, but it is usually easiest to do it beforehand— then you can just dump it on the garden and rake it out without having to carefully spread the mulch around each new plant.

A layer of shredded bark mulch in this new garden helps prevent weeds, reduce irrigation needs, and stabilize soil temperatures.

PLANTING

ONCE THE SOIL is cleared, prepared, and mulched, it is time to get planting. The process is pretty straightforward. Just remember the old adage, "Green side goes up" and you'll be halfway there. Here are some concepts to keep in mind to ensure plants have the best chance of thriving in your new garden.

TIME OF YEAR TO PLANT

Gardeners can plant a garden, in theory anyway, nearly any time of year, as long as the soil isn't frozen solid in the dead of winter. Each season has advantages and disadvantages, and the perfect time to plant will depend on your local climate. Generally, the best times to plant are in the spring or fall.

Spring planting is great because a new garden will have a full season of growing ahead of it, and cooler temperatures to get roots established before the heat of the summer. This is particularly important if you live in a climate with very cold winters. Also, let's be honest, the spring is when gardeners tend to get most excited about gardening and growing things, so it is likely when you'll want to plant the most. In cold climates, the best time to plant is just after the last frost in the spring. You can find your local average last frost date easily just by searching online, and the weeks following that date are prime planting time. It is possible to plant before the last spring frost, but gardeners may need to do so carefully. Though some perennials can survive freezing temperatures once they're established, plants from the nursery have often been grown in greenhouses and won't be acclimated to freezing temps. So, if you want to plant earlier, just make sure to ask at your local nursery if the plants have been growing outside or if they are straight from a greenhouse.

In cold, snowy climates, especially if you have heavy clay soil, springs can be very soggy, and the soil extremely saturated as it thaws, and the snows melt. With sandy soils, this is no problem. On clay soils, digging and planting then will seriously damage the soil structure, so it is best to wait for the ground to dry out a little before planting. As a test, dig up a handful of soil and squeeze it between your hands. If it squeezes into a solid ball that holds together when you poke it, the soil is too wet. Wait until the soil ball crumbles when you poke it before starting planting.

Spring is a wonderful time to plant perennials.

Fall is another ideal time to plant perennials. The still-warm soil promotes good root growth while the cooler air helps the plant retain moisture.

Fall is a wonderful and underutilized time to plant. In all but the coldest climates, perennials planted in the fall will establish beautifully. In the later summer and fall, the soil stays warm longer than the air, encouraging plants to grow nice deep root systems that will help them thrive the following summer. If you live somewhere with very hot, dry summers, fall plantings are ideal as they allow the plant the longest time to get established before facing their first drought. One of the added bonuses of fall planting is that because it is a less popular time to shop, many nurseries have fall clearance sales where gardeners can snatch up great plants for a fraction of their usual price. The main downside to planting in the fall is the potential for the plants to heave up out of the soil during freeze-thaw cycles. Keep an eye on these new plants through their first winter. If you discover the root mass of a fall-planted perennial has heaved up out of the ground, be sure to gently press it back into the ground. A layer of mulch can prevent heaving.

Gardeners can plant in the heat of the summer, but it can be hard on the plants to get established and grow roots while also facing heat and potential drought conditions. How successful summer plants will be really depends on your climate. It is challenging in the summer-dry climates of the West Coast but summer plantings will be a lot more successful in the rainier East Coast. If you plant in the summer, you will need to be very careful to keep everything watered thoroughly and regularly as these new plantings are struggling to get their roots down into the ground, until the weather cools off in the fall.

Winter planting may seem impossible, and if your soil is frozen and covered with snow, obviously it is. But in milder climates—USDA Hardiness Zones 7 and warmer—gardeners can plant from fall right through spring, and in fact, winter can be a great time to plant with cooler temperatures and shorter days putting less stress on establishing root systems.

The perfect time to plant will depend a lot on your specific climate, but don't get too hung up on planting at exactly the right time. With everything else in life, sometimes you just have to plant when your calendar cooperates. Plants are durable, and as long as you keep them watered through dry spells their first year, most plants will be just fine even if you miss the perfect planting window.

Prior to planting, lay the pots out in the area to check your spacing and plant heights.

LAYING EVERYTHING OUT

Before you put a single plant in the ground, take all your pots and place them out where they will go in the garden. Potted plants will be much smaller than their mature size in a year or two, so look up their mature spread, and use a yard stick or tape measure to ensure they are spaced properly with room to grow. If you are making a very formal garden with straight lines, use strings tied between stakes to make sure every line is straight. Take your time with this, as once things are planted, it is hard to move them. Laying everything out first gives you a chance to take a good look at it all and make any adjustments before actually putting a shovel into the soil.

Once everything is laid out and spaced properly, take some time to walk around the garden and look at it from every angle—including views from inside the home. If you are making a formal garden, make sure the straight lines look straight. If you are making an informal garden, straight lines are a problem. If, as you walk around, you notice a series of pots that are in a straight line, adjust some here and there to create a more natural, informal arrangement. This really is the last step of the design process, so take your time with this and don't hesitate to rearrange or change plans if needed. It is better to do it now than after everything is in the ground.

PLANTING

The actual mechanics of planting may seem pretty obvious, but here are a few steps to ensure it goes smoothly.

PLANTING

To remove a plant from its pot, place one hand over the top of the container, turn the pot upside down, and slide the container off the root mass.

Materials needed

- Potted plants
- Shovel or trowel
- Pruners or knife to loosen roots if needed
- Watering can or hose

Step 1: Choose the right day for planting

If possible, plant on an overcast day, or if not, plan to plant in the morning or evening. If rain is forecast for the following day or two, it will be even better. Roots exposed to the hot sun will quickly burn and die. Plants will recover faster from the shock of transplanting on a cool, cloudy day. This isn't always possible, so don't feel like you can't plant on a sunny day, but if you do get a nice cloudy one, take advantage of it.

Step 2: Move the mulch

Mulch on the soil surface is invaluable; however, if wood chip mulch is dug into the soil, it can absorb nitrogen and slow down plant growth. So before digging a hole, pull away the mulch from where you'll be planting with your hands or a rake.

Step 3: Dig the hole

With a shovel or trowel, dig a hole roughly the same size and depth as the pot your plant is currently using. In open, sunny gardens, this is usually easy. In a shade bed under a tree, it can be difficult to dig a hole between

If the roots are circling around inside the pot, loosen them with your fingers, a knife, or pruners prior to planting.

the tree roots. In these cases, choose the smallest pot sizes for your planting that you can to make your life easier and don't hesitate to shift plant positions around a little to avoid thick tree roots.

Step 4: De-pot
Generally, you can simply place your hand over the top of the container, turn the pot upside down, and slide the container off the root and soil mass. If a plant has been in a pot a long time, it can be a little hard to remove. If it won't come off easily, squeezing the side of the pot can help loosen the soil, and a gentle tug on the plant can help it come out. If a plant is really stuck, don't yank hard on the plant—you could damage it— instead get a pair of pruners and cut the plastic pot away from the roots. Once you have removed a plant from a pot, you should immediately plant it. Never pull multiple plants from their pots and then wait to plant them, as even a few minutes of exposure to the sun will harm plant roots.

A New Way to Plant

Most nursery-grown plants are grown in soilless potting mixes, which are very different from natural garden soil. Removing all the potting soil from the roots of a perennial prior to planting it is becoming a common practice among gardeners. Removing as much of the potting soil as possible allows the roots to acclimate to the native soil and establish quickly. This can be a hard practice for beginner gardeners as it feels counterintuitive to disturb the roots and remove the potting soil prior to planting. However, don't be afraid to experiment with this technique, as it is beneficial when done correctly, regardless of whether your native soil is sand-based, clay-based, or somewhere in between.

The planting hole should be roughly the same size and depth as the pot, perhaps a little wider but no deeper.

Step 5: Root prune

When the roots of plants grow out and hit the wall of a pot, they tend to turn and grow around the inside of the container, producing a thick layer of circling roots around the sides and bottom of the container. A plant like this is said to be potbound. Roots are slow to grow out of that circling pattern and into the garden soil, so it is best to cut away those circling roots. If there are just a few circling roots, you can do this with your fingers by pulling on the roots until they come loose. If there is a thick mat of roots, use a serrated knife (cheap dollar-store steak knives work great) or a pruning saw to slice away the layer of roots around the sides and bottom. This may seem extreme, but those circling roots aren't doing the plant any good and cutting them away will stimulate new roots to grow out into the garden soil.

Step 6: Bare-root
(in certain circumstances)

There are a few situations where gardeners might want to not just prune some roots, but actually remove all of the potting soil the perennials were growing in at the nursery (see sidebar on page 133). This is generally the recommendation if you have very sandy soil and are planting very drought-tolerant plants like cacti or succulents that might be prone to rot if grown in heavy, wet soil. Most nursery plants are grown in a potting mix, often mostly peat, that holds a lot of water. If that rootball full of water-retentive soil is planted into a sandy garden, you'll have a couple of problems. The soil in that rootball will hold a lot of moisture up against the base of the plant where it can cause rotting to occur, and the roots of the plant will be unlikely to grow out of that moist soil into the drier sandy soil around it. So, for plants like sedum, cacti, and other very dry-adapted species, it is best to shake off most of the potting soil from the roots and plant with the roots in direct contact with the native garden soil.

Use your hand to gently tamp the backfill soil into the hole around the plant, being careful to eliminate any air pockets. Then water the plant in immediately.

Step 7: Check the level
Place your plant in the hole and ensure it isn't too deep or too shallow. You want the soil level in the garden to be the same as what it was in the pot. Plant too deep, and you risk rotting the crown of the plant. Plant too shallowly, and the new plant will be more prone to drying out. If your planting hole isn't the right depth, either add or remove soil to get it right.

Step 8: Back fill
Take the soil you dug out of the hole and fill the gaps around the roots of the plant. You can be a little firm with this. Don't pack the soil in with all your weight, but do make sure it gets pushed down to eliminate any air pockets. Roots won't grow through air, so you want full contact between the root mass of the plant and the garden soil.

Step 9: Replace the mulch
Take the mulch you pushed aside in step 2 and push it back up around the plant. Don't cover the crown of the plant; keep it 1 inch (2.5 cm) or so away from the base of the stems to avoid problems with rot.

Step 10: Water it in
With a hose or watering can, thoroughly water the new plants. This will help the roots recover from transplant shock, but it also eliminates any lingering air pockets. If you didn't backfill carefully enough, some of the soil might collapse when you water. If so, just fill in the holes with more soil.

Step 11: Retrieve the pots
Collect the empty pots, stack them, and return them to a local nursery for reuse if they accept used plastic containers.

When You Can't Plant Right Away

There are lots of reasons gardeners might have perennials that need to be held for a while before putting them in their final garden position. These include gifts from friends, impulse purchases at nurseries, or clearance sale finds. If gardeners need to keep perennials around while waiting for the right time to plant, there are a couple of ways to hold them.

Leaving perennials in their containers works well for the short-term—ideally, no longer than a few weeks. If possible, position the pots somewhere where they get some shade in the heat of the afternoon, especially if it is during the height of the summer. Potted plants can dry out very quickly, even perennials that are very drought-tolerant in the garden, because many perennials native to places like the Great Plains beat drought by growing incredibly deep root systems—a method that obviously doesn't work in a pot. Water plants in their nursery pots once or twice a day every day during hot weather.

If you need to hold perennials for longer than a couple of weeks, and especially if you need to hold them in pots over the winter, heeling in is a simple technique to make them easier to care for. Heeling in involves digging a hole and sinking the plant—pot and all—down into the ground. Simply moving the pot below ground insulates the soil and roots from the heat of the sun, keeps them cooler, and helps them stay wet longer. Heeling in is critical if you are overwintering perennials in pots because cold snaps can be damaging to the exposed roots of a pot up above ground. Heeling in works well over winter or for a month or two during the growing season, but longer than that and the roots will start making their way out of the pot and into the soil, making them very difficult to remove again when it is time to plant. If you have plants that you know you won't be ready to put into a final location for more than a couple of months, it is best to just take it out of the pot and plant it in a temporary spot and then move it to the final garden placement when you are ready.

TEMPORARY HOLE FILLERS

When properly spaced, a newly planted perennial garden can look sparse for the first year or two. Soon enough everything will fill in and look beautiful. However, gardeners can also fill in some of those open areas with annuals and short-lived perennials to help give an instant garden effect right from the start. In addition to the visual effect of a fuller garden, keeping the ground covered helps prevent weeds from getting established.

Annuals are an obvious choice to fill in open spaces temporarily, as they'll vanish after their first year, but gardeners can use short-lived perennials like columbine (*Aquilegia*) as well. Whatever plants you choose, make sure they can fill in the open spaces without smothering or harming the perennials you want to grow. The best options will be low-growing varieties that can't shade out the taller perennials, or plants with an open, airy habit that won't cast

a deep shade over the permanent plantings. And don't be afraid to grab some pruners and cut back an annual or short-lived perennial that has gotten too big—a quick trim can keep open spaces covered while leaving room for everything else to keep growing.

AFTER CARE

Newly planted perennials need extra care through their first growing season, particularly if the weather turns hot and dry. It takes time for perennials to put down root systems into the native soil, so at first they will dry out nearly as fast as they did when growing in their previous pots. Newly planted perennials in dry weather may need watering as often as every couple of days for their first few weeks in the ground. Plan to check if they need water at least once a week through their first summer. Remember, you need to check the soil in the rootball at the base of the plant that was in the pot, not the surrounding soil. Once established,

Until perennials fill in, don't be afraid to add annual plants or tender bulbs to your garden to fill in. This gardener has added dahlias, tithonia, cannas, and a few other tender plants to the mix.

plants will have roots spread evenly over the whole garden area, but at first, they'll be limited to the soil that was in their pots when they were planted, so that soil will dry out faster than the rest of the garden.

The other key maintenance task is keeping the new garden weeded. There are more details on this in the next chapter, but always remember weed problems are the worst in a new garden, and keeping on top of them in the first year will set gardeners up for gardening success for a long time.

Optionally, by cutting off any developing flower buds gardeners can encourage the new perennials to focus on growing roots and leaves. Flowers take energy away from the plant while not helping it grow, but this is in no way an essential task to do.

Keep new plants watered well through their first season. Water deeply at least once a week, targeting the water at the base of the plant.

LABELING AND RECORD KEEPING

Once you've gotten everything in the ground, gardeners need to figure out how to keep track of what was planted. The garden will still be beautiful if you don't keep any records of what was planted, but there is a lot to be said for keeping track of the proper names of your plants as much as possible. No matter how good your memory or how good you are with names, there is no way you will keep all the names of everything you've grown in your head. And knowing those names is very useful. If you run into a pest or disease on your plants, you will need the name of the plant to look it up and figure out how to treat it. And you will probably want to buy more of a plant at some point, either to replace one that has died, or to add more of a variety you love in the garden, and, most of all, every gardener who visits is going to be pointing at flowers they like and asking, "Oh! What variety is that?"

Here are a few suggestions that gardeners can use to keep track of plants in the garden.

A List or Database

A list or database is generally the most reliable and practical method to keep track of plants. Instead of labeling each plant in the garden, simply keep a record indoors of everything that has been planted. This can be done by making a spreadsheet on your computer or by taping plastic nursery labels to the pages of a notebook or photo album. This method combines well with putting tags buried in the ground as well, as the tags outside act as a backup if for some reason you can't figure out which plant corresponds to which entry in your list. The nice thing about this method is that you can include more information and notes if you want—such as years planted, where you purchased it, and when it flowered. If you are a person who loves keeping notes and organizing information, it can be fun to keep track of how each plant has performed year after year.

A Photo Database

Since we all now carry digital cameras in our pockets all the time, when you plant something, take a picture of the label, a picture of the plant, and a wide shot showing where it is in the garden. These pictures, organized in folders, make it easy to tell exactly what is planted where, and automatically records the date you planted them as well.

You can mix and match any or all of these plant tracking methods but do make sure you do something to record what you plant, and it is better to err on the side of recording more information whenever possible. Details of where you bought something, when it was planted, and how it has performed over the years come in handy more often than you might imagine. Also, be sure to make great use of your phone camera to document the development of the entire garden as well. As your garden matures and grows, it is great fun to be able to look back at pictures of what it looked like when it was first planted and see how different plants have grown and performed over the years.

Visible Labels

Another option is sticking labels with the names of the plants in the ground next to them, like they are at the nursery. If you are going to go this route, it is best to not use the plastic nursery labels each plant came with. Though they do have the information you need on them, they do not last long; the plastic becomes brittle after just a few years of exposure to the sun. Inevitably, labels will disintegrate just when a plant has been in the garden long enough for you to forget what variety it is. Plastic nursery labels are also far from attractive, usually a bright white that stands out in the garden like a sore thumb, especially in the winter when most perennials are dormant. There are countless options for more attractive and durable labels, with metal ones being the longest lasting and the most expensive. Remember that even the longest lasting inks will fade with time as well, so it is a good idea to check your labels every few years and update any that are getting hard to read.

Buried Labels

Another approach is to keep labels with each plant, but instead of having them stick up into the air, slide them down so they are entirely underground. The plus side here is that they are not visible, so no need to worry about them being attractive, and they are out of the sun, so even cheap plastic labels will last much longer. The downside, of course, is that they can be hard to find when you need to look at them. To make them easier to find, always insert them into the ground on the same side of a plant—choose, say, the south side, and always put your labels there, so you know where to start looking for a label.

Good labels are essential. If you don't like the look of them, opt for buried labels or keep a garden journal with photos and names of each of your plants recorded in it.

CHAPTER 6

KEEPING *Things* GOING

Maintaining and troubleshooting your garden

A GARDEN IS A LIVING, dynamic thing that requires care. A well-designed perennial garden doesn't require the daily attention that a pet cat or dog does, but the garden still needs tending and maintaining over the season to keep it healthy and looking good.

Each of the tasks that a garden needs is different, but what a lot of the tasks have in common is the old adage about "a stitch in time saving nine." If gardeners plan their garden maintenance and keep on top of things like weeding and pruning, they will remain simple, easy tasks that don't take a lot of time. Let the maintenance slide, however, and the tasks can quickly build up into something that feels overwhelming to tackle. Read this chapter carefully and make sure to plan time for the care your perennial garden needs so it stays easy to maintain and looking good.

Weeding the garden early and often makes less work down the line.

WEEDING

The definition of a weed is pretty simple: It is just a plant growing where gardeners don't want it. If gardeners like the way a dandelion looks, then it isn't a weed to them. If you don't like dandelions, then they are weeds. And even the very same plant can be a weed in one part of the yard and not a weed somewhere else. Turfgrasses, for example, are certainly not weeds when growing in the lawn, but they are weeds when they creep into perennial beds. However, there are some plants that are "weedy," meaning they have attributes that make them likely to be problems in the garden. This usually means that they have extremely rapid growth that can smother other plants and they spread fast because of the ease with which they propagate from seeds or bits of roots inadvertently left behind. Remember, weeds don't always arrive in the garden spontaneously; sometimes plants that ultimately turn out to be weeds came from those for sale at a local garden center.

Controlling weeds is also, at the most basic level, pretty simple. If something gardeners don't want pops up in the garden, pull it out. But there are some skills and techniques that can help manage weeds effectively so gardeners spend less time pulling and more time enjoying the garden.

The Soil Seed Bank

The main source of weeds in the garden is going to be from seeds that are already hanging out in the soil. Many common weed species are what ecologists call *ruderal* species, meaning they thrive in disturbed habitats. In the wild, these weeds take advantage of things like falling trees, floods, or even the small disruptions from a groundhog digging a hole. The weed seeds spring quickly into life to take advantage of the newly cleared land before slower-growing perennials, trees, and shrubs can take over. One of the main ways these weed species set themselves up to take advantage of these disruptions is to produce thousands and thousands of tiny seeds that can survive for decades in the soil, waiting for the signal to germinate. And that signal, for many weed seeds, is light. Buried in the ground, or under thick plant cover, they won't spout. But exposed to light, seeds literally decades old can suddenly spring into life.

What disturbs the soil and exposes a lot of hidden weed seeds to light? Planting a new garden. The act of clearing away existing vegetation and digging holes during the planting process all triggers weed seeds to germinate. This means new gardens often have a wave of weed seeds germinating, but gardeners can make the soil seed bank a short-term problem by disturbing the soil in your garden as little as possible, and keeping any bare soil covered with mulch. When you **do** have to disturb the soil to plant something new or divide a perennial, plan to check the area a week or two afterward for new weed germinations and pull them out before they become a problem.

Weed Early and Often

Small weeds, just germinated, can be pulled out of the soil with just a quick pinch of the fingers. Wait a couple of weeks, however, and weeds will be huge plants that are hard to pull out of the ground, and possibly already flowering and producing seeds to drop all over the garden. So, the best practice is to walk through the garden often and do some quick weeding. In a newly planted garden, there might be a significant number of weeds to pull, but if you keep on it early and often, you'll exhaust the upper layer of the soil seed bank, the perennials will fill in the space, and the weekly weed check will become a weekly garden walk with very little weeding involved at all. But don't skip those weeding walks. Weeds are like credit card debt—easy to manage at first, but quickly cascading into a crisis if left unchecked.

FERTILIZING

One traditional gardening task gardeners can generally ignore in the modern perennial garden is fertilizing. As discussed in chapter 2, the goal is not to grow the biggest, lushest plants, but to recreate conditions for these plants where they would have grown in the wild. After the initial preparation of the soil, all the perennial garden needs to thrive is usually just adding mulch and letting the plant material mostly decompose in place to return nutrients to the soil. Gardeners may want to add a little fertilizer—following the advice on a soil test about the quantities and type—to a newly planted garden to help get plants growing and filling in faster. But there is no need to keep fertilizing once everything has matured. Excessive fertilization in a mature garden just makes more garden work—more staking and pruning, more dividing—as most plants outgrowing their spaces.

WATERING

In general, it is recommended to choose plants that will thrive in your climate without needing supplemental water. But there are some circumstances when you'll need to add either manual or automatic irrigation to help plants thrive, especially if you live in a hot or dry climate or are experiencing a drought. Watering thoughtfully and properly will help you use the least water possible to keep plants healthy.

Hand-watering is time consuming, but it allows you to target water directly to the root zone of the plant.

Water in the Early Morning or Evening

The goal of watering is to make sure that the moisture goes down into the soil, not evaporating in the air, so avoid watering during the heat of the day when possible. If you do a lot of irrigation, setting it up on a timer can be the best way to easily deliver water during the coolest times of the day.

Water the Soil, Not the Plants

Water in the soil can soak in and be taken up by plants, while water splashed up in the air and onto leaves mostly just evaporates without doing much good. Wet foliage is also more prone to fungal diseases. Drip irrigations lines are the ultimate way to direct water straight to the soil and not onto plants. Gardeners can also direct the flow carefully this way when watering by hand with a hose or watering can. Traditional sprinklers that spray water up into the air are far less efficient and are a particularly bad choice if you live in a dry climate with water-use restrictions.

Invest in Good Equipment

Getting the cheapest possible sprinklers and hoses can end up costing you money in the long run if you irrigate frequently. Poor quality irrigation systems will have fittings that leak, sprinklers that lose a lot of water to misting, or parts that break early when gardeners need them the most. A good irrigation system will have tight fittings, pressure-regulated sprinklers to deliver water efficiently, and a programmable timer. If gardeners really want the top of the line, they can add sensors that monitor the weather so the irrigation won't run when it rains or when high winds will blow sprinklers off course.

Drip irrigation and soaker hoses are the most efficient way to deliver water to plants, but installation can be costly and may require a professional.

Water Deeply

Perhaps the most common mistake novice gardeners make is watering too little at one time. Run a hose over a section of the garden for a few minutes and all that is done is get the very surface of the soil wet. This is not productive because water at the soil surface will easily evaporate into the air, but more importantly, plants will grow roots up towards moisture in the soil. If gardeners only get the first inch (2.5 cm) of the soil wet, then the perennials will keep their roots mostly in the top of the soil where they will be more—not less—susceptible to drought. To get a sense of how long gardeners need to irrigate to really get water deep in the soil, run the sprinklers or hand-water as usual, wait an hour for the water to soak down, and take a trowel or shovel and dig a small hole in the soil. If just a narrow layer of wet soil is sitting over the top of dry soil, you need to irrigate longer.

New Plantings

Newly planted perennials should be watered regularly for their first year during dry weather. This is critically important because many perennials—especially those native to grasslands—have adapted to survive drought and dry weather by sending roots down very deep into the soil. It takes time for newly planted perennials to develop deep roots. Water new plantings deeply to encourage them to develop deep root systems.

Regularly irrigated plants will also grow bigger and faster than perennials grown on the dry side, so irrigation during the first year can help new plantings fill in and mature more quickly. But, like fertilizer, extra water can also make plants grow too tall, requiring more staking, so once they are mature, extra irrigation can be more of a hinderance than a help.

Deep-rooted perennials are more resilient than shallow-rooted lawns when it comes to withstanding drought conditions.

Droughts

Even if you choose plants well-suited to your normal weather patterns, unusual drought years will arrive that will test the limits of the most well-designed garden. However, don't stress about every dry spell too much. Healthy, well-established perennials—even if they wilt and look pretty sad—can recover just fine from a drought year. Wilting can look scary, but it is part of plant coping strategies to combat the effects of drought by letting their leaves droop out of the direct sun. If plants wilt some during the heat of the day, but then perk up again as the temperatures drop in the evening, they will be okay. If they stay wilted in the evening, that is the time to start irrigating to keep them alive.

It is also a good idea to wait as long as you can to start watering in a drought. Plants grow in response to the conditions they are in, so if gardeners irrigate deeply at the beginning of a droughty period, plants will grow very large and lush, which will actually make them more vulnerable to damage from a drought later on. Dry conditions early will encourage plants to grow smaller, tougher leaves that are better able to resist drying out.

Counterintuitively, if it has been dry and rain is finally in the forecast, this can be a great time to do some watering. When the surface of the soil is very dry—especially if the garden has clay soil—it can be very hard for the soil to absorb water. So sometimes rare downpours during a drought will mostly just run off the soil surface rather than doing some good by soaking in. Irrigating before a rain event will help the soil take up all that precious moisture and let the rain soak deep into the soil where it is protected from evaporation.

Prioritize your irrigation, particularly during water-use restriction times. Focus both on the plants most likely to suffer during a dry spell, and on the plants that will be the hardest to replace. A prized clematis grown from cuttings given to you by your grandmother—that's irreplaceable, so keep it watered. Some short-lived columbines that were planted to fill in an open space—let them go; they won't be around that long anyway.

Accept the Losses

Sometimes, plants will fail in a drought year, and that is okay. Climates are changing, and for many places, that may mean more heat and drought. So, take a dry year as a chance to refine your plant selections and make your garden more resilient. If something dies out during a dry year, well, maybe it isn't such a good choice for your climate after all. Look around the garden—and other gardens in the area—during the driest weather and see what is thriving. Now you will have a list of what you might want to plant more of so that during the next dry spell you won't have to water so much, and the garden will still look great.

MULCHING

Bare soil, except in the driest of desert climates, is pretty rare in nature. Plants of some kind will grow nearly everywhere, covering the ground with their leaves and stems, and below the living parts, there is a layer of the old leaves and stems that are slowly decomposing and returning nutrients to the soil. The layers of living and dead plant material protect the soil from the drying sun, keeping it from eroding by the wind and washing away by the rain. By planting your perennial bed densely, you will soon achieve the same result: The ground will be totally covered by living and dead plant material. However, when planting a new bed, or moving and dividing new plants, there will be periods when the soil is exposed while the plants mature. Exposed soil is bad for the plants, bad for the soil, and bad for gardeners because weeds will take that empty space and fill it very quickly.

So the answer is mulch, and lots of it. Mulch a new bed when you plant it. About once a year afterward, you should check the depth and top up that mulch with new material as needed. This will take a lot of mulch at first, but the quantity will decrease, and less and less will be needed as the garden matures. There are two rules to applying mulch: Cover the ground, and don't cover the crowns of perennials. Mulch placed directly on top of perennials can smother them and promote disease.

Shredded leaves make a wonderful mulch for perennial plantings.

Mulch can be really any form of dead plant material. Bark or wood chips are the most common mulch materials, but fallen leaves work just as well. Lawn clippings can be used as mulch, but they should be mixed 50/50 with another material like leaves or wood chips. Pure lawn clippings can pack down very tightly and stop the rain from soaking into the soil. The best mulches are free and local and are more likely to **not** contain an unwelcome bounty of weed seeds. There is no reason to spend money on mulch in a plastic bag shipped from out of state when neighbors are throwing away big bags of leaves gardeners can take for free and spread over the garden as mulch. Another alternative is to get a load of wood chips for free from a local tree company or a load of compost from a city yard waste program.

Shredded bark mulch is an ideal choice for perennial plantings and pathways. Be sure to keep it off plant crowns.

One challenge in applying mulch in some parts of the country is the expanding spread of Asian jumping worms. Gardeners are used to thinking of earthworms as a great thing in the garden, but Asian jumping worms can consume organic matter—like mulch—incredibly rapidly and transform soils into dry lumps that don't hold water. Adding more mulch to a jumping worm infestation is like adding fuel to the fire. One strategy in this situation is to try different mulching materials. Grass, straw, hay, and pine needle mulches seem to be the least palatable to these worms. Try all the different mulch options you can, and then keep using the one that sticks around the longest in your garden.

DEADHEADING

Deadheading is the practice of cutting off flowers after they have faded and before they can develop into seed heads. This is an optional maintenance task that can help a garden look neat and tidy but isn't required. Many perennials flower petals drop cleanly away after bloom and are followed by seedheads that are quite attractive and provide excellent food for birds. There is no need to deadhead these plants. But other plants cling to their petals as they fade, making an ugly mess of brown petals. So in these cases, the choice to deadhead or not is just an aesthetic one and you should do whatever looks best to you.

There are a few times, however, when deadheading is for more than just looks. Deadheading prevents a plant from setting seed, so it can stop a perennial from becoming a weed. Some perennials self-sow in the garden too aggressively. Gardeners may love columbines or hollyhocks, but don't necessarily want them sprouting up everywhere. One option is to deadhead 90 percent of the plants, leaving a few to self-sow, but not so many that they become obnoxious. If gardeners are growing a potentially invasive species, you should always deadhead it if there is some reason that it can't be removed from the garden entirely.

Producing seeds requires energy from a plant, so deadheading can help focus that energy back to the plant. For most healthy, well-established perennials, the energy required to produce seeds is small enough that it makes no difference, but it can be important for some plants. Many short-lived perennials and biennials will be more likely to come back for another year if they are deadheaded, and gardeners might consider deadheading perennials during their first year in the garden to help the plants focus on growing deeper roots.

Finally, some spring- and early summer-flowering perennials will be more likely to push out another flush of blooms in later summer or the fall if they are deadheaded after their first flowering. This isn't always true, and if you can't find information about whether a plant will respond to deadheading or not, gardeners can always experiment by deadheading half your plants and leaving the other half. Then watch to see if there is a difference in how the two groups perform.

Deadheading involves removing spent flowers and flower stalks as they fade.

PINCHING

Pinching is the practice of cutting off the very tips of the new growth of a perennial. It is called pinching because you do it to new growth that is so tender and fresh that you don't even need shears to do it, you can just pinch off the growth with your fingers. When you pinch a perennial early in the growing season, it forces new growth out from the dormant buds below, causing more branching and making a plant grow shorter and fuller, producing more—but smaller—flowers. This can be a great treatment to transform an overly tall, lanky plant into a tidier and more compact one.

Not every plant can be pinched successfully. Generally, this technique will work great with perennials that bloom in late summer and fall, as they have a lot of growing to do before they start making flower buds. Spring bloomers, on the other hand, may already have tiny flower buds developing when you pinch them, even ones that are too small to see. Pinching a peony, for example, would just prevent it from flowering rather than making the plant more compact.

A very similar method to this technique is sometimes called the *Chelsea Chop*. For this method, instead of carefully pinching out the tips of branches, grab a pair of hedge shears and chop the plant back by about one third of its height. The name Chelsea Chop comes from the United Kingdom, where the famous Chelsea Flower Show is held at the end of May, which is the right time of year to pinch or chop summer or fall-blooming perennials in the UK climate. In the United States, late May is about the right time of year for northern gardeners, while those in the South would do better to aim for April.

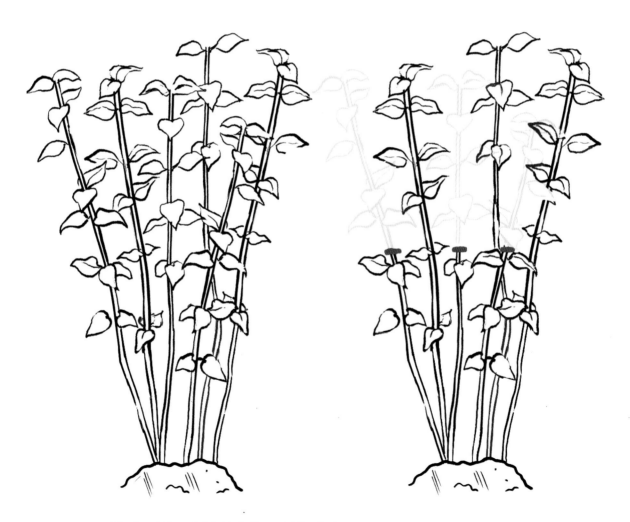

To pinch a plant, use your thumbnail and forefinger to pinch off the terminal portion of the stem just above a set of leaves. You can also use a pair of plant snips to do the job.

Just a few days after pinching, the nodes begin to form new growth, which will go on to develop two sets of flower buds where there once was one.

The plant shown at left in this illustration is unpinched. The middle illustration shows the same plant with half of its stems pinched back to half the plant's height. The illustration at right shows the full plant pinched back halfway.

Preen your plants regularly to remove dead foliage, yellow leaves, and other unsightly growth.

There are many ways to support taller perennials. Shown here is an adjustable round grow ring supported by a central bamboo stake. In the back left corner of the photo is a peripheral staking system using bamboo stakes and twine.

PREENING

Preening can be one of the most relaxing and rewarding ways to prune your plants. Get a nice pair of comfortable pruners or scissors and a tub to collect the trimmings, and just go slowly over your plants pulling off brown leaves, trimming off old seedheads that are no longer attractive, cutting back broken stems, and clipping out anything that has fallen over a path or just looks out of place. Each individual cut or trim may be small, but the effect of grooming an entire garden can be magical, giving the whole space an extra tidy shine before an invitation is extended to the garden club for a tour or just when gardeners feel like puttering around in the garden but not taking on any heavy lifting.

STAKING OR CAGING

Some plants just don't stand up well and there are many reasons for it. Some of the possible causes are in the troubleshooting section later in this chapter. But if gardeners do have a plant that just won't hold itself up high, staking or caging the perennial will give it the support it needs to look good. There are lots of ways to stake and materials that can be used, but however plants are staked, there is one key thing to remember: Always stake a plant *before* it starts falling over—the earlier, the better. Some gardeners stake plants like delphiniums when they are initially planted and it's easiest to drive in the stake then without damaging the roots or foliage. When completed while the plants are standing upright, the staking is invisible, and the plants will look utterly natural. But once a perennial has sprawled all over a walkway, trying to tie it

Peony rings are classic plant support structures that keep peonies and other plants with heavy flowers from flopping to the ground.

back into an upright position is nearly impossible. Staking is a lot about planning, timing, and paying attention. If gardeners venture into the garden and find a perennial has collapsed under its own weight, start making plans to prevent that from happening the next year. Make a note on the calendar to get out and stake that plant earlier during the next growing season. And remember that what usually pushes plants over the edge is a heavy rain, so if you are behind on staking and a thunderstorm is in the forecast, get out there and provide support before the rains arrive, not afterward.

When tying plants to supports, always use biodegradable twine, so you don't have to worry about dropping pieces on the ground. Cotton, jute, or sisal twine is a perfect tying material.

Stakes are simply lengths of wood, bamboo, or even metal pushed down into the ground until they are sturdy, and then plants are tied to them. The ideal stake should be a little shorter than the mature height of the plant, so that the stake will be covered by leaves once the plant is mature. For perennials with just a few stems, like a lily, simply tie each stem to a stake. For bushier plant forms, gardeners can loop a length of twine around the whole mass of the perennial and tie the twine back to a stake.

Cages and hoops are usually metal rings that can be put over a plant early in the season so the plant grows up through it, and then plants can lean against the rings for support. These rings are super easy to use because gardeners don't have to tie the plants to them, and once the plant grows up through them they are practically invisible. There are two key factors to using them effectively. First, put the cages or hoops out early, before the plant shoots have grown tall enough to reach the ring, so they can grow up through them naturally. And second, make sure the first ring is tall enough to reach more than halfway up the mature height of the plant, supporting the plant well. Putting in cages and hoops that are too low means that the tall, top-heavy plant stems will just flop down over the edge of the rings unsupported.

CUTTING BACK

Cutting back is a part of maintaining the perennial garden that has changed a lot in the past couple decades. In fact, this section would probably be called "fall cleanup" if this book had been written twenty years ago.

The old method was to go out in the fall, once perennials have gone dormant, and cut off all the brown stems and leaves, leaving nothing behind. The garden was then all raked smooth and left bare for the winter. This is an outdated technique. Today we know that the best practice is to leave as much of the perennial plants standing and in place for as long as possible.

Leave perennial gardens stand through the winter. They'll provide winter interest for you and habitat for wildlife. Come spring, cut the plants down if you must, leaving the debris in place where it falls. As it decomposes, it nourishes the soil.

Nourishing the Soil

In nature, old stems and leaves just gradually make their way to the ground where they slowly decompose, acting as a natural mulch to conserve water and slowly decomposing to return their nutrients to the soil. Leaving as much of the herbaceous stems and leaves as possible in the garden will mimic that effect, meaning gardeners will need to add less mulch and fertilizer to keep plants happy. If you do need to trim back a plant for aesthetic reasons, try to just drop the removed plant material right there on the soil surface rather than throwing it in a yard-waste bin or compost pile.

Winter Protection

Old stems and leaves will form an insulating layer over the dormant crown buds of a perennial and can make a big difference in helping a marginally hardy plant make it through the winter unharmed. If you have cold winters, and particularly if you are growing plants that might wish your winters were a little warmer, leave the plant material standing as a natural insulating blanket.

Perennial gardens do not need to be swept clean of leaves, dead stems, and other debris. In fact, it's healthier for plants and insects to leave this material in place.

Insects

Many native insects, from bees to beetles to caterpillars, use the layers of dead stems and leaves as a spot to hibernate for the winter. Some even love to hang out in the hollow centers of old plant stems. Leaving that material in place as much as possible keeps your garden ecosystem full of great homes for the many beautiful and useful insects who live there.

If you do cut back stems for practical or aesthetic reasons, try to do it as little as possible and never cut a plant right back to the ground level. If your grasses are interplanted with daffodils, cut them back just enough that the daffodils can show over the tops. If you don't like the look of last year's echinacea stems while this year's stems are flowering, cut them back halfway so they are covered by the thick foliage at the base of the plant. The more plant growth gardeners can leave in place, the better it is for the local ecosystem.

There is an exception to this, however. Pest insects and some diseases also like to overwinter in downed plant stems, so if gardeners are facing an outbreak of some particular plant pest or disease, consider doing a thorough fall cleanup of the plants showing the worst infestations to try to reduce the problem for the next growing season.

For any of these reasons, gardeners may want to do a little cutting back in the spring to make the garden look its best. How much of this is necessary really depends on the plant. Some perennials, like hostas and ferns, will pretty much just drop their leaves to the ground and never need any cleaning up. Others, like some ornamental grasses and echinacea, have stems that will stand pretty strong through the next summer, and trimming them back will give a tidier look to the garden.

This is a place where less is more in the garden, and where gardeners can learn over time how much is really needed to be cut back. After doing your spring cutbacks, take pictures of how much you left standing, and then remove more over the coming weeks. Note how fast the new growth covered the old stems. Were any ephemerals failing to show off beautifully because you left too much standing? Make notes of what worked, what didn't work, so you can decide if you want to leave more or less behind next year.

DIVIDING

We discussed dividing perennials as a way to propagate them in chapter 4, but dividing perennials can also be a part of keeping your garden thriving long-term. As perennials mature, they will slowly expand, the crown getting bigger with each passing year. In a new garden, this is only a good thing, but as the years go by, it may become a problem gardeners will need to deal with—especially if the center of the clump dies out. There are a few reasons that gardeners may find themself needing to divide perennials.

Fast-growing and fast-spreading species can take over the space that slower-growing varieties were using. To put the plants back in-bounds, gardeners can dig up the overly aggressive species, divide them, and just replant one small division. You can put the other divisions elsewhere in the garden, pot them up to give to friends, or just compost them. If you aren't fond of this chore there are other solutions. Gardeners can, of course, just let nature take its course and allow the most vigorous plants to take over the garden design. Or, if it is not a variety you particularly enjoy, you can remove the more vigorous plants entirely and replace them with a slower-growing species. One strategy that takes some experience to pull off successfully is to design your beds so that each area includes plants that have similar vigor levels. Slow growers paired with other slow growers will do great and coexist nicely, and super vigorous plants faced with equally muscular neighbors won't be able to push each other around either.

Many of our native pollinators take shelter or build their brood chambers inside of hollow plant stems.

Aesthetics

Seedheads, leaves, and stems in various shades of brown and tan are beautiful and are a huge part of making the perennial garden look attractive and interesting through the winter months. But by spring, gardeners may want to go out with some sheers and cut back some of the standing stems for a few reasons. Some tall perennials and grasses that looked beautiful in the fall may have been crushed flat by the snow and just look messy now. Maybe your summer-blooming perennials are interplanted with spring-blooming bulbs or ephemerals, and the standing stems would cover up the blooms. Or you might just not like the look of new growth mixing with the old, faded stems.

A donut-shaped crown is a sure sign that a perennial needs to be divided.

Gardeners may also need to divide plants to fend off the dreaded doughnut effect. Some perennials, as they grow and expand, will tend to die out in the center, producing a doughnut of healthy growth around a dead, empty center. To remedy this, dig up the whole clump, slice off some vigorous outer pieces, and replant them in the original space.

Division can also help prolong the lives of short-lived perennials, as many of these plants can have their lifespans extended indefinitely if they are regularly lifted and divided into new, young, vigorous plants. Gardeners can also simply let these plants fade away and replace them with longer-lived species, or grow new individuals from cuttings or seeds if you don't want to bother with dividing them.

How frequently you'll have to divide perennials depends on the particular species and how fast it grows. Slow-growing, long-lived species like baptisia and many ornamental grasses may never need to be divided, as they don't spread very much and are not prone to producing dead doughnut centers. A fast-growing shasta daisy in fertile soil may need to be divided as often as every three to five years to eliminate dead centers and keep them from taking over space you didn't intend for them. Short-lived primroses and columbines may need to be divided every two or three years to keep them from fading away.

TROUBLESHOOTING

Diseases such as this powdery mildew sometimes strike even the most well-tended perennial garden. Choosing resistant varieties is always your first line of defense.

SOMETIMES THINGS DO go wrong in the garden. Pests, diseases, freakish weather—if you've been gardening long enough, you'll eventually run into problems. It is impossible to give advice in this book on every possible problem gardeners might encounter, but what follows will give you the tools to figure out what you can do for a lot of common problems.

When things do go wrong in the garden, remember that it is perfectly normal. The occasional plant getting diseased or dying doesn't mean you are a bad gardener or have failed somehow; death is an inevitable part of life, as are the occasional bouts with diseases and pests. The secret to being a successful gardener is in how you respond to these challenges.

Before getting into the details of the types of problems gardeners might encounter, remember that one solution, always available, is to remove the affected plant and replace it with something else. For the occasional difficulty this isn't necessary, but if you are experiencing the same troublesome problem over and over again and spending a lot of time and money trying to remedy it, this may be a sign that you are trying to grow a plant that just isn't well-suited to your conditions. Sometimes being a good gardener means not fighting a problem off, but choosing plants that won't have problems in the first place.

FLOPPING

One of the most annoying problems in a perennial bed happens when a plant won't keep itself standing upright and collapses when hit by a strong wind or heavy rainstorm.

Often the core cause of collapsing plants is overly rich growing conditions. In the wild, most plants grow in fairly lean conditions, and the abundant fertility and moisture in a garden can cause plants to grow bigger, taller, and faster, producing tall stems that are not able to hold themselves up. If you are adding fertilizer and irrigation, dialing both of these back can help plants stay shorter and stronger—with less flopping.

Too much shade is another big cause of floppiness as plants stretch, trying to out-grow whatever is casting that shade so they can reach the light. Those tall, stretched out plant stems then very often come crashing to the ground later in the season. Moving these plants to a sunnier location will usually fix the problem.

Some plants—especially the many gorgeous perennials that have evolved on grasslands like the Great Plains— grow in the wild packed in tight together with countless other plants. In the garden, gardeners may want to space them out more so each individual plant can grow huge and happy, but this can cause problems. Tight spacing creates competition for water and nutrients that keeps plants growing smaller, and weaker plants can lean on the stronger ones around them to keep them standing upright. If you love growing prairie natives and they are sprawling everywhere, consider adding many more plants to keep them standing tall.

Finally, some varieties of plants are just floppier than others. One of the biggest culprits is selections that have very large, double flowers with extra petals. Peonies are a familiar example. Wild peonies just have a single row of petals on each flower and usually hold themselves up just fine. Most selected peony varieties for the garden have double flowers packed with petals that are just too heavy for the plants to hold up. So, if a plant in the garden won't stand up, look to replace it with a variety with single flowers or a form that doesn't grow as tall. A big focus of modern plant breeding is on selecting shorter, more compact forms, so gardeners can often find new, nonflopping introductions for most groups of popular plants.

Tall perennials prone to flopping should be staked early in the growing season.

Sometimes, of course, gardeners can't make the changes that would keep plants standing up. If your soil is naturally fertile and you have a lot of rainfall, if you have fallen in love with a peony with huge heavy blooms the stems just can't hold up, or if you don't have anywhere with quite enough sun in your garden, the only solution is to stake and prune! Refer to the maintenance section earlier to find ways to prop plants up or encourage them to grow a little shorter and bushier.

DEER, RABBITS, AND OTHER MAMMALS

One of the most frustrating problems in a perennial garden is damage done by hungry mammals. Unlike insects, which usually just nibble here and there and can be tolerated and managed, visitors like deer and groundhogs have big appetites and can devastate a garden fast. Pests like deer and rabbits are often the worst in urban and suburban gardens, and less so in rural areas. In rural areas, these animals are more likely to be scared of humans and have lots of other wild places to go to feed. In more populated areas, these animals are familiar with people and they are much harder to scare off. Consequently, if gardeners live in the suburbs, you may have to work harder to keep your plants safe. Here are some specific techniques you can use to fend off these unwanted visitors.

Fencing/Barriers

Often the most effective way to prevent problems with these types of visitors is to simply make it impossible for them to access the garden. Fences can be a big expense if you have a large area to protect, but when installed correctly, a good fence is the ultimate solution for truly eliminating the problem of browsing mammals.

The key to deploying fencing successfully is to tailor it to the pests in your area. To exclude deer, you will need a fence that is fully 6 to 8 feet (1.8–2.4 m) tall, as they are champion jumpers. For most other mammals, including rabbits and groundhogs, just a foot or two (30–60 cm) is enough.

Wild rabbits are quite fond of many perennials, asters and yarrow in particular. Surround plants with low fencing or use granular deterrents to keep their damage to a minimum.

To keep larger animals, including pets, out of the garden, a fence is essential.

In addition to animals jumping over, gardeners have to consider pests going under the fence. Rabbits will squeeze through the smallest openings, and pests like groundhogs and gophers are great at digging underneath. There are two ways to stop this. One is to dig a trench and extend the fence material 1 foot (30 cm) or more underground. An easier solution is to lay wire mesh—like chicken wire or landscape cloth—horizontally on the ground on the outside of the fence. When animals try to dig at the edge of the fence, they'll hit the wire mesh and stop. The wire mesh can be covered with mulch to make it visually disappear while still acting as a barrier to stop digging.

There is a wide array of fencing materials to choose from, including plastic netting, wire mesh, and wood. Plastic is affordable but won't last very long, while wood is more expensive but also can be a nice visual addition to your garden. Whatever you choose, make sure any openings are small enough that pests can't fit through.

A simple chicken wire cage around a plant is often enough to minimize feeding damage from mammals.

Repellent Sprays

There are many repellent sprays for deer and rabbits available for the garden, and they can work if they are used properly. However, they will work best if gardeners have very light or short-term pressure from pests. In the short-term, sprays may seem like a cheaper option then fencing, but the cost can add up very rapidly. To have success with repellent sprays, they must be applied often, usually every week or two, and more often if there has been heavy rain or plants are putting on a lot of new growth.

One of the biggest problems with repellent sprays is that, over time, your local animals can learn to ignore them. These sprays don't harm the animals, they merely smell or taste bad, and when the deer get hungry enough, they'll try nibbling things anyway. Once these pests learn to ignore a bad smell, that spray won't work for you again. And missing a regular application of the repellents can help the pest learn to ignore the spray, as the fading scent/taste is easier for pests to get used to. Rotating through different products with different active ingredients will help prevent this. Most repellent sprays use either hot peppers, garlic, or rotten eggs as active ingredients. If you switch between those three different ingredients it will be harder for the animals to get used to them and the repellent will keep them away longer.

Dogs

Dogs aren't a perfect repellent, but if you have a dog out in your garden a lot of the time, it can certainly help deter visiting mammals. This often works best in combination with fencing. Deer may hesitate to jump over even a fairly low fence if they know there is often a dog on the other side.

Resistant Plants

If gardeners can't fence in a garden, choosing plants that local mammals don't like to eat is usually the best option. In general, plants that have strongly scented foliage are less likely to be eaten, and there are many references that will give lists of deer- and rabbit-resistant plants for your area. Remember, however, to take all descriptions of a plant as being deer- or rabbit-resistant (even those in this book!) with a grain of salt. Tastes vary a lot between different areas and populations, so a plant that is rabbit-proof in one garden may be rabbit food in another. As well, hungry animals will eat plants they used to ignore, so as deer overpopulation increases, gardeners may find more and more of their plants on the deer grazing menu. Learn from experiments on what is eaten in your garden and talk to the gardeners in your neighborhood to get ideas for good resistant plants that might work.

Choosing plants resistant to troublesome animals is important. This baptisia has noted deer and rabbit resistance, and there are many other perennial plants with the same quality.

BARRIERS FOR MAMMAL PESTS

SPECIES	BARRIERS/FENCING	NOTES
Deer	Must be 6 to 8 feet (1.8–2.4 m) tall to stop them from jumping over it. They're less likely to jump an opaque fence than one they can see through.	Deer are extremely overpopulated in much of the United States and eating more and more species they used to avoid.
Rabbits	1- to 2-foot (30–61 cm)-high fences are sufficient, but rabbits can squeeze though openings as small as 1 inch (2.5 cm) wide. Chicken wire at the base of tall deer fences works well.	Rabbit populations tend to boom and crash as they breed and then predators move in. If there are tons this year, there may well be hardly any the next year.
Groundhogs	Bury the base of the fence at least 18 inches (46 cm) deep or lay the base flat on the ground 1 foot (30 cm) out from the fence to prevent groundhogs from digging under.	Groundhogs feed in the area, but trapping and removing them is rarely effective, as new groundhogs will move into the abandoned holes. To prevent this, fill in the hole opening and cover it with a sheet of chicken wire.
Voles	Voles burrow underground and eat roots. Fences don't work but gardeners can protect plants by wrapping wire mesh around the root ball when planting. Sharp-edged gravel in the planting hole can discourage them as well.	Do not confuse voles with moles. Moles eat insects, not plants, and are essentially harmless in the garden. In most of the United States, voles are a minor pest. In the Southeast, the local species of vole has a voracious appetite.
Squirrels	Squirrels cannot be fenced out. Chicken wire or hardware cloth laid flat on the ground can prevent them from digging.	Squirrels eat mostly bulbs and rhizomes when they are newly planted. Often if you can use a repellent or wire mesh to protect the plants the first year, the squirrels will leave them alone after that.
Gophers	Bury fencing in a trench at least 18 inches (46 cm) deep to prevent digging under it. Just 6 inches (15 cm) of fencing sticking up above the ground is sufficient to keep them from climbing over it.	Gopher wire is sometimes installed horizontally, flat on the ground, buried under 2 inches (5 cm) of soil. This works well for lawns but is not practical for a perennial garden.

INSECT PESTS

We've talked a lot in this book about welcoming and celebrating the insect visitors to our gardens, but sadly some insects are problems and need extra intervention to keep them from ravaging our plants. The most serious pests are usually non-native invasive insects because they often do not have effective predators among our native insects and so can quickly reach very damaging population levels.

What gardeners don't want to do is run out with a bottle of insecticide the moment they see something munching on plants. That's the old way of gardening and will wreak havoc on your local ecosystem. The current model for managing pests is called *integrated pest management*, or IPM. This relies on identifying pests, learning about their life cycles and potential damage they can do, relying first on promoting natural predators and choosing resistant plants, and only using insecticides as an absolute last resort. In a vegetable garden, that option of last resort may come more often than in a perennial garden, as there is a much greater diversity of ornamental plants to choose from, meaning gardeners can almost always simply choose selections that are not affected by particular pests.

Identification

The first thing to do when you notice an insect on your plants is to figure out what it is. This has gotten much easier to do now in the age of cell phones. Various apps will help quickly identify a range of common insects, and gardeners can also type a quick description of the insect (such as "shiny green beetle") into an online image search, and then scroll through the results until you find the insect that matches what you saw in the garden.

Learn About the Insect

Once you have the insect name, a quick search online will turn up lots of information about it. Lean heaviest on university Extension sites and sites produced by botanic gardens or reputed gardening publications over the clickbait that often gets the first couple of hits on a search engine. Most of the time, your mystery insect will turn into a fascinating new resident of your garden—pollinators, predators on other insects, butterflies and moths, and other interesting garden residents. Occasionally, you'll find an insect that is going to feed on the leaves, stems, or flowers of your plants.

Insects play a vital role in the ecosystem of your garden. Some insects, like this milkweed tussock moth caterpillar, are specialized feeders that require a single host plant species to feed (*Asclepias*). Other insects are more generalized feeders, relying on a broad range of host plants to feed. While some gardeners may think this tussock moth caterpillar is a "pest," it is not. This is a North American native insect that coevolved with milkweed in the same manner as the monarch butterfly. Why is one caterpillar seen as a pest and the other as a treasure? Learn to identify the insects you find in your garden before passing judgement.

Decide If It Is a Problem

Just because an insect feeds on your plants does not mean you need to do something about it. Most of these insects will remain in small numbers, with populations being kept low by the other insects and birds that fill your garden. In agricultural IPM they talk about the concept of an economic threshold—the point at which a pest is doing so much damage that it is costing the farmer money. For your perennial garden, gardeners can think about having an ornamental threshold, or the point at which the pests are stopping your garden from doing what you want to it to do, which is look beautiful. A few holes in leaves here and there doesn't rise to that level. A pest that can kill entire plants, like the red lily beetle, or strip plants of their leaves and flowers, like the Japanese beetle, does require action. If the description of an insect refers to it as a common garden pest, keep an eye on it and watch and see if the population starts growing. If you learn that it is a non-native pest, keep a much closer eye on it. These species are much more likely to require intervention to keep them from becoming a big problem.

Research Control Methods

Once you decide that a pest is a problem you need to deal with, do some research into the ways you can control it. For some pests, especially in a small garden, simply handpicking them off the leaves can be very effective. For others, planting flowers that encourage parasitic wasps may be enough to knock the population back. If the pest is only bothering one specific variety in the garden, consider just replacing that plant with something less palatable.

Using a Pesticide

If there is no option for control other than a pesticide, be sure to choose and deploy the pesticide in a way that will minimize the damage to your garden ecosystem. The worst choices are what are called broad-spectrum insecticides, which are compounds that kill a range of different species. Whether they are organic, like neem oil, or synthetic, like Sevin, broad-spectrum insecticides can devastate all the other insects, including pollinators, that visit your garden. The best treatments are targeted, with compounds that will kill only your pest and leave others unharmed. For example, instead of spraying an insecticide over your garden to kill mosquitoes, you can buy mosquito dunks that can target just mosquito larvae in standing water, reducing the problem while leaving other insects alone. How can you tell if a treatment is targeted? Just look at the label. If the label has a long list of pests it kills, treat this as a red flag. The best treatments will list just the specific insect you are having problems with and nothing else.

Thankfully, many common pest woes on perennials are largely aesthetic, including this damage from a four-lined plant bug on the leaf of a shasta daisy. Few pests will outright kill a plant.

A GUIDE TO COMMON PESTS OF PERENNIALS

COMMON PERENNIAL GARDEN PESTS	IDENTIFICATION	DAMAGE
Japanese beetles	Fat, white grubs underground when immature and shiny, green beetles as adults	Japanese beetle larvae eat roots and can strip plants of leaves and flowers as adult beetles.
Slugs	Slimy creepers found in damp, shady areas	Slugs chew holes in leaves, can kill seedlings completely, and can make mature plants very unattractive.
Four-lined plant bug	Shiny red when immature, yellow-green with black stripes as adults	Adults make round, dark, sunken holes in leaves that can be confused with fungal diseases. Damage is rarely serious, but unattractive.
Red lily beetle	Bright red beetles as adults. Larvae cover themselves with feces and look like slimy, brown lumps	Red lily beetles are a non-native invasive species that feeds voraciously on true lilies (*Lilium*) and some related plants.
Spotted cucumber beetle	Greenish-yellow beetles with black spots	Spotted cucumber beetles feed on a range of plants, chewing large holes in leaves. They can spread diseases of cucumbers and squash, and are less serious on ornamental plants.
Aphids	Small, usually wingless, soft insects usually found in large clusters	Aphids suck sap from plants, weakening them and sometimes spreading viruses and other diseases. Rarely a serious problem in healthy ecosystems.
Vine weevil	Dark brown or black beetle; fat, white grubs as larvae	Vine weevils feed on the roots and crowns of perennials at, or just below, the soil level. The larval stage is the most damaging. Most common in cool, moist climates.
Leaf miners	Larvae burrow between the surfaces of a leaf, making wandering discolored paths in the foliage	Larva burrow between the surfaces of a leaf, making wandering discolored paths over the foliage.
Flea beetles	Tiny jumping black beetles	Makes many tiny, small holes or brown spots on foliage. Unsightly on mature plants, but can seriously harm very small plants and seedlings.
Asian jumping worms	Invasive worms that thrash and jump when disturbed	Asian jumping worms rapidly consume organic matter and degrade soil, making it bad at holding water and prone to erosion.

TREATMENTS

- Encourage predators: Plant peonies and goldenrod to provide nectar to two different predatory wasps that have been introduced into the United States to kill Japanese beetles.
- Handpicking: Hold a bucket of soapy water under a plant and tap the leaves and flowers; most of the Japanese beetles will drop into the water and die.
- Milky spore: This is a targeted fungal disease that kills beetle larvae but not other insects. Spread it on the lawn to knock back the population. Most effective if you can convince your neighbors to use it as well.

- Make beetle humps: Build up slightly raised areas and plant with a grass or sedge to make a habitat for predatory beetles that hunt slugs.
- Bait: Slug pellets containing iron phosphate are less toxic to other organisms than those made with metaldehyde.

Fall pruning: Eggs are laid in masses inside plant stems in the summer and hatch the next spring, so cutting back and destroying plants that were heavily infested in the fall will remove most of the eggs.

- Inspect lily leaves as soon as they emerge for brown or orange egg masses, then continue to monitor and handpick larvae and adults.
- Predatory wasps that feed on lily beetles have been introduced in the United States and hopefully will begin reducing populations.

A range of beneficial wasps, beetles, and flies attack cucumber beetles, so keeping a diverse, healthy ecosystem will keep populations at a minimum.

Lacewings, ladybugs, and many other predators feed on aphids. A strong spray from a hose will knock aphids to the ground and kill them. Large groups are easily crushed by hand or wiped away with a soapy cloth.

Beneficial nematodes are a targeted, biological control that can reduce larval populations. More toxic pesticides targeting the adult beetles should only be used as a last resort.

Trim off and destroy damaged foliage to tidy the plant and kill the leaf miners.

- Beneficial nematodes can reduce populations of larvae in the soil.
- Apply row covers to protect vulnerable plants until they are big enough to tolerate damage.

- If gardeners don't have a jumping worm infestation, carefully inspect all plant material, soil, compost, and mulch to avoid introducing them.
- Use hay, straw, grass, or pine needle mulch instead of leaves.
- A fungus treatment, such as BotaniGard, can reduce populations.

Foliar diseases, like this septoria leaf spot on a *rudbeckia*, can be a challenge to control. Good air circulation is essential, as is removing diseased foliage as soon as it is spotted.

Viral pathogens, including the aster yellows that is causing the deformed flower growth on this coneflower, are usually incurable and require immediate plant removal before the virus can spread.

Foliar Diseases

Perennials may contract a range of mostly fungal diseases on the foliage. These range from mildews to rusts to various leaf spots. Foliar diseases will typically show up as some kind of discoloration (white, reddish, tan, or brown) on the leaves, followed by the leaves drying up and falling off. In almost all cases, foliar fungal diseases are not terribly serious, and what gardeners do about them really depends on aesthetics. Many phlox, for example, will get mildew on their leaves in the second half of the summer, causing the lower leaves to first become covered with a whitish film, and then turn brown and fall off. If that phlox is planted where other perennials block the view of the damaged leaves, you can simply ignore it. The plant will carry on perfectly happily even with the mildewed leaves.

But the purpose of a perennial garden is to be beautiful, so if the diseased leaves are on full display, there are a few options to take action. In general, more air circulation, more sun, and positions where the morning dew dries faster will reduce foliar fungal diseases, so you can try moving plants to a drier, more open location. There are more disease-resistant selections available of many perennials, so gardeners can look for tougher varieties. And, of course, you can simply move the infected plant behind other plants where the diseased leaves won't be visible. It is possible to use fungicidal sprays to treat these plants, but spraying is not recommended as a long-term solution. Beneficial fungi are a key part of healthy soil, and using lots of fungicides can damage them.

VIRUSES AND MYCOPLASMAS

While foliar diseases are ugly but rarely very serious, viruses and mycoplasmas are often harder to spot but much more serious. These are systemic infections in plants that are usually incurable and often fatal to the plants. Most often, they show up as irregular, mottled discolorations on foliage and or stems, or strange distortions of the normal flower form. If you find these symptoms in your garden, you should pull out and destroy the infected plants immediately, as viruses can often be spread by mites and aphids to other plants in the garden. If gardeners ever see virus symptoms on plants at a nursery, stay clear, and don't shop there again. Some viruses are most commonly spread by bad practices in nurseries, and gardeners should shop at places that are doing the work to make sure they are selling healthy plants.

Sometimes mycoplasmas, while still deadly, are quite attractive, at least at first. A common one in trilliums causes interesting-looking green streaks to appear in the flowers, while aster yellows, which affects many species in the daisy family, can distort blooms in interesting and sometimes beautiful ways. But don't be fooled—mycoplasmas are fatal and the plants should be pulled before the disease can spread.

Viral diseases are less common these days as modern horticultural and nursery practices have limited their spread, and you will very likely never see these diseases in your garden, but if you do, don't hesitate to remove them.

Root Rots

Another common group of diseases are the root rots. These are the hardest to see, and very often fatal. If a plant is wilting, but you check and the soil is wet, this is a very good sign that something is rotting the roots. Root rots are most often the result of growing plants in the wrong conditions. Too wet soils are a common cause, as is growing plants in soils of a different pH than what they are adapted too. Alkaline soils, in particular, are less hospitable to many root rots than acidic soils, so plants native to alkaline soils may be more susceptible to these diseases if grown in acidic conditions.

If you see a plant wilting in moist soil, the best course of action is to simply dig it out and replace it with something else—replanting the same variety in the same location will likely just result in the same outcome. If a plant is very special to you and hard to replace, you can try and save it. Do this by digging up the plant, rinsing away all the soil, and trimming back any roots that are soft and mushy. Dust the cut surfaces with a fungicide and put the perennial in a pot filled with new potting media. Water it well and keep it in partial shade while it tries to grow new roots. If the plant recovers, plant it in a new location in the garden, somewhere with better drainage or soil chemistry better suited to its preferences.

Nutrient Deficiencies

If plants aren't getting the nutrients they need, they can suffer. The most common symptoms of this are yellowing of the leaves—often with the veins remaining green. There are some differences in the way leaves look depending on which nutrients are deficient, but the reality is that even for professionals it is impossible to definitively tell which nutrients a plant needs just by looking at it.

Guessing based on how a plant looks is likely to send you off buying fertilizers or soil amendments that you don't need. So, if you see a plant growing slowly with yellowing leaves, get a soil test. Most often in the perennial garden, the underlying cause will be soil acidity (pH) levels, with many plants adapted to acidic soils showing iron and other nutrient deficiencies if grown on soils that are too alkaline. Get a soil test, and then either amend your soil to fix the pH or nutrient deficiency, or switch to plants that are adapted to what your soil is naturally.

Too Much or Too Little Sun

Full sun and deep shade are easy to recognize and plant for, but the in-between locations—part shade/part sun conditions—can be tricky, and sometimes gardeners will put something where it is getting more or less sun than it really needs. Remember that sun levels change over time as trees grow or fall down.

Plants getting too much sun will show damage to their leaves—either browning leaf edges or bleached out, damaged patches in the center of the leaf. If a plant suddenly receives more light because gardeners moved it or a tree was removed, sun damage may be short-term. Plants grow leaves adapted to the light levels they are in, so after a sudden change in light levels, plants will take time to grow new, sun-adapted leaves. Keeping plants well irrigated and providing some shade in the heat of the afternoon can help mitigate the damage while they adjust. Sun damage and drying out go hand-in-hand, so you can help plants tolerate more sun by irrigating and planting a windbreak, but generally the best solution is to move the plants to a more shaded spot.

The first sign that a perennial is getting too little sun is generally a lack of flowering, and as light levels drop, a lanky, open growth habit and general lack of vigor will result. There might be an increase in foliar diseases as well. Lots of perennials best adapted to full sun will survive in shade, they just won't be very vigorous or flower much. Deciding if a plant has enough sun to stay in its current location is often mostly an aesthetic one. Are you happy with the way it looks? Are you liking the amount of flowers it is producing? If yes, it can stay. If no, it is time to move it to a sunnier spot or choose a new plant better adapted to shade.

Hosta plants located in full sun often show signs of foliage burn in the summer. Remember to site plants in appropriate conditions.

A late spring frost has "zapped" the foliage of this *heuchera*. Frost damage on perennials can simply be trimmed off.

Late or Early Freezes

In spring and fall, warm weather can sometimes suddenly turn cold and freezing. Gardeners might fear that this will damage your plants, but the reality is that it almost never will. Unlike most plants commonly grown as annuals, which hail from tropical and subtropical regions and can't handle the frost, the perennials hardy in your climate will handle the vagaries of the weather just fine. If there is a really extreme weather event and new growth gets damaged, this is usually not a serious problem either. Just trim off any damaged foliage and stems and let the new growth emerge to cover it. If you do have a plant that is regularly getting damaged by early or late freezes, you can cover it with an old cloth (not plastic) sheet to add some insulation, but the best option is usually to replace it with something better adapted to your conditions.

Aggressive Spreaders

When gardeners first start a perennial garden, the best plants seem to be those that grow the fastest—rapidly covering the ground and filling in fast. But, with time, you may start thinking of those fast growers as problems. Overly aggressive plants can choke out more precious plant commodities and threaten to turn your beautifully diverse garden into a monoculture.

More concerning are plants that aren't just spreading over the ground but are also popping up as seedlings around the garden. Spreading by seed is a key factor in a plant becoming invasive in an ecological sense. Not every plant that self-seeds in your garden will become invasive, as seeding in the garden is quite different from successfully seeding into wild areas, but if a non-native plant is seeding around, do check for it on invasive plant lists in your state and surrounding areas, and consider removing it.

If a plant is spreading too much, grab a shovel and dig it out. If it is difficult to remove all the roots because they are growing intermixed with other perennials, dig out what you can, and then remove all the growth above ground. Most perennials will resprout from the roots, but if you keep regularly cutting them off at the ground level as they grow, it will kill them. Gardeners may not need to discard the plant completely. Sometimes too aggressive plants are just right if combined in a bed with other aggressive growers, both of which can hold their own. Or perhaps there is a small space for it that is hemmed in by concrete driveways and sidewalks where it can't run very far. You can also give it as a gift to another gardener—just be sure to warn them of its spreading ways, and **never** gift a plant that is on invasive species lists. A native plant that is way too aggressive for a small, urban garden might be just right for a gardener in a rural area with lots of space to fill.

If a plant is spreading by seeds, the simplest solution is deadheading. Simply cut off all the flowers as they fade, and gardeners can stop the plant from producing seeds in the first place. Do not rely on this to control a plant that is on invasive species lists, however. It is easy to get busy and miss deadheading some flowers, and you don't want to be responsible for it spreading into and damaging native habitats.

One example of an aggressive spreader is the chameleon plant (*Houttuynia*). It may look like a pretty groundcover, but it packs an invasive punch and is extremely difficult to get rid of.

RIGHT-SIZING *Your* GARDEN

AS THE GARDEN MATURES and you work to maintain it and deal with any problems that arise, be sure to step back and ask yourself how you feel about the amount of time you are spending working on it. Working in a garden to make it look its best can be satisfying and enjoyable, but it can also be tedious, tiresome, and hard to fit into your life. If the garden is feeling overwhelming, make it smaller or replace plants you have to spend a lot of time on with varieties that don't ask much from you. If, on the other hand, you are loving being out in the garden, looking forward to a weekend with your hands in the dirt, that is a sign that your garden space should be bigger. The perfect size and corresponding amount of work it takes is different for each person and will change for you as an individual as you go through different stages of your life. Scaling your gardening ambitions to what you can practically and pleasurably take care of is key to any successful garden maintenance program.

CHAPTER 7

PLANT PROFILES

THE PLANT PROFILE SECTION looks at some of the most popular and widely adapted perennial plants for a range of climates, conditions, bloom times, and gardening styles.

This list is by no means exhaustive. It would be easy to fill multiple volumes with just plant profiles, but the following plants are a good starting point to begin your journey into gardening with perennials.

The information provided for each plant covers the key points of its attributes and cultural requirements, but space is limited, so it isn't possible to cover every detail. Most of the time, this basic information is all gardeners will need to select the right plants for the garden and keep them happy and thriving, but if you fall in love with a group of plants or run into a problem you can't seem to solve, you may want to seek out more information to supplement what is in this chapter.

Finally, there is an old saying in gardening circles: "Plants don't read books." Yes, plants don't always follow the rules. If you have exceptionally rich soil, you may find most of your plants grow bigger than the sizes listed here. If your local deer population is particularly hungry, you may find them nibbling on plants that are generally considered deer-resistant. But that is part of the fun of gardening; every year you'll learn new things and discover new plants you didn't think would thrive in your garden. Be open-minded and willing to experiment.

PERENNIAL ICON KEY

There are icons used in each of the plant profiles to help share important information succinctly. Here is a key to their meanings:

☼	Full sun
⛅	Partial sun
●	Shade
🌡	Low heat tolerance
🌡	Medium heat tolerance
🌡	High heat tolerance
🐰	Deer/rabbit resistance
💧	Low water use
💧💧	Medium water use
💧💧💧	High water use
⬆	Upright growth habit
🔄	Rounded growth habit
↔	Groundcover growth habit
🌾	Attractive seedheads
🧴	Fragrance
🐝	Pollinator friendly

Achillea millefolium

Common name(s): Yarrow
Height: 2'–3' (30–61 cm) | **Width:** 2'–3' (30–61 cm)
Bloom time: Summer | **Lowest hardiness zone:** 3
Pruning: Cut back in spring as desired
Propagation: Division, seed | **Dormant:** Winter or evergreen
Native region: North America, Europe, and Asia

YARROW IS NATIVE to pretty much the entire Western Hemisphere, which gives you a sense of just how adaptable and durable this perennial is. It makes a spreading mat of very finely cut, ferny foliage, and then sends up tall stems topped with flat masses of small flowers. Wild plants typically have white flowers, but selected forms range from red to pink to yellow and warm orange shades in between. The blooms are beautiful and incredibly popular with pollinators and are a particularly good food source for beneficial wasps and flies that will help control pest insects. After the flowers fade, leave the seedheads up if you like the look, or deadhead and possibly get a rebloom later in the summer.

❋ **QUICK TIP** Yarrow clumps tend to die out in the center after a few years and are best divided regularly to maintain their vigor.

Aconitum carmichaelii

Actaea racemosa

Common name(s): Monkshood
Height: 2'–4' (61–91 cm) | **Width:** 1'–1.5' (30–46 cm)
Bloom time: Fall | **Lowest hardiness zone:** 3
Pruning: Cut back in spring as needed
Propagation: Division and seed | **Dormant:** Winter
Native region: Central China

THIS IS A DURABLE, long-lived perennial that ends the year with rich, blue flowers that have an unusual, hooded shape that gives the plant its common name. Blue flowers are wonderful any time of the year, but these are particularly marvelous contrasting with the dominant yellow and red tones of fall. Though monkshood can grow in sun or partial shade, afternoon shade will help it thrive where summers are hot. Like many long-lived perennials, it can take a few years to establish, so be patient as they bulk up and start showing off.

❋ **QUICK TIP** All parts of this plant are extremely toxic. This makes it immune to damage by deer and rabbits, but it is not a good choice for gardens with children.

Common name(s): Black cohosh
Height: 4'–6' (1.2–1.8 m) | **Width:** 2'–3' (61–91 cm)
Bloom time: Midsummer | **Lowest hardiness zone:** 3
Pruning: Cut back in spring, if desired
Propagation: Division and seed | **Dormant:** Winter
Native region: Eastern North America

SHADE GARDENS IN SUMMER can be lackluster after the spring ephemerals have faded and there is nothing but foliage, which is beautiful but always looks the same. That is why you need black cohosh to get things moving again by sending up incredible tall spires of fragrant white flowers. The blooms are everything cool, elegant, and beautiful—just what a summer day needs. The typical wild form of this species has quite attractive jagged green leaves, but if that isn't enough for you, numerous selections have dark—almost black—leaves that make an incredible contrast with the white blooms.

❋ **QUICK TIP** This plant used to be considered part of the genus *Cimicifuga*, and you may still see it under that name in some references.

Adiantum pedatum

Agapanthus

Common name(s): Northern maidenhair fern
Height: 1'–2' (30–60 cm) | **Width:** 1'–2' (30–60 cm)
Bloom time: NA | **Lowest hardiness zone:** 3
Pruning: None needed | **Propagation:** Division
Dormant: Winter | **Native region:** Eastern North America

THIS IS ONE of the most beautiful and delicate-looking ferns, with airy fronds that slowly spread to form colonies. But don't be fooled by that fragile appearance. This is a tough, problem-free plant. Despite the common name, this species has a native range reaching all the way into Alabama and Louisiana and adapts to a range of climates provided it has moist soil and shade. The western (*Adiantum aleuticum*) and southern (*A. capillus-veneris*) maidenhair ferns are great closely related species for gardeners on the West Coast and Deep South.

The fine texture of this fern looks amazing when paired with the bold foliage of classic shade plants like hosta and brunnera.

❋ QUICK TIP If the frond tips turn brown in the summer, the culprit is usually too much sun or too little water. Consider moving maidenhairs into more shade or irrigating through dry spells.

Common name(s): Lily of the Nile
Height: 1'–4' (30–120 cm) | **Width:** 2'–3' (61–91 cm)
Bloom time: Midsummer
Lowest hardiness zone: 6–8, depending on species
Pruning: Cut faded flower stems | **Propagation:** Division
Dormant: Winter dormant or evergreen,
depending on species
Native region: South Africa

IN HOT, DRY CLIMATES, this perennial is a tough-as-nails performer with attractive masses of strappy foliage topped by round heads of blue flowers in summer. There are countless hybrids and cultivars within this genus. Flower color is typically blue, but can range to white or dark purple, and heights vary from little 1-foot (30 cm) varieties to towering 4-foot (1.2 m) specimens. All of them are exceptionally drought-tolerant and make wonderful cut flowers. Traditional varieties are evergreen and only hardy to about Zone 8, but there is an increasing range of hybrids with hardier, deciduous species that can survive winters in Zone 6.

❋ QUICK TIP Wet soils during cold winters are particularly lethal to agapanthus, so give them excellent drainage if they are growing at the edge of their cold hardiness range.

Agastache

Common name(s): Hyssop, hummingbird mint
Height: 2'–4' (61–120 cm) | **Width:** 2'–3' (61–91 cm)
Bloom time: Summer
Lowest hardiness zone: 4–6, depending on cultivar
Pruning: Deadhead and cut brown stems in spring, if desired
Propagation: Cuttings and seed | **Dormant:** Winter
Native region: North America

AGASTACHE IS A GENUS with its biggest center of diversity in western North America. They all have wonderfully fragrant foliage and showy flowers over a very long period in the summer. Those blooms are incredibly attractive to pollinators, both bees and hummingbirds. Most of the species and hybrids are short-lived, especially if grown in the wetter climates of Eastern North America. Anise hyssop (*Agastache foeniculum*), with blue flowers, is native as far east as New England, and so handles rainy climates better than most other selections. Since agastache are short-lived, they are good options to use as fillers in a new garden, providing flowers until the slower-maturing perennials fill in.

❋ **QUICK TIP** Agastache are easy to root from cuttings, so if gardeners make a habit of propagating them every couple of years, they can have them in the garden forever despite their short-lived nature.

Agave

Common name(s): Century plant
Height: 1'–5' (30–150 cm), depending on species
Width: 1'–5' (30–150 cm), depending on species
Bloom time: Rarely bloom
Lowest hardiness zone: 7–10, depending on species
Pruning: None needed | **Propagation:** Division
Dormant: Evergreen
Native region: Western North America

DRAMATIC, LIVING SCULPTURES, agaves are widespread in the dry climates of western North America and are wonderful additions to the garden anywhere they are hardy. The most common varieties have beautiful blue-green leaves edged with dramatic spines, often in a dark, contrasting color. This is definitely not a plant to put next to a walkway as their spines are very sharp. Though, the spines do make them resolutely immune to damage by deer, rabbits, and other mammals. Despite their desert origins, agaves can tolerate a surprising amount of shade. What they cannot handle is wet soil, particularly in the winter. In wet conditions, they will simply rot.

❋ **QUICK TIP** Agaves live for decades before flowering, then sending up a huge flower spike the hummingbirds will visit in droves. After flowering, the plant will die, so enjoy the show and think about what to plant there next.

Alcea

Common name(s): Hollyhock
Height: 5'–7' (1.5–2.1 m) | **Width:** 1'–3' (30–91 cm)
Bloom time: Early summer | **Lowest hardiness zone:** 3
Pruning: Deadhead after flowering
Propagation: Seed | **Dormant:** Evergreen
Native region: Western Asia

HOLLYHOCKS ARE A CLASSIC, old-fashioned cottage garden plant rarely seen in gardens today. When you do see one in full bloom, it is easy to fall in love with them. Especially winsome is the low mound of crinkly green foliage that explodes into enormous spires of huge, showy flowers buzzing with every pollinator in the neighborhood. However, there are downsides. Hollyhocks are short-lived, often little more than biennial, and the leaves are prone to a rust disease that is quite unattractive though rarely actually serious. Choosing varieties of the fig-leaf hollyhock (*Alcea ficifolia*) mitigates—but doesn't entirely solve—both those problems. If gardeners love hollyhocks, the best way to enjoy them is to plant them where other plants can hide the rusty leaves, and plan to resow seeds every year or two.

✳ **QUICK TIP** Hollyhocks do great in lean, rocky, or sandy soils, so they can be the perfect choice for a difficult spot where little else will thrive.

Alchemilla mollis

Common name(s): Lady's mantle
Height: 12"–18" (30–46 cm) | **Width:** 1'–2' (30–61 cm)
Bloom time: Early summer | **Lowest hardiness zone:** 3
Pruning: Can cut back after flowering
for a tidier look, if desired
Propagation: Division and seed
Dormant: Winter or evergreen
Native region: Eastern Europe

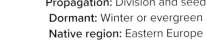

THIS LITTLE PERENNIAL fills the shade garden with beautiful leaves covered with fine hairs that give them a soft textured and silvery-green color. Even more exciting, the leaves make water bead up on them like little jewels. In early summer, those magical leaves are topped by a cloud of countless tiny yellow-green flowers. The blooms look great in the garden and are wonderful cut flowers as well. In the garden and in a vase, lady's mantle is a plant that would win the Oscar for Best Supporting Actor. It isn't the star of the show, but it shines in the corners and makes everything around it look even better.

✳ **QUICK TIP** Though generally considered a shade plant, lady's mantle will do well in full sun in cool-summer climates.

Allium 'Millenium'

Alstroemeria

Common name(s): Millenium ornamental onion
Height: 1'–2' (30–61 cm) | **Width:** 1' (30 cm)
Bloom time: Midsummer | **Lowest hardiness zone:** 4
Pruning: None needed | **Propagation:** Division
Dormant: Winter
Native region: Hybrid of European species

ALL SEASON LONG, this incredibly durable, adaptable perennial makes a carpet of glossy, rich green, grasslike foliage. Then, in midsummer, right when the garden is feeling a little tired, it starts opening round flower heads of pinky-lavender blooms. The flower display is so intense that it can completely cover the plant, the foliage hardly visible, and the blooms are always buzzing with bees and other pollinators. As the flowers fade, they develop into tan seedheads that will keep looking good well into winter. About the only thing this plant can't tolerate is very wet, boggy soils.

❋ **QUICK TIP** Millenium has an oniony smell if you crush the foliage, which you probably won't notice but this does keep deer and rabbits from nibbling on it.

Common name(s): Peruvian lily
Height: 1'–3' (30–91 cm) | **Width:** 1'–3' (30–91 cm)
Bloom time: Summer
Lowest hardiness zone: 5–8, depending on species
Pruning: None needed | **Propagation:** Division
Dormant: Winter | **Native region:** South America

GARDENERS MAY BE more familiar with this plant from seeing it in bouquets from a florist than in a garden, but the same profuse blooming and long-lasting flowers that make it a great cut flower also make *alstroemeria* a stand-out performer in the perennial border. The garden varieties are complex hybrids of many species from South America and vary widely in size and color. Historically, most alstroemeria hybrids were not very cold-tolerant, but breeding from Cornell University in Ithaca, New York has introduced a series of Zone 5 hardy hybrids, starting with the excellent (and fragrant) cultivar, 'Sweet Laura'. Today there is an alstroemeria for nearly every sunny garden. Just remember to give them good drainage if they are growing at the edge of their hardiness range.

❋ **QUICK TIP** Alstroemeria can be slow to establish, so don't judge them by their first year in the ground. They take their time to settle in, then start showing off hard!

Amsonia hubrichtii

Andropogon gerardii

Common name(s): Hubricht's bluestar
Height: 3' (91 cm) | **Width:** 3' (91 cm)
Bloom time: Early summer | **Lowest hardiness zone:** 4
Pruning: None needed | **Propagation:** Division and seed
Dormant: Winter
Native region: Southcentral North America

THE NAME BLUESTAR refers to the flowers of this plant, which are very pretty, soft blue stars in little clusters in early summer. But the real feature of this plant is the foliage. Individual leaves are narrow threads that are silky soft, the whole plant making a rounded cloud of delicate foliage that feels wonderful to brush past. In the fall, the leaves turn a rich, golden yellow that rivals the best fall color of any tree and lasts for a very long time. If your fall garden is boring, plant some amsonia.

✳ **QUICK TIP** Amsonia is very drought-tolerant thanks to an extremely deep root system, but it takes time for those roots to develop, so water through dry spells for the first couple of years in the garden.

Common name(s): Big bluestem
Height: 4'–6' (1.2–1.8 m) | **Width:** 2'–3' (61–91 cm)
Bloom time: Early fall | **Lowest hardiness zone:** 4
Pruning: Cut back in spring
Propagation: Division and seed | **Dormant:** Winter
Native region: Central North America

BIG BLUESTEM IS ONE of the dominant native grasses of the Great Plains and is a dramatic and imposing presence in the perennial garden. It can grow taller than most people, and will stand tall without flopping as long it is in full sun and not grown in overly moist or fertile soils. New selections of the species emphasize foliage color. 'Windwalker' has silvery-blue foliage in the summer, and 'Blackhawks' is so dark it is almost black, and so makes an incredible backdrop for plants with white or yellow blooms. The tall stems fade to tan with the arrival of cold weather and provide great beauty and structure to the garden over the winter.

✳ **QUICK TIP** Big bluestem is great interplanted with spring bulbs, as they will bloom before it comes into growth in the spring.

Anemone hupehensis
(aka *Eriocapitella hupehensis*)

Antennaria

Common name(s): Japanese anemone
Height: 2'–3' (61–91 cm) | **Width:** 2'–3' (61–91 cm)
Bloom time: Later summer and fall.
Lowest hardiness zone: 4
Pruning: Cut back brown stems in the spring
Propagation: Division | **Dormant:** Winter
Native region: Asia

Common name(s): Pussytoes
Height: 6" (15 cm) | **Width:** 1' (30 cm)
Bloom time: Early summer | **Lowest hardiness zone:** 3
Pruning: None needed | **Propagation:** Division
Dormant: Evergreen
Native region: North America, Europe, and Asia

A STAR OF THE LATER summer and fall garden, Japanese anemone sits quietly, not making much of an impression most of the year, before exploding with delicate blooms in shades of pink or white as the growing season winds down. Equally happy in full sun or partial shade, Japanese anemones are commonly seen in older gardens because once established, they are very long-lived and reliable. This is a plant that can also spread quite aggressively once established, so it may not be a good choice for a small garden, but if you have the space to let it run, a big patch in full bloom is breathtaking.

✳ QUICK TIP Because Japanese anemones don't bloom in the spring when most gardeners are shopping, these plants may be hard to find at your local nursery, so don't hesitate to find a mail-order source.

WHEREVER YOU ARE in North America, there is almost certainly a native species of antennaria in your area. There are dozens of species, sometimes hard to tell apart, but they all have pretty much the same game plan: a low carpet of beautiful silvery foliage that spreads almost flat to the ground, topped in the spring by little clusters of fuzzy, white (or occasionally pink) flowers that look, indeed, a lot like the toes of a kitten. They are denizens of usually hot, dry, well-drained spaces, and so are perfect choices to cover difficult ground. They look wonderful spreading with hardy succulents and cacti over dry, sandy soils.

✳ QUICK TIP Pussytoes thrive planted in the cracks between paving stones, and will outcompete weeds there, saving gardeners from a tedious chore.

Aquilegia

Common name(s): Columbine
Height: 1'–3' (30–91 cm) | **Width:** 1.5' (46 cm)
Bloom time: Early summer | **Lowest hardiness zone:** 3
Pruning: Cut back in summer if foliage gets ragged
Propagation: Seed | **Dormant:** Winter
Native region: North America, Europe, and Asia

COLUMBINES MAKE DELICATE mounds of foliage topped by some of the most intricate flowers in the garden. Each bloom is a cluster of five long trumpets filled with nectar for pollinators surrounded by five flaring petals. The most commonly sold varieties at garden centers are hybrids of the European species, *Aquilegia vulgaris*, but North America is home to some of the most beautiful species in this group, from the red-and-yellow *A. canadensis* native to eastern North America, to the dozens of species from the West, including the dreamy blue Colorado columbine (*A. caerulea*). Columbines are generally easy to grow, but they are also typically quite short-lived, only persisting in the garden for a few years unless they are allowed to self-seed.

✳ **QUICK TIP** Leaf miners make tunnels in columbine leaves that can be unattractive. If gardeners don't like the look, just cut the plants back to the ground after flowering and they will flush out new, pristine leaves.

Aralia cordata 'Sun King'

Common name(s): Golden Japanese aralia
Height: 3'–6' (91–180 cm) | **Width:** 3'–6' (91–180 cm)
Bloom time: Late summer | **Lowest hardiness zone:** 4
Pruning: Cut back as needed in spring
Propagation: Division and seed
Dormant: Winter | **Native region:** Japan

IF GARDENERS WANT BIG, bold, brilliant foliage, this is the plant for the garden. This Japanese aralia has large leaves with dramatic coarse textures and a bright golden-yellow color that really lights up a shade garden. The leaf color will be the brightest yellow in part sun and will green out a little—but still be beautiful—in deeper shade. The leaves are the real show here, but once the plant matures, they'll be joined by clusters of white flowers that develop into very attractive black berries in the fall. This long-lived perennial can take quite a few years to reach its mature size, so plan ahead for the transformation of the small plant size straight from the nursery to the giant it will eventually become.

✳ **QUICK TIP** The new growth of this plant is harvested and cooked much like asparagus in Japan, so if you have a mature plant it can double as an ornamental and a vegetable.

Arisaema triphyllum

Common name(s): Jack-in-the-pulpit
Height: 1'–2' (30–60 cm) | **Width:** 1' (30 cm)
Bloom time: Spring | **Lowest hardiness zone:** 4
Pruning: None needed | **Propagation:** Division and seed
Dormant: Summer, fall, and winter
Native region: Eastern North America

A COMMON SIGHT in native woodlands in eastern North America and a wonderful addition to shade gardens, the Jack-in-the-pulpit emerges early in the spring with attractive dark green leaves and a very unusual flowering structure that gives it its common name. After flowering, the leaves fade, and, once plants are mature, the flowers are followed by big heads of brilliant red berries in mid to late summer. If you love the look of this plant, there are a host of other species in the genus from Asia that are also beautiful and interesting garden plants. Jack-in-the-pulpits lack the brilliant colors of most flowers, but they have a subtle and unique beauty all their own.

✳ QUICK TIP Jack-in-the-pulpit plants produce only male flowers when young, then develop female flowers as they mature, so it may take a few years for your plants to start producing their beautiful berries.

Aruncus dioicus

Common name(s): Goat's beard
Height: 2'–5' (61–150 cm) | **Width:** 2'–4' (61–120 cm)
Bloom time: Spring | **Lowest hardiness zone:** 4
Pruning: Cut back in spring, if desired
Propagation: Division and seed
Dormant: Winter
Native region: North America, Europe, and Asia

DO YOU LOVE ASTILBE, but wish you had a version that was native, bigger, and more dramatic? Goat's beard may be the plant for you! The big plumes of tiny white flowers are gorgeous in the spring, and the ferny foliage looks good all summer long. Though usually grown in part shade, this perennial will also take full sun as long as it has plenty of water in the summer, especially in northern gardens. If you love the look of goat's beard, but don't have room for such a large plant, dwarf goat's beard (*Aruncus aethusifolius*) is a very similar species, but only gets 1 foot (30 cm) or so tall and wide.

✳ QUICK TIP Goat's beard comes in male and female forms. They are both beautiful, but the male forms tend to flower a little more heavily.

Asarum

Asclepias tuberosa

Common name(s): Wild ginger
Height: 6" (15 cm) | **Width:** 1'–2' (30–61 cm)
Bloom time: Spring | **Lowest hardiness zone:** 4
Pruning: None needed | **Propagation:** Division
Dormant: Winter or evergreen
Native region: North America, Europe, and Asia

Common name(s): Butterfly weed
Height: 1'–2' (30–61 cm) | **Width:** 1'–2' (30–61 cm)
Bloom time: Summer | **Lowest hardiness zone:** 5
Pruning: Cut back as needed in the spring
Propagation: Division and seed | **Dormant:** Winter
Native region: Eastern North America

PRETTY MUCH ANY woodland in the Northern Hemisphere has native wild gingers growing in it. In eastern North America, *Asarum canadense* dominates, while several species, including *A. arifolium* and *A. shuttleworthii,* are in the South. On the West Coast, *A. caudatum* takes over, and there are many species native to Europe and Asia as well. They are all durable, easy-to-grow, pest-resistant groundcovers for shade with attractive bold foliage that is mostly evergreen (though *A. canadense* disappears for the winter). If you are looking for a native alternative to invasive groundcovers for the shade instead of using English ivy, vinca, and pachysandra, try wild gingers—they are a fantastic option.

✳ **QUICK TIP** Get down to the base of your wild gingers in the spring, and you might spot their beautiful but hidden flowers that are pollinated by ground-dwelling beetles.

IF YOU WANT INTENSE summer color, it is hard to beat the glowing orange (or rarely yellow) flowers of butterfly weed, which blooms over a very long period of late summer and will keep going even longer if gardeners deadhead the faded flowers. The common name comes from the fact that many butterflies will visit the flowers, and the leaves—like other milkweed species—are the key food source for monarch butterfly caterpillars. This species has thick, fleshy roots that store a lot of water and make it very drought-tolerant when established but it does not do well in heavy, wet soils.

✳ **QUICK TIP** Do you love butterfly weed but have incompatible wet soils? Consider swamp milkweed (*A. incarnata*), which has beautiful pink blooms that are fragrant as well.

Aspidistra attenuata

Astilbe

Common name(s): Cast iron plant
Height: 2'–3' (61–91 cm) | **Width:** 2' (61 cm)
Bloom time: Winter | **Lowest hardiness zone:** 7
Pruning: Trim old leaves as needed
Propagation: Division | **Dormant:** Evergreen
Native region: China and Japan

WANT SOMETHING FOR a difficult, dark, shady spot? Something you just can't kill? Well, the common name of this plant literally is cast iron plant! As long as winters aren't too cold, this is a plant that will fill a dry shady area with bold green leaves. The flowers are very cool looking too, but produced at the leaf bases where you probably won't notice them. Individual leaves on a cast iron plant can persist for several years and sometimes look a bit ratty near the end of their life—periodically going through and cutting off the tired ones will keep your clump looking its best. Cast iron plants are slow growing, so think of them as a long-term investment in the garden.

❋ QUICK TIP If you really love aspidistras, look for the variegated forms. They can be pricy and hard to find, but are very beautiful and collectible.

Common name(s): Astilbe
Height: 1'–3' (30–91 cm) | **Width:** 1'–3' (30–91 cm)
Bloom time: Early summer | **Lowest hardiness zone:** 4
Pruning: Cut back in spring, if desired
Propagation: Division | **Dormant:** Winter
Native region: Asia

CLASSIC BLOOMERS for the shade garden, astilbe start the summer with big plumes of tiny flowers mostly in shades of pink. Before and after they bloom, they have attractive, cutleaf, almost fernlike foliage. Astilbe prefer soil that stays evenly moist through the summer and can suffer in dry conditions. They will grow in full shade, but the heaviest flowering is in partial shade, or even nearly full sun in gardens with cool summers and consistently moist soil. There are countless hybrids of astilbe, most focused on different colors of flowers, but new breeding also has focused on foliage color, with ones that are dark chocolate brown or bright gold.

❋ QUICK TIP If your astilbe dies back during an unusual summer dry spell, don't despair. They can go dormant early and come back into growth next spring.

Athyrium filix-femina

Common name(s): Lady fern
Height: 1'–3' (30–91 cm) | **Width:** 1'–2' (30–61 cm)
Bloom time: NA | **Lowest hardiness zone:** 4
Pruning: None needed | **Propagation:** Division
Dormant: Winter
Native region: North America, Europe, and Asia

DELICATE, LACY FRONDS make this fern look fragile, but the fact that it is native to pretty much all of the Northern Hemisphere and that ferns are some of the most ancient plants in the fossil record points to the fact that this is, in fact, a quite tough, adaptable plant that will thrive in nearly any shady garden. Lady ferns are a particularly great combination with native spring ephemerals, as the ferns will come up after the ephemerals have finished and fill the space left by your fading trilliums and bluebells. If you want a lady fern with more pizzazz, look for the closely related Japanese painted fern (*Athyrium niponicum* var. *pictum*) with silver and red patterned fronds.

✳ **QUICK TIP** If your fern fronds are developing crispy brown edges, it means they either need more shade, more moisture, or some combination of the two.

Baptisia australis

Common name(s): False indigo
Height: 2'–4' (61–120 cm) | **Width:** 3'–4' (91–120 cm)
Bloom time: Early summer | **Lowest hardiness zone:** 3
Pruning: Trim brown stems as needed in spring
Propagation: Division and seed | **Dormant:** Winter
Native region: Central and Eastern North America

ONE OF THE TOUGHEST and longest-lived perennials gardeners can grow, baptisias are slow to mature, taking a few years to reach their full potential, but then boast beautiful foliage, elegant spires of blooms in early summer, and attractive seed pods afterward. Very deep root systems give them excellent drought tolerance once they are established, but young plants may need supplemental water while their roots develop. Baptisias can fix nitrogen in the soil, making their own fertilizer, and so they can thrive in very lean, poor soils. *Baptisia australis*, with purple flowers, is the most commonly grown species, but there are other species with yellow or white blooms, and an ever-increasing array of hybrids with more diverse color forms.

✳ **QUICK TIP** Baptisias have a vase-shaped growth habit, so they combine beautifully in the garden with low-growing plants and groundcovers.

Begonia grandis

Common name(s): Hardy begonia
Height: 1'–2' (30–61 cm) | **Width:** 1'–2' (30–61 cm)
Bloom time: Summer into fall | **Lowest hardiness zone:** 6
Pruning: None needed
Propagation: Seed, division, and bulblets
Dormant: Winter | **Native region:** Asia

BEGONIA **IS A HUGE GENUS,** with many of the species being beloved in gardens for their showy flowers and beautiful foliage, but most of them require very mild winters to survive. This species is the one cold-hardy member of the group, sometimes thriving even up into Zone 5 in areas with good, deep snow cover. It has attractive, bold, red-backed leaves and produces large numbers of pink flowers from late summer into fall, right when most shade gardens are in desperate need of something new. At the base of the leaves, it produces small structures called *bulblets*, which can be collected to propagate more plants.

✳ **QUICK TIP** If you garden in Zone 8 or warmer, a whole host of other begonia species and varieties will be hardy for you and can add tons of interest to your shaded garden.

Berlandiera lyrata

Common name(s): Chocolate flower
Height: 1'–2' (30–61 cm) | **Width:** 1'–2' (30–61 cm)
Bloom time: Summer and fall | **Lowest hardiness zone:** 4
Pruning: Trim as needed if habit gets messy
Propagation: Seed | **Dormant:** Winter
Native region: Western North America

CHOCOLATE FLOWER is a slightly sprawling perennial with silvery green leaves and cheerful yellow daisy flowers produced over a very long period from summer into fall. This little plant has a lot going for it, but the one feature that really makes it stand out is that the flowers smell like chocolate. It is a wonderful—though hunger-inducing—addition to a garden. It can be used simply to bring cut flowers into the house. This is a desert species and does best in lean, dry soils. It can be grown in wetter climates, but it will be very short-lived and develop an open, sprawling growth habit. If it gets too rangy, just trim it back to encourage new, more compact, growth.

✳ **QUICK TIP** Don't sleep on the seedheads that follow after the flowers. They are exceptionally beautiful as well even if they don't smell like dessert.

Bletilla striata

Common name(s): Chinese ground orchid
Height: 1'–2' (30–61 cm) | **Width:** 1' (30 cm)
Bloom time: Early summer | **Lowest hardiness zone:** 5
Pruning: None needed | **Propagation:** Division
Dormant: Winter | **Native region:** East Asia

IF YOU THINK ORCHIDS have to live in the house except in tropical regions, think again. There are a lot of orchids native to temperate regions around the world, though often they have very exacting habitat requirements that make them tricky to cultivate in a garden. But this orchid is downright easy to grow in a partially shaded garden, slowly spreading with time to make dramatic clumps. The blooms in early summer are classic orchid flowers, bright pink, and so elegant garden visitors will think you are a gardening wizard. No need to tell them how easy this plant is to grow. After the blooms, the broad, pleated leaves remain extremely attractive for the rest of the year.

❋ **QUICK TIP** If you love this plant, look for the beautiful, variegated forms and selections with different flower colors. They're all generally easy to grow, though some selections are a little less cold hardy.

Bouteloua gracilis

Common name(s): Blue grama grass
Height: 2' (61 cm) | **Width:** 2' (61 cm)
Bloom time: Summer | **Lowest hardiness zone:** 3
Pruning: Cut back in spring before new growth emerges
Propagation: Division and seed | **Dormant:** Winter
Native region: Western North America

A VERY BEAUTIFUL, fine-textured, almost airy grass, this plant mixed with other perennials will produce an instant soft, romantic meadowy feel. And in summer, the flowers and seedheads emerge up above the leaves and seem to dance in the air on almost invisibly slender stems. In the typical forms, the seedheads are brown, but in the very popular 'Blonde Ambition' cultivar, they are a light golden tan that is even more beautiful. This is a grass native to very dry climates, so it is perfect for waterwise gardens, but will suffer in heavy wet soils.

❋ **QUICK TIP** Planted thick and mown to a few inches tall, this grass makes a wonderful native, drought-tolerant lawn.

Brugmansia

Common name(s): Angel's trumpet
Height: 3'–6' (91–270 cm) | **Width:** 3'–4' (91–120 cm)
Bloom time: Summer | **Lowest hardiness zone:** 8
Pruning: Cut back any dead growth in the spring
Propagation: Cuttings | **Dormant:** Winter
Native region: South America

IN TROPICAL REGIONS, this plant develops into a woody shrub, but in the warmer parts of North America it can be grown as a perennial, dying back to the ground each winter then shooting up to grow and flower again each summer. Brugmansias love lots of heat, lots of fertilizer, and lots of water, and when they get all of that, they'll reward you with waves of truly enormous trumpet-shaped blooms in shades of white, yellow, or pink. But the best feature of all is the fragrance. During the day, gardeners will enjoy the sweet scent from the trumpets, but as evening falls, scent production goes into overdrive, pumping out an intoxicating aroma that will fill the garden.

❋ **QUICK TIP** Love brugmansia but have winters a little too cold for it? Deep mulch piled over the plants in the fall can help, or you can dig them up and store them in a cold basement.

Brunnera macrophylla

Common name(s): Siberian bugloss
Height: 1' (30 cm) | **Width:** 1'–2' (30–61 cm)
Bloom time: Spring | **Lowest hardiness zone:** 3
Pruning: None needed | **Propagation:** Division and seed
Dormant: Winter | **Native region:** Central Europe

THE LARGE, BOLD, heart-shaped leaves are the main reason you'll want to grow this species. In the wild, the leaves are typically plain green with occasional silver spots, but most forms sold to gardeners have dramatic silver patterns covering most of the leaf. That silver foliage is a wonderful way to brighten up a dark, shaded area and looks incredible when paired with delicate ferns. As great as the leaves are, the flowers are well worth enjoying too. The blooms are airy clouds of small true-blue flowers in spring. One plant in bloom is nice, but big masses of them flowering together are absolutely magical. Plants will slowly spread to form a groundcover, and will often self-seed when happy.

❋ **QUICK TIP** Seedlings that pop up will sometimes lack the silver color of named cultivars, so weed out seedlings with plain green leaves to keep your garden silver.

Calamintha nepeta

Common name(s): Calamint
Height: 1'–2' (30–61 cm) | **Width:** 1'–2' (30–61 cm)
Bloom time: Summer and fall | **Lowest hardiness zone:** 5
Pruning: Cut back stems in spring, if desired
Propagation: Cuttings, division, and seed
Dormant: Winter | **Native region:** Europe

AT THE BEGINNING of the summer, calamint starts blooming with countless small white or light blue flowers and just doesn't stop. It just keeps blooming and blooming and blooming right up until the first frost in the fall. The individual flowers are small, and the effect is an airy filler that knits a garden together and makes everything around it look better. The small flowers are extremely attractive to bees and provide a consistent food source for pollinators all summer long. The whole plant has a strong, herbal scent that releases if gardeners brush past the plant. The scent keeps deer and rabbits from nibbling.

❋ **QUICK TIP** Calamint is a great choice for difficult spots where you can't irrigate as it is drought-tolerant and doesn't need rich soil to thrive.

Callirhoe involucrata

Common name(s): Purple poppy mallow
Height: 1' (30 cm) | **Width:** 1'–3' (30–91 cm)
Bloom time: Summer | **Lowest hardiness zone:** 4
Pruning: None needed | **Propagation:** Seed and cuttings
Dormant: Winter | **Native region:** Central North America

RICH, SATURATED FLOWERS that are a deep purple-red with a white center that almost seems to glow make this plant a dramatic beauty. Those flowers keep coming all summer, making a very long-lasting display. A deep, drought-resistant root system makes it a great choice for dry, difficult spots, and the low, spreading growth habit allows it to mingle with other plants and fill in any open areas in a perennial garden. The deep root system does not transplant well once established, so do not attempt to divide this plant, just start more from seeds or cuttings if you want more of it—which you probably will.

❋ **QUICK TIP** Plant this at the edge of a retaining wall or raised beds, and the stems will trail down beautifully.

Campanula

Common name(s): Bellflower
Height: 6"–3' (15–91 cm), depending on species
Width: 1'–2' (30–61 cm), depending on species
Bloom time: Summer
Lowest hardiness zone: 3–5, depending on species
Pruning: Cut back in spring, if desired
Propagation: Seed, division, and cuttings
Dormant: Winter
Native region: North America, Europe, and Asia

THE GENUS *CAMPANULA* is huge, with over 500 species. They nearly all have blue, bell-shaped flowers, though a handful of whites and pinks slip through here and there, and it seems like an absurd number of them are beautiful garden plants. In general, they do best in areas with cooler summer temps. At one extreme, there are small alpine species like *Campanula carpatica* and *C. portenschlagiana,* which form low-growing carpets that completely cover themselves with blooms and are best suited to rock gardens and tumbling over the edges of stone retaining walls. Tall species like *C. persicifolia* make tall spires of blooms and running species like *C. punctata* are very beautiful but should be used with caution in small gardens, as they can take over large areas quickly.

❋ **QUICK TIP** Most campanulas will do best where they get a little shade in the heat of the afternoon.

Canna

Common name(s): Canna lily
Height: 3'–6' (91–180 cm) ∣ **Width:** 2'–3' (61–91 cm)
Bloom time: Summer ∣ **Lowest hardiness zone:** 7–8
Pruning: Cut back in spring
Propagation: Division and seed ∣ **Dormant:** Winter
Native region: Tropical Americas

GARDENERS MIGHT FALL in love with cannas for their bold foliage. The leaves are huge, tropical looking, and can be green, dark purply brown, or even striped orange or yellow. Or you might be taken by their intensely colored flowers, usually in shades of yellow, orange, and red. Or you might love the way they grow rapidly through the hottest days of the summer, quickly filling an empty garden or making a living privacy fence.

If cannas aren't hardy in your area, the thick rhizomes can be dug and stored in a cool basement over the winter, or try overwintering them in a warm spot next to the south wall of a building where they may surprise you by coming back year after year.

❋ **QUICK TIP** Many canna species are native to wetlands, so though they thrive in ordinary garden soil, they are great choices for difficult wet areas.

Carex pensylvanica

Chelone

Common name(s): Pennsylvania sedge
Height: 8" (20 cm) | **Width:** 1'–2' (30–61 cm)
Bloom time: Summer | **Lowest hardiness zone:** 3
Pruning: None needed | **Propagation:** Division
Dormant: Evergreen
Native region: Eastern North America

Common name(s): Turtlehead
Height: 2'–3' (61–91 cm) | **Width:** 1'–2' (30–61 cm)
Bloom time: Late summer | **Lowest hardiness zone:** 5
Pruning: Cut back in spring, if desired
Propagation: Division, cuttings, and seed
Dormant: Winter | **Native region:** Eastern North America

THIS LITTLE PERENNIAL sedge is easy to overlook, but incredibly useful in the garden. It looks like a low-growing grass and can be mown and used as a lawn alternative in areas too shady for traditional turf, but its true superpower is the way it grows when it is interplanted between taller-growing perennials in a sunny garden. There it will gently weave itself in between the other plants, never smothering or harming them, just filling the space as a living mulch and preventing weeds from popping up. Interplanting with sedges is a strategy some top landscape designers use to minimize maintenance, and it works just as well in the home garden.

✳ QUICK TIP *Carex* is a huge genus, and there are many other species worth exploring, especially to give the effect of ornamental grasses in the shade.

CHELONE **IS A GENUS** of four very similar-looking species, each with attractive glossy dark foliage topped in late summer with spikes of unusual, snapdragon-like pink (or rarely white) flowers. The closed flower shape reserves the pollen and nectar for their preferred pollinators, the large bumblebees that can pull the flowers open. In the wild, they tend to grow in very wet soils in light shade, but they'll adapt to full sun and normal soils in the garden. The beautiful foliage and tight growth habit makes them a perfect choice for more formal garden designs.

✳ QUICK TIP *Chelone* are a great choice for difficult spots like rain gardens that can both flood and get dry as the plants take a wide range of conditions in stride.

Chrysanthemum

Common name(s): Mum
Height: 1'–3' (30–91 cm) | **Width:** 1'–3' (30–91 cm)
Bloom time: Fall
Lowest hardiness zone: 4–7, depending on variety
Pruning: Cut back in spring, as desired
Propagation: Cuttings and division
Dormant: Winter | **Native region:** East Asia

CHRYSANTHEMUMS ARE ONE of the oldest cultivated flowers in the world, with records of them being grown in China as early as the fifteenth century BCE. In North America, they are mostly sold as disposable potted plants in the fall, but there is a huge range of diversity within this group that is well worth exploring and adding to the garden. The common potted mums are usually only hardy to Zone 7 or so, but there are many hardier selections that will be reliable perennials in all but the very coldest gardens. Flowers range from tiny pompoms to huge, elegant spider forms, and all are pest- and problem-free and very easy to propagate via cuttings.

✳ QUICK TIP To maximize beauty and ecological value, choose mums with open daisylike flowers, which will attract hundreds of pollinators.

Chrysogonum virginianum

Common name(s): Green and gold
Height: 3"–4" (7.6–10 cm) | **Width:** 1'–2' (30–61 cm)
Bloom time: Summer | **Lowest hardiness zone:** 5
Pruning: Deadhead, if desired
Propagation: Division and seed
Dormant: Winter | **Native region:** Eastern North America

ONE OF THE BEST native groundcovers, this little plant makes a rich carpet of low green leaves that are topped with yellow daisy flowers over a very long period. In hot summer climates, the bloom may slow down in midsummer, but in cooler climates it just flowers nonstop. This is a very adaptable plant; it is probably best in partial shade in moist soils, but it can grow in quite deep shade (though flowering will be reduced there) and will even take full sun if the soil is consistently moist. Works great as an edging at the front of the bed or is an easy way to fill in a shady area where turf won't thrive.

✳ QUICK TIP The faded flowers can look messy, but they are easy to quickly deadhead with a pair of hedge clippers.

Colocasia esculenta

Conoclinium coelestinum

Common name(s): Elephant ears
Height: 3' (91 cm) | **Width:** 3' (91 cm)
Bloom time: Summer | **Lowest hardiness zone:** 7
Pruning: None needed | **Propagation:** Division
Dormant: Winter | **Native region:** Southeast Asia

Common name(s): Blue mistflower
Height: 1'–3' (30–91 cm) | **Width:** 1'–4' (30–120 cm)
Bloom time: Late summer and fall
Lowest hardiness zone: 5
Pruning: Cut back in spring, if desired
Propagation: Division, cuttings, and seed
Dormant: Winter | **Native region:** Eastern North America

ELEPHANT EARS are amazing plants that give a lush, tropical look to the garden. They love hot, wet conditions and thrive in the Southeast. Originally spread around the world as a crop cultivated for their edible tubers, the huge dramatic leaves have made them increasingly popular in the ornamental garden. Leaves can be green, dark purple, or glowing yellow, with new breeding ever increasing the diversity of this group. Just be aware that some of the new selections are not quite as cold hardy as the older varieties. Elephant ears don't flower often in gardens, but that is beside the point. These plants are all about the leaves.

✳ **QUICK TIP** Want even **more** tropical drama? Look for *Colocasia gigantea*! It is a little less cold-tolerant, but individual leaves can reach 4 to 5 feet (1.2–1.5 m) in length.

IN LATE SUMMER—when the garden is often looking tired and a little worse for the wear—and continuing well into the fall, this durable perennial puts out endless clusters of fuzzy lavender-blue flowers. The flowers are a great contrast to the yellow and orange colors that can dominate the fall garden, and pollinators love them just as much as gardeners. The blooms are always popular with bees and a good fueling spot for migrating butterflies. The only downside is that this plant can spread fairly aggressively by rhizomes, so put it in a space where it has room to roam.

✳ **QUICK TIP** In warmer climates (Zone 7 and above) consider the closely related *Conoclinium greggii*, which is even more heat-loving and doesn't spread as much.

Coreopsis verticillata

Cyclamen hederifolium

Common name(s): Threadleaf coreopsis
Height: 2' (61 cm) | **Width:** 2'–3' (61–91 cm)
Bloom time: Summer | **Lowest hardiness zone:** 3
Pruning: Deadhead to encourage reblooming
Propagation: Division, cuttings, and seed
Dormant: Winter | **Native region:** Eastern North America

GARDENERS WILL FIND a range of coreopsis for sale at your local garden center, with little daisy flowers in shades of yellow, orange, or red. Countless new hybrids are introduced each year, but this species, particularly in the cultivars 'Moonbeam' (pale yellow flowers) and 'Zagreb' (rich yellow blooms), remains one of the best. Lots of coreopsis are very short-lived, performing more like annuals than perennials, but this species will stick around, spreading to make big mats of delicately textured foliage topped with cheery yellow flowers over a long period of the summer. Trim off the faded blooms, and they'll even rebloom in late summer.

✳ **QUICK TIP** Coreopsis make great cut flowers, so don't hesitate to take some indoors to enjoy in a vase.

Common name(s): Ivy-leaved cyclamen
Height: 3"–4" (7.6–10 cm) | **Width:** 6" (15 cm)
Bloom time: Fall | **Lowest hardiness zone:** 4
Pruning: None needed | **Propagation:** Seed
Dormant: Summer | **Native region:** Central Europe

IVY-LEAVED CYCLAMEN is an incredibly useful perennial because it grows a bit backward. During the summer, when most plants are in full growth, it is totally dormant, sitting underground as a little corm. Then, in the fall, as most of the garden is going dormant, it springs into growth, sending up a mass of pink or white flowers followed by silver-patterned leaves. The leaves stay up all winter long before fading away at the end of the next spring. So, if your winter shade garden looks bare, gardeners just need some cyclamen to fill the winter with color before ceding that space to other perennials come spring.

✳ **QUICK TIP** Don't confuse this very cold-tolerant cyclamen with the much more common florist cyclamen (*Cyclamen persicum*), which is also beautiful, but only hardy to Zone 8 or 9.

Dalea purpurea

Common name(s): Purple prairie clover
Height: 1'–3' (30–91 cm) | **Width:** 1' (30 cm)
Bloom time: Summer | **Lowest hardiness zone:** 3
Pruning: Cut back in spring, if desired
Propagation: Seed | **Dormant:** Winter
Native region: Central North America

OVER A LOW MASS of narrow foliage comes tall, wiry stems topped with intensely purple flower heads—like little bottle brushes. The flowers sway beautifully in the wind, bringing great motion to the garden. Once established, a deep taproot gives this plant incredible drought tolerance but this does make mature plants difficult to move or divide. As a legume, this perennial can also fix nitrogen—essentially making its own fertilizer—so it is a great plant for very difficult, lean, rocky soils. Mix this with some ornamental grasses to create the meadow garden of your dreams.

✳ **QUICK TIP** In extremely dry climates, consider the related species *Dalea frutescens*, which is a desert native and makes a low mound covered with bright pink flowers.

Delosperma

Common name(s): Ice plant
Height: 1"–2" (2.5–5 cm) | **Width:** 1' (30 cm)
Bloom time: Summer
Lowest hardiness zone: 6–8, depending on variety
Pruning: None needed
Propagation: Division and cuttings
Dormant: Evergreen | **Native region:** Africa

ICE PLANTS MAKE a ground-hugging carpet of succulent foliage, and then explode into sheets of bloom in the summer. Some cultivars, like the gorgeous 'Fire Spinner', will bloom once at the beginning of the summer, while others—and many of the newer hybrids—keep flowering all summer long. Winter hardiness varies quite a bit within this group, but often what kills them in cold climates is not freezing in low temperatures, but rotting out in the cold, wet soils of spring. This means many species that are perfectly hardy in the cold, dry Intermountain West may rot out in the wetter soils of the East. Giving them excellent drainage will go a long way to helping them thrive in rainy climates.

✳ **QUICK TIP** Hardy succulents are perfect plants to share with friends because they are so easy to propagate—trim off a bit, stick it in the ground, and it will root and grow.

Delphinium

European hybrid

Common name(s): Delphinium, larkspur
Height: 1'–6' (30–180 cm), depending on variety
Width: 1'–3' (30–91 cm) | **Bloom time:** Spring and summer
Lowest hardiness zone: 3
Pruning: Cut back in spring, as needed
Propagation: Seed and division | **Dormant:** Winter
Native region: North America, Europe, and Asia

DELPHINIUM **IS A BIG GENUS BELOVED** by gardeners for its incredible spires of true-blue flowers. While the most familiar form of this genus to most gardeners are the stunning and often finicky to grow European hybrids, there are many species of *Delphinium* native to North America that make fantastic—and easier to grow—garden plants.

KEY GROUPS

European Hybrids
Derived primarily from the species *Delphinium elatum*, these plants can be absolutely stunning, with towering spires of huge flowers. However, these hybrids demand very rich, fertile soil, even moisture, and cool temperatures. If you have the cool-summer climate for them, look for the 'New Millennium' series, bred in New Zealand, which are by far the best selections in this group.

Delphinium exaltatum
Native to Eastern North America, this is a tall summer-blooming perennial, similar to the European hybrids but with smaller flowers, and much more heat-tolerance, with their native range reaching down into Alabama.

Delphinium tricorne
Another eastern native, this is a spring ephemeral, with 1- to 2-foot (30–61 cm) spikes of rich blue flowers in the spring before going dormant. They're very adaptable and easy to grow.

Delphinium carolinianum
This is the dominant species in the plains of the Central United States, coming up early to bloom in the prairies before the grasses get tall. It is a perfect choice for drier, warmer conditions.

Western species: From the Rockies on to the West Coast is home to many species of delphinium, most of which are sadly very rarely cultivated. *D. menziesii*, and *D. variegatum* are two beautiful ones well worth searching out, as is *D. nudicale*, which has brilliant red flowers.

❋ **QUICK TIP** Plants of many of the best native delphiniums are hard to find for sale, so seeds are often the best way to get these gorgeous varieties in your garden.

Delphinium tricorne

Dianthus

Common name(s): Pinks, carnation, sweet William
Height: 3"–18" (7.6–46 cm) | **Width:** 6"–1' (15–30 cm)
Bloom time: Spring and summer
Lowest hardiness zone: 3
Pruning: Deadhead after blooming
Propagation: Seed and cuttings | **Dormant:** Winter
Native region: Eurasia

DIANTHUS HAVE BEEN garden staples forever, with old gardens rarely without having some sweet William (*Dianthus barbatus*) seeding around and carnations (*D. caryophyllus*) being a fixture at every florist shop. But both of these classics have flaws as garden plants, typically for being short-lived. A wave of new breeding though has brought us an ever-expanding palette of gorgeous, long-lived dianthus with beautiful double, often very fragrant, flowers that bloom for a very long period over a compact mound of foliage. Dianthus will perform best in full sun and when growing in well-drained soils. Most dianthus suffer in the hot, humid summers of the Southeast, but there are a few that will thrive there. Get advice from a good local nursery on the best choices for your area.

✳ **QUICK TIP** The less fragrant a dianthus flower, the longer it lasts, so if gardeners want great scent, you'll lose a little in bloom power.

Dicentra

Common name(s): Bleeding heart
Height: 1'–2' (30–61 cm) | **Width:** 1'–2' (30–61 cm)
Bloom time: Spring | **Lowest hardiness zone:** 3
Pruning: None needed | **Propagation:** Division and seed
Dormant: Winter | **Native region:** North America and Asia

THE MOST FAMILIAR bleeding heart in most gardens is the related Asian species, *Lamprocapnos spectabilis*, but gardeners shouldn't miss out on the beautiful species native to North America, *Dicentra eximia* from the East and *D. formosa* from the West. Both have intricate bleeding heart flowers over very attractive ferny foliage and keep flowering for a long time, especially if temperatures stay cool. A little more off the beaten path are the spring ephemeral species, like *D. cucullaria*, which emerges early with ferny foliage and beautiful flowers before vanishing back underground for the summer.

✳ **QUICK TIP** The unique flower shape of bleeding hearts evolved to specifically be pollinated by large bees, especially bumblebee queens coming out of hibernation in the spring.

Digitalis

Common name(s): Foxglove
Height: 2'–3' (61–91 cm) | **Width:** 1' (30 cm)
Bloom time: Summer | **Lowest hardiness zone:** 4
Pruning: Cut back in spring, if desired
Propagation: Seed and division
Dormant: Winter | **Native region:** Europe

THE MOST CLASSIC and familiar foxglove is *Digitalis purpurea*, which is an incredibly beautiful plant with tall spires of pink or white flowers but is very short-lived in the garden, usually performing as a biennial. Far more practical for most perennial gardens is the hybrid form *D. × mertonensis*, which is somewhat shorter, with spikes of large pink bell-shaped flowers, and, best of all, is a long-lived, easy-to-grow perennial. If you get bit by the foxglove bug, there are quite a few other species well worth growing, all with tall spires of beautiful blooms, but gardeners may have to grow them from seed to really explore the genus.

❋ **QUICK TIP** Foxgloves have a powerful toxin (they are also used to make heart medicine), which makes them resolutely immune to damage by deer and rabbits.

Echinacea

Common name(s): Coneflower
Height: 1'–4' (30–120 cm) | **Width:** 1'–2' (30–61 cm)
Bloom time: Summer | **Lowest hardiness zone:** 4
Pruning: Cut back in spring, if desired
Propagation: Seed and division
Dormant: Winter | **Native region:** Central North America

IT USED TO BE the only echinacea in gardens was *Echinacea purpurea*, with its pink or white flowers. Then Jim Ault at the Chicago Botanic Garden hybridized the common garden staple with the rare yellow species, *E. paradoxa*, and the coneflower world changed forever. Today gardeners can get echinacea in every shade of yellow, white, orange, red, and pink and cultivars now have big flowers, small flowers, fragrant blooms, and double forms with extra layers of showy petals. An unfortunate reality though is that many of these varieties are short-lived in the garden. Pinching off flower buds the first year can help them get established and be sure to look for side-by-side evaluations at botanic gardens to sort through the many varieties and find the best echinacea cultivars.

❋ **QUICK TIP** Echinacea love to self-seed, but if gardeners grow a mix of colors together, the seedlings tend to revert to pink.

Echinocereus

Common name(s): Hedgehog cactus
Height: 1' (30 cm) | **Width:** 1' (30 cm)
Bloom time: Spring
Lowest hardiness zone: 5–7, depending on species
Pruning: None needed | **Propagation:** Cuttings and seed
Dormant: Evergreen
Native region: Western North America

ECHINOCEREUS ARE ONE of the most beautiful and adaptable groups of cacti, and some of the most cold-hardy species out there. Good drainage is key for them surviving the coldest winters in wet climates, and in dry climates they are easy to grow and trouble-free as well. In addition to being beautiful living sculptures, these cacti have incredible flowers. *Echinocereus triglochidiatus* and *E. coccineus* have huge, bright red flowers, while *E. reichenbachii* has enormous magenta blooms. And if you hate cactus spines, *E. reichenbachii* has small, not very aggressive spines. There is also a spineless form of *E. triglochidiatus* but be warned that without the spines to protect them, rabbits find cacti extremely tasty.

✳ QUICK TIP If you love cacti, but garden in a wet climate, grow them in containers that you can move under an eave or into a shed to protect them during the wettest times of the year.

Echinops ritro

Common name(s): Globe thistle
Height: 3'–4' (91–120 cm) | **Width:** 2' (61 cm)
Bloom time: Late summer | **Lowest hardiness zone:** 3
Pruning: Cut back in spring, if desired
Propagation: Seed, division, and root cuttings
Dormant: Winter | **Native region:** Europe

THE WORD "THISTLE" in a common name may turn you off, but give globe thistle another look. The spiny foliage is quite attractive and dramatic (and keeps deer and rabbits from nibbling) and the round balls of blue flowers are dramatic and quite unlike anything else you will grow. The flowers are a huge hit with pollinators, especially beneficial wasps that help control garden pests. The blooms make very long-lasting cut flowers as well, lasting nearly indefinitely if you dry them. Nothing much bothers this plant as long as gardeners don't plant it in soggy soil, which can cause it to flop or rot out.

✳ QUICK TIP Spiny foliage can be annoying to work around, but it is a surefire way to prevent damage from browsing mammals.

Epilobium canum

Common name(s): Hummingbird trumpet, California fuchsia
Height: 4"–6" (10–15 cm) | **Width:** 1'–2' (30–61 cm)
Bloom time: Late summer | **Lowest hardiness zone:** 3
Pruning: Usually none needed
Propagation: Cuttings and division | **Dormant:** Evergreen
Native region: Western North America

FORMERLY INCLUDED IN the genus *Zauschneria*, this plant provides incredible flowering for dry gardens. Slowly spreading to make a low carpet, in late summer and into fall it explodes into bloom with hundreds of bright orange-red trumpets which, as the common name suggests, will be a huge hit with your local hummingbirds.

This and related species are fantastic plants for dry western gardens, but will struggle and be significantly less cold-tolerant in wetter gardens in the East. Raised beds with sand and gravel will help it thrive where it rains often, but it never quite flowers as heavily in rainy conditions as it does in dry sites.

✳ **QUICK TIP** This plant can spread rapidly, so don't plant it where it can smother smaller perennials.

Epimedium

Common name(s): Barrenwort, bishop's hat, fairy wings
Height: 1'–3' (30–91 cm) | **Width:** 1'–3' (30–91 cm)
Bloom time: Spring | **Lowest hardiness zone:** 5
Pruning: Trim old leaves in the spring
Propagation: Division | **Dormant:** Winter or evergreen
Native region: Eurasia

EPIMEDIUMS ARE A BIG, diverse group, with more species and hybrids regularly being introduced to the nursery trade. They have beautiful, delicate-looking leaves, often with beautiful jagged edges, spots, or simply flushed with purple—especially when they first emerge in the spring. The flowers are delicate, intricate things that dance in airy clouds on wire-thin stems. When established, epimediums are notably drought-tolerant and are a great choice for difficult dry shade locations. When choosing the right epimedium for your garden, remember that some are clumpers, which will stay where you put them, just slowly bulking up over time, and some are spreaders, which will run and grow to form a groundcover.

✳ **QUICK TIP** To best show off the beautiful new growth of epimediums, trim away the old leaves in the spring before they break dormancy.

Erigeron glaucus

Common name(s): Fleabane
Height: 1'–2' (30–61 cm) | **Width:** 1'–2' (30–61 cm)
Bloom time: Summer | **Lowest hardiness zone:** 6
Pruning: Deadhead spent flowers
Propagation: Cuttings, seed, and division
Dormant: Evergreen
Native region: Western North America

***ERIGERON* IS A BIG GENUS,** with a lot of beautiful plants in it. All bear small daisy flowers, but maybe the best for the garden are from the West Coast of North America, especially this species, which is a durable, drought-tolerant, beautiful perennial that just flowers and flowers and flowers. The similar *Erigeron speciosus* is a fantastic plant as well, as are most members of this genus.

Some gardeners may be put off by the flowers because they look similar to the slightly weedy *E. annuus*, but don't let that prejudice stop you from enjoying this wonderful perennial.

❋ QUICK TIP Long-blooming perennials like this erigeron will often benefit from deadheading to keep the floral production coming all summer.

Eriogonum

Common name(s): Wild buckwheat
Height: 6"–2' (15–61 cm) | **Width:** 1"–2" (2.5–5 cm)
Bloom time: Summer | **Lowest hardiness zone:** 5
Pruning: None needed | **Propagation:** Seed and cuttings
Dormant: Mostly evergreen
Native region: Western North America

IF YOU ARE GARDENING in a dry climate and aren't growing *Eriogonum*, you've really got to reconsider your choices. This genus is huge, with over 200 species, spread over nearly every part of the western half of North America. Once established, they are some of the toughest, most drought-tolerant perennials you can grow, and produce incredibly long-lasting flower clusters over a very long period. Yellow is the dominant color of the genus, but there are some pinks, reds, and oranges to be found as well. Popular species include *E. alleni*, *E. umbellatum*, and *E. grande*, but there is a long list of great *Eriogonum* to explore.

❋ QUICK TIP If you really get into this genus, check out the Eriogonum Society to connect with other lovers of these very cool plants.

Eryngium

Common name(s): Sea holly
Height: 2'–3' (61–91 cm) | **Width:** 1'–2' (30–61 cm)
Bloom time: Summer | **Lowest hardiness zone:** 5
Pruning: Cut back in spring, if desired
Propagation: Division, root cuttings, and seed
Dormant: Winter | **Native region:** Europe

FROM A MASS OF COARSE and somewhat spiny—as the common name suggests—leaves comes tall spikes of some of the coolest flowers in the perennial garden. Each flower head is a rounded cone of blue flowers, surrounded by a jagged collar of silver-blue bracts. Eryngium are arresting, different, very dramatic, and make for incredible cut flowers. Eryngiums do best in well-drained soils and thrive in dry conditions and, as the name suggests, are very salt tolerant, making them a good choice for seaside gardens. They will grow in richer garden soils but will probably need staking.

✳ **QUICK TIP** Eryngium tend to be short-lived, so regularly propagating them by root cuttings can ensure you always have some in the garden.

Euphorbia corollata

Common name(s): Flowering spurge
Height: 2' (61 cm) | **Width:** 2' (61 cm)
Bloom time: Summer | **Lowest hardiness zone:** 4
Pruning: Cut back in spring, if desired
Propagation: Division, cuttings, and seed
Dormant: Winter | **Native region:** Eastern North America

THIS LITTLE PLANT GROWS wild in dry spots all over Eastern North America, and when seeing it in the wild gardeners might not be impressed, but move it into the garden and it quickly shows just how beautiful it can be. Over a very long period in the summer, it produces a big cloud of tiny white flowers—think baby's breath, but more elegant and on a native plant. The flowers keep coming and coming, and then, in the fall, it does something few perennials do—it puts on a really great display of fall color as the leaves turn a bright orange that would rival any maple.

✳ **QUICK TIP** Plants in the *Euphorbia* genus have milky, caustic sap that makes them deer- and rabbit-proof, but can irritate the skin, so wear gloves when handling.

Eutrochium purpureum

Common name(s): Joe-Pye weed
Height: 4'–6' (1.2–1.8 m) | **Width:** 3'–4' (0.9–1.2 m)
Bloom time: Late summer | **Lowest hardiness zone:** 4
Pruning: Cut back in spring
Propagation: Division, seed, and cuttings
Dormant: Winter | **Native region:** Eastern North America

A HUGE PERENNIAL that will make a statement in the garden, tall selections of Joe-Pye weed growing in good conditions may well end up taller than you are. In late summer, the plants top themselves with a layer of fluffy, silvery-pink flowers that will attract what seems like every pollinator in a 20-mile (32 km) radius. Joe-Pye weed is a fantastic, long-lived, durable perennial, and honestly the biggest problem for most gardeners is that it is just too big of a plant. Luckily, new dwarf selections, like the very popular 'Little Joe' cultivar, will fit in nearly any garden.

✻ **QUICK TIP** Joe-Pye weed will grow in almost any soil and is a particularly good choice for soggy or seasonally flooded areas where other perennials might rot out.

Fragaria virginiana

Common name(s): Wild strawberry
Height: 6" (15 cm) | **Width:** 2'–3' (61–91 cm)
Bloom time: Spring | **Lowest hardiness zone:** 4
Pruning: None needed | **Propagation:** Division and seed
Dormant: Winter | **Native region:** North America

THIS IS ONE of the wild ancestors of the hybrid garden strawberry, and it does indeed produce tasty—if very small—fruits, but that's just one of the many reasons to grow this perennial in your garden. Wild strawberries spread quickly to make a beautiful groundcover and are great at forming a living mulch around the feet of taller perennials. The white flowers are pretty in the spring, the berries are both beautiful and delicious, and the leaves turn a nice orange-red color in the fall. But perhaps best of all, wild strawberries are one of the best wildlife plants you can grow. In most places, gardeners will find dozens of different species of butterflies and moths using strawberries as a food plant for their caterpillars, and of course any berries you don't eat the birds happily will finish off.

✻ **QUICK TIP** West Coast gardeners should try their local native species, the other wild ancestor of garden strawberries, *Fragaria chiloensis*.

Fuchsia magellanica

Gaillardia x grandiflora

Common name(s): Hardy fuchsia
Height: 2'–3' (61–92 cm) | **Width:** 3'–4' (91–120 cm)
Bloom time: Summer | **Lowest hardiness zone:** 7
Pruning: Trim as needed to control size
Propagation: Cuttings
Dormant: Evergreen or winter dormant,
depending on climate
Native region: South America

Common name(s): Blanketflower
Height: 2'–3' (61–91 cm) | **Width:** 1'–2' (30–61 cm)
Bloom time: Summer | **Lowest hardiness zone:** 3
Pruning: Cut back in spring, as needed
Propagation: Cuttings and seed
Dormant: Winter | **Native region:** Western North America

GAILLARDIA BRINGS COLOR, color, and more color to the perennial garden. The brilliant red-and-yellow flowers start early in the summer and keep coming right through until frost. Pollinators will come for the flowers, and goldfinches and other birds love to eat the seeds that develop afterward. The biggest weakness to this plant is that it simply does not live very long. In heavy, wet soils expect it to perform more like an annual, and even in drier soils don't expect individual plants to persist more than a few years. However, it is easy to propagate, and when happy it can self-sow to perpetuate itself.

YOU MAY THINK OF FUCHSIAS as residents of annual hanging baskets, but this species is actually quite cold-tolerant and a workhorse perennial with an incredibly long flowering season throughout the summer. In addition to selections of *Fuschia magellanica*, there are quite a few hybrids using it and other species that are hardy to Zones 7 or 8. In milder winters, these plants can behave almost as a small shrub, while in the colder end of their range, they'll die back to the ground each winter. The biggest weakness to these plants is that they typically are not very heat-tolerant, so they tend to struggle in the Southeast, despite being winter hardy there.

❋ **QUICK TIP** There are numerous cultivars of this species, including some that tone down the colors to a softer yellow, or a deep, rich red that fits with a more muted color scheme.

❋ **QUICK TIP** If gardeners are looking for a living hummingbird feeder, you've found your plant. Their constant flowering makes them a perfect nectar source.

Gaultheria procumbens

Common name(s): Wintergreen
Height: 3"–6" (7.6–15 cm) | **Width:** 1' (30 cm)
Bloom time: Summer | **Lowest hardiness zone:** 3
Pruning: None needed | **Propagation:** Division
Dormant: Evergreen
Native region: Eastern North America

CRUSH THE LEAVES of this plant, and you'll recognize the scent instantly—this is the original source of the familiar wintergreen flavoring. These days, the taste in your gum is an artificial version, but this is the real deal. As long as it has acidic soils, this woodland native can survive in deep shade, making a beautiful carpet of rich evergreen leaves, topped by white flowers in the summer and brilliant red berries all winter long. Surprisingly, the berries, through edible, are incredibly bland. The leaves are the real source of the wintergreen flavor.

✳ **QUICK TIP** If you have wintergreen growing in the garden, pull off a leaf and chew it while you work—the familiar taste is cool and refreshing.

Geranium

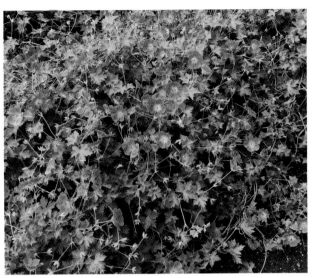

Common name(s): Cranesbill
Height: 1'–2' (30–61 cm) | **Width:** 1'–2' (30–61 cm)
Bloom time: Spring and summer
Lowest hardiness zone: 5
Pruning: Cut back in spring, if desired
Propagation: Cuttings and division | **Dormant:** Winter
Native region: North America, Europe, and Asia

PERENNIAL GERANIUMS are classic garden plants that offer a lot of beauty for very little work. They are pretty adaptable but do best with a little shade in hot climates, and wherever they are grown, they offer an abundance of pretty, five-petaled flowers. The hybrid 'Rozanne' is a standout performer, blooming nonstop all summer and well into the fall, and 'Biokovo' is a great choice for dry shade, with fragrant foliage and beautiful soft pink flowers. And though most geraniums hail from Eurasia, there are some species native to the United States, like *Geranium maculatum*, which is a great spring ephemeral for the shade garden.

✳ **QUICK TIP** Geraniums are generally fairly deer- and rabbit-resistant, and those with the strongest scent to their foliage are the least appetizing to hungry grazers.

Geum triflorum

Common name(s): Prairie smoke
Height: 6"–2' (15–61 cm) | **Width:** 1' (30 cm)
Bloom time: Spring | **Lowest hardiness zone:** 3
Pruning: Cut back in spring, if desired
Propagation: Division and seed | **Dormant:** Evergreen
Native region: Northern North America

THIS LITTLE PRAIRIE native is pretty in the spring when it puts up small, nodding pink flowers over a clump of attractive foliage. But the real show starts after the blooms fade and transform into seedheads. These seeds develop clusters of long silky threads that have a silvery pink color and float like a cloud over the plant, giving it the common name of prairie smoke. Plant a mass of this in the garden, and you won't be able to resist stroking the silky-soft seeds or taking picture after picture of them, especially when they are backlit by the sun.

✳ **QUICK TIP** To enjoy these incredible seedheads even longer, cut some, and hang them until they dry to use in long-lasting arrangements.

Gillenia trifoliata

Common name(s): Bowman's root
Height: 2'–4' (61–120 cm) | **Width:** 1'–3' (30–91 cm)
Bloom time: Early summer | **Lowest hardiness zone:** 4
Pruning: Cut back as needed in spring
Propagation: Seed and division
Dormant: Winter | **Native region:** Eastern North America

THIS PERENNIAL FORMS an attractive, almost shrublike clump of foliage, with dark reddish stems that contrast with the fresh green leaves. In early summer, that clump is topped by a very long-lasting cloud of small white (rarely pink) flowers. Flowering is heavier in full sun than partial shade, but it makes a great display in both settings. The beauty of the flowers is rivaled by the leaves in the fall, when they turn a rich orange color, as good as many actual shrubs. When established, gillenia is quite drought-tolerant, so it is a good choice for difficult dry shade locations.

✳ **QUICK TIP** *Gillenia stipulata* is a closely related plant, similar in most aspects but with more dramatically cut, jagged-looking foliage.

Hakonechloa macra

Common name(s): Japanese forest grass, Hakone grass
Height: 1'–1.5' (30–46 cm) | **Width:** 1'–1.5' (30–46 cm)
Bloom time: Summer | **Lowest hardiness zone:** 5
Pruning: Cut back in spring if desired
Propagation: Division | **Dormant:** Winter
Native region: Japan

ONE OF THE VERY FEW true grasses that will thrive in the shade, this perennial makes very elegant fountains of arching foliage that anchor a shade garden and make a great contrast to the other leaf forms typically found in a shade garden. The plain green form is almost never seen for sale; instead, the most common cultivars in the trade are 'Aureola', which has gold-striped leaves, and 'All Gold', which has solid golden-yellow foliage. Both are beautiful and will light up a dark corner of the garden. Far less common, but worth searching out, is the selection 'Beni-kaze', which is green in the summer but takes on a nice red color in the fall.

❋ QUICK TIP Japanese forest grass can be a bit slow to mature in cool, northern gardens, but is well worth the wait once fully grown in.

Hedychium

Common name(s): Ginger lily
Height: 3'–5' (91–150 cm) | **Width:** 3'–4' (91–120 cm)
Bloom time: Late summer | **Lowest hardiness zone:** 7
Pruning: Cut back in spring | **Propagation:** Division
Dormant: Winter | **Native region:** Southeast Asia

THE HOT, HUMID SUMMERS of the Southeast can leave a perennial garden looking pretty tired and worn. Unless, of course, you grow ginger lilies. These vigorous perennials thrive in the heat, making tall stands of dramatic tropical foliage, and then, in late summer, they produce big spikes of gorgeous flowers. There are quite a few species and hybrids to explore. *Hedychium coccineum* has huge heads of bright orange or red flowers, while *H. coronarium* has large, pure white, and incredibly fragrant blooms. All of them will grow in partial shade, though flowering will be the heaviest in sun and rich soils.

❋ QUICK TIP Some ginger lilies, particularly *H. coronarium*, are classic "pass-along plants" and more likely to be acquired as gifts from other gardeners than purchased at nurseries.

Helenium autumnale

Common name(s): Sneezeweed, Helen's flower
Height: 3'–5' (91–150 cm) | **Width:** 2'–3' (61–91 cm)
Bloom time: Summer and fall
Lowest hardiness zone: 3
Pruning: Cut back before flowering to reduce flopping and cut back after flowering to encourage rebloom
Propagation: Division, cuttings, and seed
Dormant: Winter | **Native region:** North America

FROM LATE SUMMER INTO AUTUMN, this plant covers itself in cheerful daisies. There are numerous hybrids and cultivars of this species, with flowers in shades of yellow, orange, or red. Deadheading will help prolong the flower display and keep it going right up until frost. This plant is quite tolerant of wet soils, so it is a great choice for rain gardens or other low areas that might temporarily flood after a storm. On fertile soils, it can grow too tall and floppy, in which case an early summer cutting back will help a lot, or look for dwarf varieties to plant.

❋ **QUICK TIP** Though native to nearly the entire North American continent, heleniums have long been far more popular in Europe than here in its native land. It is high time to change that!

Helianthus

Common name(s): Perennial sunflower
Height: 4'–6' (1.2–1.8 m) | **Width:** 3'–4' (0.9–1.2 m)
Bloom time: Summer and fall | **Lowest hardiness zone:** 4
Pruning: Cut back in spring, if desired
Propagation: Division, cuttings, and seed
Dormant: Winter | **Native region:** North America

THE MOST COMMON SUNFLOWER in gardens is the annual species, but there are a wealth of perennial sunflowers that deserve to be a bigger part of any garden. In general, the perennial sunflowers are tall plants with abundant yellow daisy flowers in summer and fall, with deep, drought-proof root systems, and few serious pest or disease problems. Even better, sunflowers are sometimes called a keystone species for the sheer number of butterflies, moths, and pollinators they support. With many species to choose from, you might consider *Helianthus salicifolius* 'First Light', which produces an unbelievable abundance of flowers, *H. multiflorus* 'Flore Pleno', which has double blooms like yellow pom-poms, or *H. maximiliani*, which is an incredible performer in arid climates.

❋ **QUICK TIP** Don't forget to cut some of your sunflowers for a vase! They make great cut flowers to enjoy indoors.

Helleborus

Hemerocallis

Common name(s): Lenten rose
Height: 1'–2' (30–61 cm) | **Width:** 1'–2' (30–61 cm)
Bloom time: Late winter and spring
Lowest hardiness zone: 4
Pruning: Cut back old foliage before flowering
Propagation: Division and seed
Dormant: Evergreen | **Native region:** Europe

Common name(s): Daylily
Height: 1'–5' (30–150 cm), depending on variety
Width: 1'–4' (30–120 cm) | **Bloom time:** Summer
Lowest hardiness zone: 3–5, depending on variety
Pruning: Cut back faded flower stems
Propagation: Division | **Dormant:** Winter or evergreen
Native region: Asia

THE GREAT FEATURE of hellebores is that they will almost certainly be the very first plant in your garden to start flowering, and they carry on blooming through late frosts and even snows without missing a beat. The ever-expanding range of hybrids provides blooms in shades of pink, purple, white, green, almost black, and even yellows and oranges. The flowers tend to hang down, but newer selections have blooms that face out so you can see the beautiful petals more easily. The foliage is excellent too, glossy, dark, and evergreen, with some hybrids showing silvery or even pinkish patterns on the leaves. It is generally best to cut off the old leaves in late winter to better show off the flowers and new growth.

❉ QUICK TIP Though generally grown in shade, hellebores can thrive—and flower incredibly heavily—in full sun, particularly in cooler climates.

NEARLY EVERY PERENNIAL garden has at least one daylily in it, and it is easy to see why. Huge, profuse, incredibly showy flowers from a very durable, easy-to-grow, problem-free plant. Other than deer nibbling on them, not much bothers a daylily. Hot, dry, full sun? No problem. Wet, soggy soils? Fine. From just a few species with yellow or orange flowers, modern plant breeders have created a truly staggering diversity of flowers shapes, colors, and forms. If you can imagine it, a daylily flower probably does it. Just be aware that there are lots of new hybrids that have beautiful flowers on ugly, tattered-looking plants. Avoid buying plants based on a photo of a single flower when possible.

❉ QUICK TIP Daylily flowers are both beautiful and edible, a bit like lettuce, with the lighter colors usually tasting the best.

Hepatica americana

Common name(s): Liverwort
Height: 6" (15 cm) | **Width:** 1' (30 cm)
Bloom time: Spring | **Lowest hardiness zone:** 4
Pruning: None needed | **Propagation:** Seed and division
Dormant: Evergreen | **Native region:** Eastern North America

MOST OF OUR NATIVE woodland wildflowers are beautiful in the spring but then go completely dormant for the summer, which can leave a native shade garden looking pretty bare for a lot of the year. But not hepaticas. Their spring floral display is beautiful, and the leaves that follow stay up all summer, and even through the winter. The cheerful little flowers range in shades of white, blue, or pink, and in some forms the leaves are even beautifully patterned with silver and brown. This native plant is woefully underappreciated in gardens, but any searching gardeners have to do to find a source will be well worth your time.

❋ **QUICK TIP** Hepaticas don't like being smothered, so rake fall leaves off their crowns, and don't mulch too deeply around them.

Hesperaloe parviflora

Common name(s): Red yucca
Height: 3'–5' (0.9–1.5 m) | **Width:** 3' (0.9 m)
Bloom time: Summer
Lowest hardiness zone: 5 (if kept dry)
Pruning: Deadhead, if desired
Propagation: Seed and division | **Dormant:** Evergreen
Native region: Western North America

A REMARKABLY TOUGH PLANT that will adapt to nearly any conditions, provided it isn't too wet—even surviving very cold winters provided it has excellent drainage. The quite attractive foliage is long, narrow, and succulent, but the real show here are the flowers. Tall stems are covered with bright red blooms that just keep coming throughout the summer and are just as big a hit with hummingbirds as they are with gardeners. If you don't like bright red, there are selections with pink or yellow flowers as well. If you garden in a dry climate, don't want to irrigate, but still want beautiful flowers, this is the plant for you.

❋ **QUICK TIP** Hesperaloes can take a couple of years to get established before they flower. Be patient—once they settle in, the show is worth it!

Heuchera

'Smoke and Mirrors'

'Electric Plum'

'Caramel'

Common name(s): Coral bells
Height: 6"–2' (15–61 cm) | **Width:** 6"–2' (15–61 cm)
Bloom time: Summer or fall | **Lowest hardiness zone:** 4
Pruning: None needed usually | **Propagation:** Division
Dormant: Evergreen | **Native region:** North America

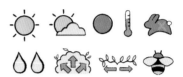

ONE OF THE PREMIERE FOLIAGE PLANTS for shade (though they can grow in full sun in cooler climates), talented plant breeders have transformed the mostly plain green leaves of the wild heucheras into a truly astonishing range of colors, ranging from near black through reds and oranges, bright yellow-greens, and many marked and spotted with silver. Though the foliage is the main feature of most heucheras, some have attractive flowers as well. *Heuchera sanguinea* has bright red flowers that hummingbirds love, and *H. villosa* has big clouds of small white blooms. Some modern hybrids combine both good flowers and foliage on one fantastic plant.

As beautiful as heucheras are, they can be frustrating as too many of the new hybrids have not been properly selected to thrive over the long term in the garden. Many gardeners joke that they are just expensive annuals, surviving just one year after planting. One excellent resource is the in-depth evaluation of plants done at the Mt. Cuba Center in Delaware. Their report is available online and can help guide your shopping to the most vigorous cultivars, especially for gardeners living on the East Coast. Heuchera plants also need to be divided every few years to maintain their vigor.

✳ **QUICK TIP** Heuchera leaves make beautiful and unexpectedly long-lasting additions to flower arrangements. Cut some, and they'll probably outlast all the flowers in the vase.

Hibiscus

Common name(s): Hardy hibiscus, rose mallow
Height: 3'–6' (91–180 cm) | **Width:** 3'–4' (91–120 cm)
Bloom time: Summer | **Lowest hardiness zone:** 5
Pruning: Cut back dead stems as desired in spring
Propagation: Cuttings, division, and seed
Dormant: Winter | **Native region:** Eastern North America

IF YOU WANT TROPICAL-LOOKING DRAMA, look no further than the hardy hibiscus. These plants produce about the biggest flowers gardeners can grow, with individual blooms reaching the size of a dinner plate. The wild species grow extremely tall, but modern breeding has produced a whole range of more compact hybrids topping out at about 3 feet (91 cm) that fit more easily into most gardens. If the huge flowers aren't enough for you, there are also selections with dark purple-red foliage to up the drama even more. In the wild, these hibiscus grow in wet, marshy conditions, but they thrive in average garden soils as well.

❋ **QUICK TIP** Hardy hibiscus are very slow to wake up and emerge in the spring, so be patient, and interplant them with spring ephemerals or bulbs to fill in the space until they get growing.

Hosta

Common name(s): Hosta, plantain lily
Height: 6"–4' (15–120 cm) | **Width:** 6"–4' (15–120 cm)
Bloom time: Summer | **Lowest hardiness zone:** 3
Pruning: Deadhead flowering stems as desired
Propagation: Division | **Dormant:** Winter
Native region: East Asia

HOSTAS ARE PERHAPS the most widely planted shade perennial in North America. The foliage is the big draw here—big, bold, and in an ever-expanding range of sizes, textures, and colors. Hosta tolerate both heat and cold, can thrive both in deep shade and near full sun (especially in cooler climates), and tolerate dry shade once established. Hostas are easy to divide and share with friends but require essentially no maintenance. Gardeners can trim off the faded flower stems if they want, but the leaves will just turn yellow and then seem to vanish in the fall, always looking tidy with no cleaning up. The only real weakness of hostas is that they are tasty. Deer love them, and in the Southeast, voles will devour the roots overnight.

❋ **QUICK TIP** Don't overlook hosta blooms. They can be pretty, especially hybrids descended from *Hosta plantaginea*, which has large, fragrant blooms.

Hylotelephium spectabile

Iris

Common name(s): Sedum, stonecrop
Height: 1'–2' (30–61 cm) | **Width:** 1'–2' (30–61 cm)
Bloom time: Late summer | **Lowest hardiness zone:** 3
Pruning: Cut back in spring
Propagation: Division and cuttings
Dormant: Winter | **Native region:** East Asia

Bearded iris

Common name(s): Flag
Height: 6"–4' (15–120 cm) | **Width:** 1'–2' (30–61 cm)
Bloom time: Spring and early summer
Lowest hardiness zone: 3–6 (depending on the species)
Pruning: Deadhead spent flowers,
cut back brown foliage in the spring
Propagation: Division and seed
Dormant: Evergreen or winter dormant
Native region: Europe, Asia, Eastern North America,
Western North America, or Central North America,
depending on species

THIS PLANT—particularly the cultivar 'Herbstfreude' or 'Autumn Joy'—has long been one of the most popular garden perennials in North America, and for good reason. The succulent foliage is tough, drought-tolerant, and attractive. The big heads of pink flowers give a burst of color in the fall when it is most needed, and the seedheads that follow look fantastic all winter long, even in areas with heavy snowfall. As if all that wasn't enough, the flowers are extremely attractive to pollinators as well. The enormous popularity of this plant has brought a lot of new selections to the market, so gardeners can find forms with darker flowers, rich purple foliage, and variegated leaves. Though, to be honest, the classic selection 'Herbstfreude' or 'Autumn Joy' is still pretty hard to beat.

❋ QUICK TIP Though this plant thrives in dry conditions, it does not demand them, and will grow in nearly any soil that isn't actually a wetland.

THE *IRIS* GENUS has something for every garden, with species that thrive in everything from sun to shade and from standing water to drylands. What all the irises have in common are gorgeous flowers in every color imaginable.

KEY GROUPS

Louisiana Hybrids of species native to wet areas of Southeastern United States, these gorgeous plants have flowers in rich, saturated colors and thrive in wet soils.

Lamium maculatum

Pacific Coast Hybrids of species native to the West Coast, these low-growing irises are perfectly adapted to the wet winters and dry summers of their native range and have some of the most intricately patterned blooms of the genus.

Iris cristata Native to woodlands in Eastern North America, this species forms a low, grass-like groundcover for shade, topped with purple flowers in spring.

Japanese This wetland species has a long history of breeding in Asia, and blooms in early summer with huge flowers that can reach 6 inches (15 cm) across.

Bearded This group of European species and hybrids are incredibly drought-tolerant and easy to grow. Their long history of breeding has produced a staggering array of varieties, ranging from the elegantly simple forms of the species to modern hybrids with enormous, ruffled blooms in every color except true red.

Siberian This durable group of Eurasian species and hybrids grow in nearly any condition. The flowers are mostly in shades of purple, though new hybrids are expanding the color range. They have notably beautiful foliage that could pass for ornamental grass when out of bloom.

❋ **QUICK TIP** Irises make great cut flowers, so pick a few stems to enjoy up close in a vase.

Siberian iris

Common name(s): Spotted deadnettle
Height: 3"–6" (7.6–15 cm) | **Width:** 1'–2' (30–61 cm)
Bloom time: Summer | **Lowest hardiness zone:** 3
Pruning: None needed | **Propagation:** Division
Dormant: Evergreen (except in very cold winters)
Native region: Eurasia

A USEFUL LITTLE GROUNDCOVER for shady areas, lamium spreads rapidly to make a carpet of silver-marked leaves, topped in early summer with purple, pink, or white flowers. The typical wild form of the species has green leaves with just a stripe of silver down the middle, but most cultivars that gardeners find for sale have nearly solid silver leaves with just a thin margin of green. The leaves are the main reason to grow this plant, but the flowers can be quite pretty as well and are always a big hit with your local bees. The biggest problem with lamium is that it can be too vigorous, especially in cool climates, so don't plant it next to small plants it can overwhelm.

❋ **QUICK TIP** For even more foliage color, look for the cultivar 'Aureum', which has bright golden-yellow foliage.

Lavandula

Common name(s): Lavender
Height: 2'–3' (61–91 cm) | **Width:** 2'–3' (61–91 cm)
Bloom time: Summer | **Lowest hardiness zone:** 4
Pruning: Trim as needed to maintain shape
Propagation: Cuttings and seed
Dormant: Evergreen | **Native region:** Mediterranean region

LAVENDER IS ONE OF THE MOST iconic scents in the world—both the leaves and the flowers have a fresh, clean aroma that is soothing and sometimes even used in cooking. The lavender plant is what is called a subshrub, performing mostly as a perennial, but developing woody stems over time, and the occasional hard pruning is helpful to keep them shapely. All lavenders demand excellent drainage and will die if in wet soils over the winter. English lavender (*Lavandula angustifolia*) is tops for fragrance, but the fussiest and least heat-tolerant. French lavender (*L.* x *intermedia*) is probably the most adaptable, while Spanish lavender (*L. stoechas*) is the best for very hot climates.

✳ QUICK TIP Plant lavender next to paths where you and visitors to your garden will brush against the foliage to release the incredible scent.

Lewisia cotyledon

Common name(s): Bitterroot
Height: 6" (15 cm) | **Width:** 6" (15 cm)
Bloom time: Summer | **Lowest hardiness zone:** 5
Pruning: None needed | **Propagation:** Seed and cuttings
Dormant: Evergreen
Native region: Western North America

NATIVE TO THE SLOPES of the Rocky Mountains, this little plant is one of our most beautiful natives. The rosette of succulent leaves is quite attractive, and in early summer they are topped by sprays of gorgeous flowers in rich, saturated shades of pink, yellow, and orange. Lewisia is strikingly drought-tolerant, with both succulent leaves and thickened roots to store water, and gardeners in the Intermountain West will find it easy to grow—even prone to self-sowing. In wetter climates, this plant struggles, however. Wet soils reduce cold hardiness significantly, and hot, humid weather is the kiss of death. In rainy climates, the hybrids between *Lewisia cotyledon* and *L. longipetala* are better choices, having smaller flowers but with much more tolerance of humidity, heat, and cold.

✳ QUICK TIP Lewisias are usually grown from seed, each one coming up a little different, but this plant is easy to root from cuttings to make an exact duplicate of a favorite plant.

Liatris spicata

Common name(s): Blazing star, gay feather
Height: 2'–4' (60–120 cm) | **Width:** 1'–2' (30–60 cm)
Bloom time: Late summer | **Lowest hardiness zone:** 3
Pruning: Cut back in spring, as desired
Propagation: Division and seed
Dormant: Winter | **Native region:** Eastern North America

A DRAMATIC AND ARCHITECTURAL PLANT, liatris sends up tall, narrow spires densely packed with bright magenta flowers. The flowers are incredibly beautiful, and a perfect contrast in form if gardeners are finding their garden design too filled with rounded shapes. In addition to their beauty, liatris are famous for their ability to attract butterflies, and are a particular favorite of monarch butterflies. *Liatris spicata* is the most widely grown, but there are dozens of other species, all North American natives. The flowers all look very similar but vary in height and climatic preferences. Dry climate gardeners should look for *L. punctata*, the most drought-tolerant of the group.

QUICK TIP **Liatris have good drought tolerance thanks to deep root systems, but this takes time to establish, so be sure to irrigate through dry spells during their first year.**

Lilium

Asiatic hybrid

Common name(s): Lilies
Height: 2'–6' (61–180 cm) | **Width:** 1'–2' (30–61 cm)
Bloom time: Summer
Lowest hardiness zone: 4–6, depending on variety
Pruning: Cut back stems in spring as desired
Propagation: Division and seed | **Dormant:** Winter
Native region: North America, Europe, and Asia

TRUE ARISTOCRATS OF THE GARDEN, lilies are a huge, incredibly diverse group, with elegant flowers, often intense fragrance, and sometimes a slightly high-maintenance disposition.

KEY GROUPS

Asiatic This group of hybrids boasts the widest color range of all the true lilies, coming in nearly every color except blue. Generally, these are growing on compact plants, with up-facing flowers that are lacking any fragrance.

Oriental With huge, intensely fragrant blooms in shades of white or pink, oriental lilies are wildly popular and great cut flowers. They can also be a bit fussy to grow, really performing their best in climates with cool summers.

(Continued on next page)

Liriope spicata

(Continued from previous page)

Trumpet Large, incredibly fragrant, trumpet-shaped blooms give this group its name. These lilies have great vigor, but often need to be staked to hold up their heavy heads of blooms.

Intersectional Hybrids Modern technology has produced a whole slew of new hybrids between these groups. The "OT" hybrids—crosses between oriental and trumpet lilies—are particularly popular, producing incredibly vigorous plants that can tower to 8 feet (2.4 m) tall and produce hundreds of flowers.

Lilium formosanum Not used much in breeding, this species is one of the most heat-tolerant and a great choice for the Southeast. The typical form can reach 7 feet (2.1 m) tall with fragrant, white blooms. There is also a tiny variety called *L. formosanum* var. *pricei,* which only reaches 1 foot (30 cm) or so tall.

Native Lilies Though not grown as much as their Asian counterparts, there are some beautiful North American native lilies. Most of them have nodding, brilliantly colored, orange-and-red flowers. The eastern species *L. michiganense, L. michauxii, L. superbum,* and *L. philadelphicum* are all gorgeous and worth growing, and West Coast gardeners should look for their local *L. columbianum* and *L. pardalinum.*

✳ QUICK TIP Watch for the invasive scarlet lily beetle, which was introduced to eastern Canada from Europe and is slowly moving across the continent.

Common name(s): Lily turf
Height: 8"–18" (20–46 cm) | **Width:** 1'–2' (30–61 cm)
Bloom time: Late summer | **Lowest hardiness zone:** 4
Pruning: Cut back brown foliage in spring as needed
Propagation: Division | **Dormant:** Evergreen
Native region: East Asia

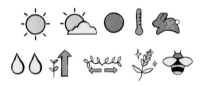

THOUGH NOT A TRUE LILY, nor turf, the common name lily turf sums up this plant well. It makes a carpet of narrow, grasslike leaves that stand in for turf quite well, particularly in spots too shaded for a traditional lawn. As a bonus, in late summer it gives you spikes of attractive purple flowers, which are followed by little back berries. Though evergreen, the old foliage can get fairly beat-up looking by the end of the winter, so it is usually best to give it a haircut in the spring before the new leaves emerge to freshen it up.

✳ QUICK TIP There are quite a few other cultivars of *Liriope muscari* that give a similar grasslike effect, but in smaller or taller forms.

Lilium canadense

Lobelia cardinalis

Common name(s): Cardinal flower
Height: 2'–4' (61–120 cm) | **Width:** 1'–2' (30–61 cm)
Bloom time: Summer | **Lowest hardiness zone:** 3
Pruning: Cut back as needed in the spring
Propagation: Division and seed
Dormant: Winter | **Native region:** Eastern North America

THIS PERENNIAL PROVIDES some of the brightest red flowers out there—an intense, glowing red that is a telltail sign this plant is pollinated by hummingbirds. If you don't love intense red, the closely related *Lobelia siphilitica* has rich blue flowers, and numerous hybrids have resulted in cultivars with a range of flower colors, and some with dark foliage. In nature, these plants tend to grow in wet, boggy areas, but they do perfectly well in standard garden conditions as well. Individual plants tend to be short-lived, so plan to propagate them by division or seed every few years, or use them as a temporary filler in a new garden.

❋ **QUICK TIP** Don't confuse these native, perennial lobelias with *L. erinus,* which is from South Africa and is grown as an annual.

Lupinus

Common name(s): Lupine
Height: 3'–4' (91–120 cm) | **Width:** 1'–2' (30–61 cm)
Bloom time: Summer | **Lowest hardiness zone:** 3
Pruning: Cut back in spring, if desired
Propagation: Seed | **Dormant:** Winter
Native region: North America

THE MOST COMMON garden lupines are hybrids of *Lupinus polyphyllus*, a species native to the West Coast. Extensive breeding, mostly done in Europe, has transformed that wild plant into cultivars with huge spires of densely packed blooms in a range of colors. The plants are beautiful and very intolerant of hot summer weather. Better suited to many gardens is *L. perennis*, which is native to a wide swath of eastern North America. There are also other, very rarely cultivated species of lupine, like *L. diffusus,* native down into Florida, and *L. sericeus,* native to very dry parts of the West.

❋ **QUICK TIP** Almost all lupine species are short-lived perennials, but will self-sow when happy. Reducing your mulch use will give the seedlings places to germinate, or you can collect and sow the seeds yourself.

Lycoris

Common name(s): Surprise lily, red spider lily
Height: 2'–3' (61–91 cm) | **Width:** 1' (30 cm)
Bloom time: Late summer | **Lowest hardiness zone:** 5 or 7
Pruning: Deadhead after flowering, if desired
Propagation: Division | **Dormant:** Summer
Native region: Asia

THERE ARE TWO TYPES of lycoris common in old gardens in North America. The surprise lily (*Lycoris squamigera*) is found mostly in the North, has strappy foliage in the spring that quickly goes dormant, and tall stems of pink blooms that come up in late summer without any leaves. In the South, you are more likely to see the red spider lily (*L. radiata*), which is similar but with bright red blooms and leaves that come up in the fall after flowering and go dormant in the spring. Both are wonderful, very long-lived, trouble-free plants that look amazing in the garden. Interplant them with another perennial and the leafless lycoris flowers can look like they are springing magically from an entirely different plant.

QUICK TIP **Lycoris are technically bulbs but should be planted in the spring like a perennial, not in the fall like a tulip.**

Mertensia

Common name(s): Virginia bluebell
Height: 1'–2' (30–61 cm) | **Width:** 1'–2' (30–61 cm)
Bloom time: Spring | **Lowest hardiness zone:** 3
Pruning: None needed | **Propagation:** Division and seed
Dormant: Summer through winter
Native region: Eastern North America

ONE OF THE BEST spring ephemerals, Virginia bluebells explode into growth early in the spring, putting up a mass of attractive, slightly blueish leaves, topped by big clusters of (predictably) blue, bell-shaped flowers. The display is bold and bright and makes the spring garden look incredibly lush. And then, when they go dormant, those leaves turn yellow and seemingly vanish overnight. No pruning or cleanup needed, they simply melt away and cede the stage for summer-growing perennials like hostas. Forms with lavender, pink, and white flowers are not uncommon in the wild, but sadly rarely for sale. If gardeners find a source, snatch them up!

QUICK TIP **Virginia bluebell isn't just beautiful; it is tasty as well. New shoots quickly stir-fried are delicious. Just be sure to harvest in moderation so you can enjoy the blooms as well.**

Mirabilis multiflora

Common name(s): Wild four o'clock
Height: 1'–2' (30–61 cm) | **Width:** 2'–3' (61–91 cm)
Bloom time: Summer | **Lowest hardiness zone:** 4
Pruning: Cut back in spring, if desired
Propagation: Seed and division
Dormant: Winter | **Native region:** Western North America

THIS PLANT'S ABUNDANT, bright pink flowers are beautiful, and look great over its silvery-green foliage. Even better, the flowers just keep on coming nonstop all summer long. And even better than that, it can put on that incredible floral display in extremely dry climates with no supplemental water whatsoever. This plant is the ultimate proof that a xeric garden doesn't need to just be cacti and rocks. The flowers stay closed in the morning and pop open in the afternoon, so they are a perfect choice for a garden you will enjoy in the evenings after work.

✳ **QUICK TIP** It takes time for this plant to develop its drought-proof root system, so do water through dry spells the first year or two while it settles in.

Monarda didyma

Common name(s): Scarlet beebalm
Height: 2'–4' (61–120 cm) | **Width:** 2'–3' (61–91 cm)
Bloom time: Summer | **Lowest hardiness zone:** 4
Pruning: Cut back in spring, as needed
Propagation: Division, seed, and cuttings
Dormant: Winter | **Native region:** Eastern North America

THE FLOWERS OF SCARLET BEEBALM are instantly recognizable in brilliant intense red, opening in a circle at the top of the tall stems. The entire plant has a fresh, minty smell when you brush against it or rub the leaves, which is very pleasant to humans and thankfully unappealing to rabbits, deer, and other hungry mammals. Scarlet beebalm is tolerant of, but does not demand, wet soils. The downside to this plant is that it is quite large and can spread somewhat aggressively. Luckily for the owners of small gardens, there are lots of new hybrids that give an expanded color range on much more compact plants that will fit into any garden space.

✳ **QUICK TIP** In very dry climates, try *Monarda fistulos* or *M. punctata*, which have great drought tolerance and are just as beautiful.

Muhlenbergia capillaris

Common name(s): Muhly grass
Height: 3'–4' (91–120 cm) | **Width:** 3' (91 cm)
Bloom time: Late summer
Lowest hardiness zone: 7 (colder in dry climates)
Pruning: Cut back brown leaves in the spring
Propagation: Division and seed | **Dormant:** Winter
Native region: Central and Eastern North America

ONE OF THE MOST BEAUTIFUL grasses in the world, muhly grass is a typical ornamental grass in the first half of the year, but then it flowers and everything changes. The flower and seedheads are a light, airy cloud over the leaves, but the really amazing part is that they are pink. Mixed through the garden, they make an airy pink mist that is absolutely magical. Grow this if you need to spice up the end of the growing season or want a break from all the orange and yellow hues that can dominate the fall.

✳ **QUICK TIP** If *Muhlenbergia capillaris* isn't hardy for you, try *M. reverchonii* 'Undaunted', which is hardy to Zone 5.

Nepeta × faassenii

Common name(s): Catmint
Height: 1'–2' (30–61 cm) | **Width:** 1'–3' (30–91 cm)
Bloom time: Summer | **Lowest hardiness zone:** 3
Pruning: Cut back after flowering to encourage reblooming
Propagation: Cuttings and division
Dormant: Winter | **Native region:** Eurasia

CATMINT IS ONE OF THOSE workhorse perennials that always looks good, never seems to have any problems, and makes everything around it look even better. Even out of bloom, the silvery, fragrant foliage is attractive, but this is a plant that is rarely out of bloom. The soft, pale blue flowers just keep coming in flushes all summer. Giving the plant a quick trim after each bloom cycle helps it keep looking tidy and encourages rapid rebloom. Pollinators—especially bees—love the flowers, and rabbits and deer hate the scented leaves. Though it doesn't require dry conditions, catmint is impressively drought-tolerant once established.

✳ **QUICK TIP** For years, the cultivar 'Walker's Low' was the only selection gardeners would find in nurseries, but new breeding has now added smaller, heavier flowering selections better suited to small spaces.

Oenothera lindheimeri
(aka *Gaura lindheimeri*)

Common name(s): Gaura, beeblossom
Height: 2'–4' (61–120 cm) | **Width:** 1'–2' (30–61 cm)
Bloom time: Summer and fall | **Lowest hardiness zone:** 5
Pruning: Cut back to reduce flopping
Propagation: Seed and cuttings | **Dormant:** Winter
Native region: Southcentral North America

THE HUGE APPEAL of this plant is that it flowers like an annual, nonstop, all summer long—spike after spike of small flowers that dance on the wind. The blooms are usually white, though pink selections exist, and there are also forms that have attractive reddish foliage. The biggest downside to this plant is that it can be very short-lived in the garden. Regular deadheading and well-drained soils will encourage it to persist, but don't expect individual plants to last more than a few years. Luckily, it often self-sows when happy with its conditions, and gardeners can also propagate it by seeds or cuttings to ensure it is always in the garden.

✳ **QUICK TIP** Gaura's short lifespan and open, airy habit make it a perfect choice to temporarily fill spaces in new gardens while other perennials mature.

Oenothera macrocarpa

Common name(s): Evening primrose
Height: 4"–8" (10–20 cm) | **Width:** 1'–2' (30–61 cm)
Bloom time: Summer | **Lowest hardiness zone:** 4
Pruning: Cut back brown stems in spring
Propagation: Division and seed
Dormant: Winter | **Native region:** Central North America

THE GENUS *OENOTHERA* is a big one, and frankly it includes a lot of weeds. Some are very pretty weeds—like *Oenothera speciosa,* which has lovely pink flowers and a desire to consume the world—but there are some truly fantastic plants in the group as well. *O. macrocarpa* is one of the best. It makes a low carpet of leaves—beautifully silvery leaves in some forms—topped with huge clear yellow flowers that just keep coming all summer long. Dry soils suit this plant the best, and it has outstanding drought tolerance once established.

✳ **QUICK TIP** Also consider *Oenothera macrocarpa* ssp. *fremontii,* which is similar but with a finer, more delicate texture to leaves and flowers, or the wonderfully fragrant white blooms of *O. pallida.*

Ophiopogon planiscapus 'Nigrescens'

Opuntia

Common name(s): Black mondo grass
Height: 6"–8" (15–20 cm) | **Width:** 6"–1' (15–30 cm)
Bloom time: Summer | **Lowest hardiness zone:** 6
Pruning: Cut back brown leaves in spring as needed
Propagation: Division and seed
Dormant: Evergreen | **Native region:** Japan

USUALLY WHEN A PLANT is described as being black, it is actually dark purple or brown. But the leaves of black mondo grass really are about as close to black as gardeners will find in the plant world. The foliage is narrow and glossy, giving the effect of a grass, though the pinkish flowers in late summer give it away as not being a grass at all. It will slowly spread to become a low groundcover but it is never aggressive or prone to smothering other plants. Use this around plants with yellow, variegated, or silver foliage, and by contrast the very dark leaves will make all its neighbors look even brighter and more intense.

✳ **QUICK TIP** Gardeners might find this plant for sale in the annual section of the garden center, as it is a popular addition to container plantings.

Common name(s): Prickly pear
Height: 6"–15' (15–30 cm) | **Width:** 1'–2' (30–61 cm)
Bloom time: Summer | **Lowest hardiness zone:** 4
Pruning: None needed | **Propagation:** Cuttings
Dormant: Evergreen | **Native region:** North America

PRICKLY PEARS ARE ONE of the most widely adapted plants in the world, with species native to nearly every single U.S. state and Canadian province. They have classic flattened, photosynthetic stems called "pads," long spines, and tiny hairlike prickles called *glochids*. The main appeal of this cactus is the living sculpture of their stems, but opuntia also have large, beautiful flowers. The most widely distributed and adaptable species is the eastern prickly pear (*Opuntia humifusa*), which can take a lot of rain and has gorgeous yellow flowers. In drier, western climates, the range of species gardeners can grow explodes, including a range of stunning hybrids with incredible flower displays. Almost nothing will kill an opuntia, so they are a fantastic choice for difficult, hot, dry locations.

✳ **QUICK TIP** Cold-hardy cacti tend to shrivel up and deflate during the winter to avoid freezing damage. They can look like they've died, but don't worry—they'll plump back up and look great in the spring.

Origanum

Common name(s): Oregano
Height: 1' (30 cm) | **Width:** 1' (30 cm)
Bloom time: Summer | **Lowest hardiness zone:** 5
Pruning: Trim as needed to shape the plant
Propagation: Cuttings | **Dormant:** Winter
Native region: Europe

OREGANO IS MOST FAMILIAR as the edible herb essential to a good tomato sauce, but there are a slew of ornamental varieties as well, which are must haves in a dry garden. Even the typical culinary oregano (*Origanum vulgare*) is pretty attractive, with big clusters of small, pink flowers, but some of the other species and varieties are stunning. Look for 'Kent Beauty', which has flower clusters surrounded by soft pink bracts and tumbles beautifully over the edge of a container or retaining wall. 'Drops of Jupiter' has glowing bright yellow foliage that looks incredible emerging with spring bulbs, and 'Rotkugel' has dark purple bracts surrounding pink flowers that bees adore.

✳ **QUICK TIP** Drainage is key to having happy oreganos. If gardeners only have wet clay, consider growing in raised beds with sand or even containers.

Oxalis oregana

Common name(s): Wood sorrel
Height: 6" (15 cm) | **Width:** 1' (30 cm)
Bloom time: Spring to fall | **Lowest hardiness zone:** 7
Pruning: None needed | **Propagation:** Division and seed
Dormant: Evergreen
Native region: Western North America

YES, THERE ARE A LOT OF OXALIS species that are terrible weeds, but this one is a good one. The foliage makes a beautiful evergreen carpet (there are also deciduous forms, but look for evergreen varieties if possible) and it sends up sweet little pink flowers from spring right up to fall. Evergreen groundcovers for shade are incredibly useful, but the most popular ones (like English ivy, vinca, and Asian pachysandra) have turned out to be pretty seriously invasive. So, turn to this native instead. Gardeners in the East might consider their native *Oxalis violacea*, which is similar, though not evergreen.

✳ **QUICK TIP** Oxalis leaves are edible, and have a sour, lemony flavor—pleasant to snack on while out in the garden.

Pachysandra procumbens

Paeonia

Common name(s): Allegheny spurge
Height: 6"–1' (15–30 cm) | **Width:** 1'–2' (30–61 cm)
Bloom time: Spring | **Lowest hardiness zone:** 5
Pruning: None needed | **Propagation:** Division
Dormant: Winter or evergreen in warm climates
Native region: Eastern North America

Common name(s): Peony
Height: 3' (91 cm) | **Width:** 3' (91 cm)
Bloom time: Spring | **Hardiness zone:** 3
Pruning: Trim brown foliage in the spring
Propagation: Division in the fall
Dormant: Winter | **Native region:** Europe and Asia

ASIAN PACHYSANDRA (*Pachysandra terminalis*) is a popular groundcover for shade, but unfortunately it is proving to be an invasive weed, and nurseries are not allowed to sell it in some states. Luckily, there is a native alternative. The native pachysandra is much slower growing and less aggressive than the Asian species, but also a lot more attractive. The leaves are beautifully marked with silvery patches, and the white flowers in early spring are not only pretty, but quite fragrant as well. In Zone 7 and warmer, the leaves will remain green all winter; in colder climates it is more likely to be deciduous. The best feature of this plant is its ability to grow in deep, dry shade where not much else will.

✳ QUICK TIP Space plants 6 to 12 inches (15–30 cm) apart to quickly establish a nice groundcover.

PEONIES ARE SOME of the longest-lived perennials in the world. Plant one today, and it will probably still be blooming for your great-grandchildren. The huge, usually fragrant flowers come in mostly shades of pink and white, though newer hybrids add yellows to that color range. Many peonies have such huge, heavy flowers that they need staking to stand up. Single-flowered forms and the 'Intersectional' (aka 'Itoh') hybrid forms stand up better, but most traditional double forms need to be staked. Peony foliage often declines and looks ratty by the end of the summer, so plant them where late-summer perennials can take over and hide the leaves.

✳ QUICK TIP Peonies produce nectar on the outside of the flower buds. This can attract ants that eat the waxy nectar covering the buds, allowing them to open. This can be annoying, but that nectar also feeds a tiny wasp that kills Japanese beetle larvae, so planting peonies can reduce Japanese beetle problems.

Panicum virgatum

Common name(s): Switch grass
Height: 4'–5' (1.2–1.5 m) | **Width:** 2' (61 cm)
Bloom time: Summer | **Lowest hardiness zone:** 5
Pruning: Cut back in spring before new growth starts
Propagation: Division | **Dormant:** Winter
Native region: North America

SWITCH GRASS is one of the dominate species of the American tallgrass prairies, native to nearly every U.S. state, and is a very useful, adaptable ornamental grass. Switch grass has a narrow, upright form, which gives a great vertical accent to a garden design. The tall stems keep standing right through the winter—even through snow—to keep beauty and structure in the garden when most perennials have exited the scene. There is an ever-expanding selection of great cultivars of this plant to choose from. Cultivars like 'Northwind' and 'Heavy Metal' have been selected for the silvery-blue color of their leaves, while 'Shenandoah' and 'Red Flame' flush red in late summer and fall.

✳ QUICK TIP Panicum is a warm-season grass, meaning it is slow to come into growth in the spring. Take advantage of that by interplanting it with bulbs or spring ephemerals.

Papaver orientale

Common name(s): Oriental poppy
Height: 1'–3' (30–91 cm) | **Width:** 1'–3' (30–91 cm)
Bloom time: Early summer | **Lowest hardiness zone:** 3
Pruning: None needed
Propagation: Seed, division, and root cuttings
Dormant: Summer | **Native region:** Europe and Asia

INCREDIBLY LONG-LIVED PERENNIALS, oriental poppies are one of those plants that can often be seen still blooming next to the foundations of long-abandoned farmsteads. The large, coarse leaves usually emerge in the fall, the plant explodes into growth in the spring, and then, in early summer, there opens truly enormous poppy flowers, typically a bright scarlet, though white and pink forms are available as well. In full bloom, a clump of oriental poppies is traffic-stopping. After flowering, they go completely dormant, so they are best planted between things like hardy hibiscus that are slow to get growing in the beginning of the summer and can fill in where the poppies used to be.

✳ QUICK TIP Oriental poppies need cold winters to thrive, so they are a great way to celebrate the beauty of a northern climate.

Passiflora incarnata

Common name(s): Purple passionflower, Maypop
Height: 6'–8' (1.8–2.4 m) | **Width:** 3'–6' (0.9–1.8 m)
Bloom time: Summer | **Lowest hardiness zone:** 5
Pruning: Trim as needed to control growth
Propagation: Seed and cuttings
Dormant: Winter/evergreen in warm climates
Native region: Eastern North America

PASSIONFLOWERS ARE A PRIMARILY tropical group, but this native vine is the most cold hardy of the genus. The real feature of the species are the flowers, which look like something Dr. Seuss would have dreamed up. A row of rounded petals surrounds a crimped purple-and-white fringe, all topped by stamens and pistils that look like some sort of weird alien antenna. Those flowers are followed by edible fruits, which are similar to the tropical passionfruits, though smaller and less juicy. Be warned that this beautiful vine can be a bit aggressive, especially in hot climates where it can grow rapidly and spread over large areas from the roots. Plant it where it has room to run or keep the pruning shears at the ready.

✳ QUICK TIP Passionflower vines are the only host plants for the gorgeous gulf fritillary butterfly, so keep an eye out for them if you live in the southern half of North America.

Penstemon

Penstemon x mexicali

Common name(s): Beard tongue
Height: 4"–3' (10–91 cm) | **Width:** 6"–2' (15–61 cm)
Bloom time: Summer
Lowest hardiness zone: 4–7, depending on the species
Pruning: Cut back in spring, if desired
Propagation: Seed, cuttings, and division
Dormant: Winter or evergreen
Native region: North America

PENSTEMON IS A GENUS native only to North America, and there are a lot of them. Nearly 300 species have been described, native to nearly every corner of the continent, with the highest diversity in the Mountain West. The western species are an essential component of any dry garden, as they are supremely well adapted to low water conditions. Penstemons have perhaps the widest range of flower colors of any perennial from true blue, purple, pink, red, yellow to orange (there is no black or green, but that's about it). It is impossible to cover this diverse group thoroughly in this space, but here are a few species gardeners should know:

- *Penstemon digitalis* is probably the most popular of the eastern species. It is a tall perennial with white (or rarely pink) flowers. Wild native plants typically have green foliage, but the most popular garden selections have dark reddish-purple leaves.
- *P. × mexicali* is a complex hybrid of several western species. Selections come with blooms in shades of red, pink, or purple, and flower nonstop all summer over attractive glossy foliage. They are good drought-tolerant plants but do well in rainier climates as well.
- *P. heterophyllus* is the easiest to grow of the blue penstemons, putting out clouds of azure flowers in early summer, and sometimes reblooming later in the season. It prefers good drainage but is more tolerant of wet conditions than many western species.
- *P. pinifolius* is a wonderful groundcover species, making a carpet of narrow, glossy green leaves and then flowering nearly continuously with blooms that can be yellow, orange or red. Extremely heat- and drought-tolerant, this is a key plant for dry climates.

❄ **QUICK TIP** Penstemon are quick and easy to grow from seed, and that can be the best way to explore the more unusual corners of this genus.

Penstemon serrulatus

Perovskia atriplicifolia
(*syn.* Salvia yangii)

Common name(s): Russian sage
Height: 3'–5' (91–150 cm) | **Width:** 2'–4' (61–120 cm)
Bloom time: Summer | **Lowest hardiness zone:** 5
Pruning: Cut back to the ground in early spring
Propagation: Cuttings | **Dormant:** Winter
Native region: Central Asia

A VERY DURABLE, long-blooming perennial for difficult dry sites, Russian sage has silvery, fragrant foliage and lavender flowers over a very long period from the summer into the fall. Problems only develop with this plant when it is treated too well. Give it a rich soil and a lot of water, and it will get tall, floppy, and messy. Add in a little shade, and the plant gets even worse. Grow this plant in lean, dry, sunny spots for the best results. Russian sage is a subshrub and can ultimately have somewhat woody stems, so it is best to cut it down to the ground each spring to encourage a more compact, tidy growth.

❄ **QUICK TIP** Look for dwarf cultivars if the typical form is too big for the garden.

Phlomis cashmeriana

Phlox

Common name(s): Kashmir false sage
Height: 3' (91 cm) | **Width:** 1'–2' (30–61 cm)
Bloom time: Early summer | **Lowest hardiness zone:** 5
Pruning: Cut back in spring as desired
Propagation: Seed and cuttings | **Dormant:** Winter
Native region: Central Asia

THE TALL FLOWERING STEMS of this perennial are dotted with whirls of bright lavender-pink blooms that provide a fantastic vertical accent to the garden. After the flowers fade, they develop into brown seedheads that keep looking fantastic right through the winter. The blooms look romantic and beautiful enough to be part of a classic English cottage garden but are, in fact, great dry-climate perennials with excellent drought tolerance, though they will grow just fine in wetter climates as well. Even without the flowers, the bold, silvery leaves are a beautiful addition to the garden.

✳ **QUICK TIP** If you love this species, try *Phlomis russeliana*, which looks very similar, but is a bit larger with yellow flowers instead of pink.

Phlox paniculata cultivar

Common name(s): Phlox
Height: 3"–4' (7.6–120 cm) | **Width:** 1'–2' (30–61 cm)
Bloom time: Spring and summer
Lowest hardiness zone: 4
Pruning: Cut back as needed in the spring
Propagation: Division, cuttings, root cuttings, and seed
Dormant: Winter or evergreen
Native region: North America

EXCEPT FOR ONE SPECIES, *Phlox* is a uniquely North American genus and one that has become a favorite in gardens around the world thanks to their beautiful, often fragrant, flowers and wide adaptability. As an added bonus, phlox flowers are a favorite nectar source for many butterflies.

KEY GROUPS

Tall Phlox *Phlox paniculata* is the most popular, but *P. Carolina* could be included in this group as well. These are upright growing perennials that bloom with big, rounded clusters of strongly fragrant flowers. Soft pink to lavender is the default color, but cultivars now range from white, bright pink, even to purple and almost blue. Best in full sun to part shade and grown in rich soils.

Moss Phlox Called moss phlox for their low, dense green foliage, these phlox form creeping groundcovers and then explode to cover themselves in blooms in the spring. *P. subulata* is the most popular of this group, but there are many other low-growing species worth exploring like *P. bifida* and *P. douglasii*. In general, these low-growing phlox prefer drier conditions.

Woodland Phlox *P. divaricata* is the queen of this group, growing maybe 1 foot (30 cm) tall, with clusters of fragrant blue, lavender, or white flowers. *P. stolonifera* and *P. pilosa* have similar growth habits, with *P. pilosa* being the most tolerant of sunny and dry conditions. These will all take partial shade, but they will bloom most heavily with more sun.

✳ QUICK TIP Many phlox species are prone to powdery mildew on their leaves. This is unattractive but doesn't seriously harm the plants.

Phlox divaricata

Physostegia virginiana

Common name(s): Obedient plant
Height: 3'–4' (91–120 cm) | **Width:** 2'–3' (61–91 cm)
Bloom time: Summer to fall | **Lowest hardiness zone:** 3
Pruning: Cut back in spring, if desired
Propagation: Division and seed
Dormant: Winter | **Native region:** Eastern North America

SPIRES OF FOXGLOVELIKE pink or white flowers start opening in the beginning of the summer, and just keep on blooming right up until the frost. With a huge native range covering nearly the entire eastern half of North America, this is a very adaptable plant that will thrive in a range of conditions, from soggy soils to dry ones. The typical forms of the plant can spread rapidly, which is great if you have a large area to fill. In small gardens look for selections like the popular 'Miss Manners' that have a clumping, nonspreading habit.

✳ QUICK TIP Obedient plant will bloom in partial shade, though it may need staking there to prevent flopping.

Platycodon grandiflorus

Common name(s): Balloon flower
Height: 1'–3' (30–91 cm) | Width: 1'–2' (30–61 cm)
Bloom time: Summer | Lowest hardiness zone: 3
Pruning: Deadhead to prolong blooming
Propagation: Division and seed
Dormant: Winter | Native region: East Asia

CALLED BALLOON FLOWER for the puffy round shape of the flower buds right before they open, the buds open up into star-shaped flowers. Balloon flower is a long-lived perennial and generally without any pest or disease problems. There are many selections of this species, ranging from tall forms bred for use as cut flowers in Asia to very short forms only 1 foot (30 cm) or so tall that are more commonly found for sale at nurseries. Blue is the typical flower color, though white and pink forms are available, as well as double-flowered selections with extra layers of petals. The faded flower petals tend to hang on and look messy, so a quick trim after bloom makes for a tidier look and encourages rebloom.

✳ QUICK TIP Balloon flowers are easy to grow from seed and will flower their first summer, making them economical and practical plants to fill a new garden.

Podophyllum peltatum

Common name(s): Mayapple
Height: 1' (30 cm) | Width: 2'–3' (61–91 cm)
Bloom time: Spring | Lowest hardiness zone: 3
Pruning: None needed | Propagation: Division and seed
Dormant: Summer and winter
Native region: Eastern North America

THE BROAD, UMBRELLA-LIKE leaves of the mayapple are an iconic groundcover in the woodlands of Eastern North America and are equally wonderful in the garden. They come up early, making the garden feel full and lush, and then go dormant, leaving space for summer-growing perennials like hostas to fill in for the rest of the year. The large, white flowers are quite attractive, though hidden under the leaves, and are followed by very tasty fruits—if you can manage to get them before the squirrels or raccoons do. If you love mayapples, you can also look for the many species from Asia that feature beautifully patterned leaves.

✳ QUICK TIP Mayapple seeds and unripe fruits are toxic, so only eat the flesh of ripe, fragrant, yellow fruits.

Polemonium reptans

Common name(s): Jacob's ladder
Height: 12"–18" (30–46 cm) | **Width:** 12"–18" (30–46 cm)
Bloom time: Spring to early summer
Lowest hardiness zone: 3 | **Pruning:** None needed
Propagation: Division and seed | **Dormant:** Winter
Native region: Eastern North America

JACOB'S LADDER is a delicate-looking perennial with almost fernlike foliage and clouds of soft blue flowers in the spring. Unlike so many woodland natives, it is not an ephemeral—the attractive foliage stays up all summer long, so you get a beautiful foliage presence long after the flowers have gone. Gardeners can amp up that foliage display with the variegated cultivar 'Stairway to Heaven', which has a tidy white margin to the leaves that flushes pink in cool weather. This variegated Jacob's ladder is so popular that gardeners are much more likely to find it for sale rather than the plain green version.

❋ **QUICK TIP** If you love this plant, there are others in the genus to consider. Try the very shade tolerant *Polemonium caeruleum*, the fragrant hybrid 'Heaven Scent', and the dark-leaved 'Purple Rain Strain'.

Polygonatum

Common name(s): Solomon's seal
Height: 2'–3' (61–91 cm) | **Width:** 1'–3' (30–91 cm)
Bloom time: Spring | **Lowest hardiness zone:** 3
Pruning: None needed | **Propagation:** Division
Dormant: Winter
Native region: Europe, Asia, and North America

MOST SOLOMON'S SEALS have the same growth pattern—a creeping rhizome just under the soil surface that sends up tall, arching stems with broad leaves and dangling white flowers hanging below. Far and away, the most popular variety in gardens is *Polygonatum odoratum* var. *pluriflorum* 'Variegatum', which is a variegated form of an Eurasian species, each leaf outlined in white. It is an incredibly durable, easy-to-grow plant that spreads happily in nearly any garden. But the eastern North America native *P. biflorum* is just as excellent and easy to grow. If you want something for a small garden, look for *P. humile*, which forms a tiny groundcover, just a few inches tall.

❋ **QUICK TIP** Solomon's seal flowers are beautiful and fragrant, though easy to overlook. It is worth lifting up the arching stems to get a closer look at them (and a sniff).

Polystichum acrostichoides

Primula

Common name(s): Christmas fern
Height: 1'–2' (30–61 cm) | **Width:** 1'–2' (30–61 cm)
Bloom time: NA | **Lowest hardiness zone:** 3
Pruning: None needed | **Propagation:** Division
Dormant: Evergreen
Native region: Eastern North America

Common name(s): Primrose
Height: 6"–2' (15–61 cm) | **Width:** 1'–2' (30–61 cm)
Bloom time: Spring | **Lowest hardiness zone:** 3
Pruning: Deadhead as needed
Propagation: Division and seed
Dormant: Winter or evergreen
Native region: Europe, Asia, and North America

WITH A NATIVE RANGE that stretches from Nova Scotia to Florida and west into Texas, it is fair to say that this fern can successfully adapt to a range of different gardens. Dry shaded slopes? Fine. Hot summers? Love it. Cold winter? Won't miss a beat. Perhaps its very best attribute is that it will tolerate extremely dark shade, even the dense, year-round shade under conifers. Plants will grow more slowly in very deep shade, but still keep on going, putting out glossy, dark-green fronds each spring that stay evergreen right through the winter. Plants clump rather than spread, but, planted close together, they make a fantastic native groundcover for difficult sites.

✳ **QUICK TIP** Pair Christmas fern with yellow-leaved or variegated plants to give the greatest contrast to its dark green fronds.

THE MOST COMMONLY SOLD varieties of primroses are in the *Polyanthus* group, derived from hybrids of two European species. They typically form rosettes of broad green leaves topped with clusters of big flowers in a pretty staggering color range. These common forms are quite short-lived. But do a little looking—especially if you are willing to grow some from seed—and gardeners can find some wonderful varieties for cool-summer climates. The double-flowered 'Belarina' series are fantastic long-lived perennials, and Barnhaven Primroses, the primula specialists, have seed strains in some of the most incredible colors.

✳ **QUICK TIP** Primroses are usually grown from seed commercially, but they are easy to divide to make more at home. Just dig and separate them just after they've finished flowering.

Pulmonaria

Pulsatilla

Common name(s): Lungwort
Height: 1'–2' (30–61 cm) | **Width:** 1'–2' (30–61 cm)
Bloom time: Spring | **Lowest hardiness zone:** 3
Pruning: Usually none needed
Propagation: Seed and division
Dormant: Winter or evergreen
Native region: Europe and Asia

Common name(s): Pasque flower
Height: 1' (30 cm) | **Width:** 6"–1' (15–30 cm)
Bloom time: Spring | **Lowest hardiness zone:** 3
Pruning: None needed | **Propagation:** Division and seed
Dormant: Winter
Native region: Europe, Asia, and North America

ONE OF THE EARLIEST PERENNIALS to bloom in the spring, coming up when the earliest bulbs are flowering, *Pulmonaria* start the year off with clusters of blue, pink, or white flowers. Flowering is the heaviest in partial shade, but they will still grow and bloom in full shade. The flowers are pretty, but are possibly upstaged by the foliage, with is broad and patterned with silver. Some forms have silver spots, others have entirely silver leaves. The foliage sometimes gets a little mildew and can brown if grown in too much sun or in too hot of a climate.

✳ **QUICK TIP** *Pulmonaria* have bristly leaves that make them unappetizing to deer and rabbits, but the leaves can also irritate human skin, so wear gloves when working with this plant.

PASQUE FLOWER IS A VERY EARLY spring-blooming perennial with nodding, usually purple (though red, pink, white, and blue selections are available) flowers. Every part of the plant, from the ferny leaves to the flower petals themselves, are covered with fine, silky hairs that make them soft to the touch and look absolutely magical when backlit by morning or evening sun. But the standout feature of this plant is not the flowers, but the seedheads that come afterward. Each bloom transforms into a ball of seeds, each with a long, feathery tail.

The European species *Pulsatilla vulgaris* is most commonly sold, but look for the North American native *P. nuttalliana* if you can find it.

✳ **QUICK TIP** Pulsatilla will rot in heavy, wet soils, so provide good drainage for the longest-lived plants.

Pycnanthemum muticum

Ratibida columnifera

Common name(s): Mountain mint
Height: 1'–3' (30–91 cm) | **Width:** 1'–3' (30–91 cm)
Bloom time: Summer into fall | **Lowest hardiness zone:** 4
Pruning: Cut back in spring as desired
Propagation: Division, seed, and cuttings
Dormant: Winter | **Native region:** Eastern North America

THIS IS A VIGOROUS PERENNIAL with silvery, fragrant foliage that has a tendency to spread a little bit too much for small gardens. Starting in midsummer and carrying on into fall, it blooms nonstop with many clusters of small white or pinkish flowers, surrounded by fuzzy silver bracts. Humans like the flowers, but pollinators *love* them. You'll count dozens of different species visiting the flowers every day, and the bloom is particularly valuable because it comes at a time when many gardens are a bit empty and tired in the hottest part of the summer. After the flowers fade, the seedheads are fantastic as well, looking good well into the winter.

✳ QUICK TIP Pycnanthemum leaves are a natural mosquito repellent if you rub them on your skin. A bonus that'll make you smell good too!

Common name(s): Mexican hat
Height: 1'–3' (30–91 cm) | **Width:** 1'–2' (30–61 cm)
Bloom time: Summer into fall | **Lowest hardiness zone:** 4
Pruning: Cut back as it needs it, as the plant gets floppy
Propagation: Seed | **Dormant:** Winter
Native region: Central North America

THERE ARE A LOT OF PLANTS with yellow daisy flowers native to North America, but this one is unique, with a long, narrow central cone and broad showy petals that hang down. Some people see a resemblance to a sombrero in the bloom, hence the common name. In the garden the incredible value of this plant is the very long bloom season—it starts at the beginning of the summer and just keeps on going right into the fall. Like so many heavy-blooming perennials, it tends to be short-lived, especially if grown on wet soils, though it will self-seed to perpetuate itself in good conditions. Lean, dry soils will give the best performance, and it may need a little trimming if it gets too floppy in rich conditions.

✳ QUICK TIP Flowers of *Ratibida* come in either yellow or brownish-orange. The yellow tends to stand out and make the best display.

Rudbeckia fulgida

Ruellia humilis

Common name(s): Black-eyed Susan, orange coneflower
Height: 2'–3' (61–91 cm) | **Width:** 2' (61 cm)
Bloom time: Late summer | **Lowest hardiness zone:** 3
Pruning: Cut back in spring as needed
Propagation: Division and seed
Dormant: Winter | **Native region:** Eastern North America

THIS IS ONE OF THE MOST ICONIC American native plants and it is popular the world over for its incredible display of brilliant yellow daisy flowers with dark centers. The plant slowly spreads into large masses, and when in full bloom, they are traffic-stopping. The cultivar 'Goldsturm'—selected in Germany—has dominated the market for years, and while it is a beautiful plant, it is susceptible to a fungal disease called septoria leaf spot. Gardeners can reduce the disease by improving air circulation or looking for newer selections, like the fantastic 'American Gold Rush', which is more disease resistant.

✳ **QUICK TIP** There are lots of other great rudbeckias to try, like *Rudbeckia maxima* with huge blue-green leaves or *R. laciniata,* which will tower over you.

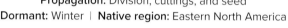

Common name(s): Wild petunia
Height: 1'–2' (30–61 cm) | **Width:** 1'–2' (30–61 cm)
Bloom time: Spring to fall | **Lowest hardiness zone:** 4
Pruning: None needed
Propagation: Division, cuttings, and seed
Dormant: Winter | **Native region:** Eastern North America

RUELLIA DON'T LOOK MUCH LIKE a petunia, honestly, but it does resemble that annual in one respect—it just keeps on flowering. The soft lavender or purple flowers start coming in late spring, and they keep on coming all summer and into fall. And unlike a lot of long-blooming perennials, it doesn't flower itself into an early grave. This isn't a short-lived plant; it'll keep coming back year after year. Now, the flowering is never over-the-top stunning—this isn't a plant that covers itself with blooms—but it is always pretty, always looking good, and is a great plant to tuck into open spots in the garden to fill in and give continuity through the growing season.

✳ **QUICK TIP** Ruellia won't tolerate soggy, wet soils, so choose well-drained locations for this plant.

Salvia

Salvia x sylvestris 'May Night'

Common name(s): Sage
Height: 1'–3' (30–91 cm) | **Width:** 1'–3' (30–91 cm)
Bloom time: Summer
Lowest hardiness zone: 4–7, depending on variety
Pruning: Deadhead and cut back in spring, as desired
Propagation: Cuttings, division, and seed
Dormant: Winter | **Native region:** North America, South America, Europe, Asia, and Africa

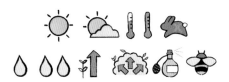

The genus *Salvia* is huge, with nearly 1,000 different species native to every continent except Australia and Antarctica. With few exceptions, salvias have good drought tolerance, fragrant foliage, and abundant flowers. Here are some species you should consider:

- *Salvia nemorosa* is a European species, and it and related hybrids are very popular garden plants. They are compact plants with spikes of small purple, pink, or white flowers in early summer with some rebloom later in the year. It is hardy to Zone 4.

- *S. azurea* is an American prairie species, hardy to Zone 5, with huge candelabras of clear, sky-blue (or rarely white) flowers in late summer and fall. It is inclined to be floppy when grown in rich soils.
- *S. greggii* and related species and hybrids from Texas and Mexico are sometimes sold as annuals, but many forms are hardy to Zone 6, especially in dry conditions. They make tidy rounded mounds covered with usually brilliant red flowers, though purple, white, pink, and soft yellow forms are available as well.
- *S. guaranitica* is often sold as an annual, but this South American sage with large, blue flowers is hardy to Zones 6 or 7. It can spread aggressively, but the huge flowers beloved by hummingbirds are worth growing it.
- *S. pachyphylla* is one of many western desert species that are fantastic for dry-climate gardening. This one is hardy to Zone 5, with silver foliage and purple flowers, surrounded by long-lasting mauve bracts.

❊ QUICK TIP Some salvias can get a bit rangy and wild looking in the summer. A quick trim and deadheading will help keep them looking tidy.

Salvia leucantha

Sanguinaria canadensis

Common name(s): Bloodroot
Height: 6" (15 cm) | **Width:** 1' (30 cm)
Bloom time: Spring | **Lowest hardiness zone:** 3
Pruning: None needed | **Propagation:** Division
Dormant: Winter | **Native region:** Eastern North America

BLOODROOT POPS UP early in the spring with cheerful white (very rarely pink) flowers and then unfurls broad, very unusually lobed leaves, which stay up looking very attractive until they go dormant in mid to late summer. The flowers are very pretty, but usually only last a day or two, so the real feature is the foliage. There is a double-flowered selection, 'Plena', that has stunning waterlily-like flowers, which last much longer than the single form and are really incredible in mass. Bloodroot spreads slowly by rhizomes and should be divided every few years, as old clumps tend to die out from the center.

✳ **QUICK TIP** The name *bloodroot* refers to the red sap of this plant. That sap can be caustic, so wear gloves when dividing if you have sensitive skin.

Sarracenia

Common name(s): Pitcher plant
Height: 6"–3' (15–91 cm) | **Width:** 1' (30 cm)
Bloom time: Spring | **Lowest hardiness zone:** 5
Pruning: Cut back old leaves in the spring
Propagation: Division and seed
Dormant: Winter or evergreen
Native region: Eastern North America

PITCHER PLANTS GROW in very nutrient-poor bogs and so have evolved to capture insects in their colorful, tube-shaped leaves in order to harvest their own fertilizer. The leaves are incredibly colorful—the better to lure insects in—with different varieties being yellow, red, or patterned with bright white. Pitcher plants need constant moisture, acidic soils, and no fertilizer to thrive. A container set in a tray of water, or a bog made with a pond liner filled with sand or peat usually works best. Tap water can be too alkaline and have too many dissolved minerals for pitcher plants, so use rainwater if possible.

✳ **QUICK TIP** A bog for pitcher plants is a perfect home for lots of other cool plants as well. Some of these are the sundews (*Drosera*), Venus flytraps (*Dionaea muscipula*), or a beautiful bog orchid (*Calopogon*).

Scabiosa columbaria

Schizachyrium scoparium

Common name(s): Pincushion flower
Height: 1'–2' (30–61 cm) | **Width:** 1' (30 cm)
Bloom time: Summer | **Lowest hardiness zone:** 5
Pruning: Deadhead to encourage rebloom
Propagation: Seed and division
Dormant: Winter | **Native region:** Europe

Common name(s): Little bluestem
Height: 2'–4' (61–120 cm) | **Width:** 1'–2' (30–61 cm)
Bloom time: Late summer | **Lowest hardiness zone:** 3
Pruning: Cut back in spring before new growth emerges
Propagation: Division and seed
Dormant: Winter | **Native region:** Eastern North America

OVER A VERY LONG PERIOD in the summer, this perennial puts up clusters of flowers on long, strong stems. The outer blooms in the cluster have larger, ruffled petals, while the inner ones are smaller. Lavender is the typical color, but there are also white and pink selections. The long stems make scabiosa popular as a cut flower, but they are also fantastic in the perennial border, and the flowers are very attractive to butterflies. Though not picky about soil conditions, they will overwinter and grow the best when growing on the dry side. Very wet soils can cause them to rot, especially during cold weather.

✳ **QUICK TIP** If plants get too large and rangy, a hard cut back in the summer will force out new, more compact, growth.

LITTLE BLUESTEM is one of the dominate species of the tallgrass prairies, and is found in open, sunny areas around eastern North America. The name *bluestem* comes from the bluish hue of the leaves, which is quite beautiful, and only gets more attractive in late summer as it flowers and takes on reddish tints as well. Over the winter, the stems turn tan and keep looking attractive until cut down in the spring. The biggest flaw to this grass is that it tends to flop over unless grown in very lean, dry conditions. Luckily, there are a lot of new selections on the market that are a little more compact and stand tall even in richer soils.

✳ **QUICK TIP** Little bluestem is slow to come into growth in the spring, so it pairs well with spring bulbs and ephemerals.

Scrophularia macrantha

Common name(s): Red birds in a tree
Height: 3'–4' (91–120 cm) | **Width:** 1'–2' (30–61 cm)
Bloom time: Summer to fall
Lowest hardiness zone: 4
Pruning: Cut back in spring, deadhead
Propagation: Division, cuttings, and seed
Dormant: Winter
Native region: Southwestern North America

A FANTASTIC PERFORMER FOR DRY, western gardens, this species has lush green foliage topped with big candelabras of intensely red flowers that bloom from early summer right up to the first frost in the fall. Each individual flower is an unusual shape that looks a little like a perching bird, giving the plant its common name. Gardeners will probably see lots of actual birds on it as hummingbirds adore the nectar-filled flowers. One of the great features of this plant is that, though extremely drought-tolerant, it looks very lush—perfect to give a greener feel to a waterwise garden.

❋ **QUICK TIP** *Scrophularia marilandica* and *S. lanceolata* are interesting relatives of this plant and native to eastern North America. Their flowers are much less showy, but pollinators love them too.

Sempervivum

Common name(s): Hens-and-chicks, houseleek
Height: 2"–6" (5–15 cm) | **Width:** 6"–1' (15–30 cm)
Bloom time: Summer | **Lowest hardiness zone:** 3
Pruning: Remove the faded flower stems
Propagation: Division | **Dormant:** Evergreen
Native region: Europe

THIS PLANT HAS CHARMING evergreen rosettes of succulent leaves that send up little offsets to spread and make a living carpet. Once an individual rosette has matured—often after several years—it will send up a tall flowering stem and then die, but it will be more than replaced by the many offsets that surround it. Sempervivum do best in sunny, dry conditions, but can take a surprising amount of shade, and even grow in fairly heavy soils as long as the soils are not absolutely soggy. About the only place they don't thrive is in the hot, humid Southeast. The leaves range from green to silver to dark red, and there even are a few bright yellow forms. Hybrids from the species *Sempervivum arachnoideum* feature spiderweb-like hairs and are fussier about conditions than most other varieties.

❋ **QUICK TIP** Coloration will change dramatically with the season and conditions, with the strongest reds in full sun, cool temperatures, and dry soils.

Silene chalcedonica

Silphium

Common name(s): Maltese cross
Height: 3'–4' (91–120 cm) | **Width:** 1'–2' (30–61 cm)
Bloom time: Summer | **Lowest hardiness zone:** 4
Pruning: Cut back in spring as needed
Propagation: Division, seed, and cuttings
Dormant: Winter | **Native region:** Europe

Common name(s): Cup plant, prairie dock
Height: 5'–10' (1.5–3 m) | **Width:** 3'–4' (0.9–1.2 m)
Bloom time: Late summer | **Lowest hardiness zone:** 4
Pruning: Cut back in spring, as desired
Propagation: Seed | **Dormant:** Winter
Native region: Central and Eastern North America

THIS IS A VERY OLD-FASHIONED garden plant not often grown today, but it is well-worth rediscovering. Generally, it is pest- and problem-free, producing heads of glowing scarlet flowers over a long period in the summer. The related rose campion (*Silene coronaria*) is another half-forgotten garden perennial, but with silver foliage and bright magenta blooms. Both plants are too tall and awkward to look good in a pot at the nursery, but plant some in your garden and you'll quickly see why they have been cultivated for so long. Plants can be somewhat short-lived, especially in poorly drained soils, but are easily propagated to perpetuate them.

❋ **QUICK TIP** Gardeners may see this plant referred to by the old genus name *Lychnis*, but *Silene* is the most accepted current taxonomic classification.

IS YOUR GARDEN FEELING TOO TAME? Is everything too small and delicate? Are you looking for something big and bold and brash? Silphiums are the answer. These are towering perennials with huge dramatic leaves. *Silphium terebinthinaceum* has enormous, nearly 2-foot (61 cm) long leaves in a cluster at the base before sending up huge, leafless flowering stems with yellow daisies at the top. *S. perfoliatum* has similar flowers but with enormous, long leaves all the way up the stem. Both grow root systems that are just as huge, giving them great drought tolerance once established, though they will grow happily in wet soils as well.

❋ **QUICK TIP** It will take a few years for a silphium to settle in and start reaching a mature size, so be patient and plan ahead for the garden real estate they will be taking up.

Sisyrinchium angustifolium

Solidago

Common name(s): Blue-eyed grass
Height: 1' (30 cm) | **Width:** 1' (30 cm)
Bloom time: Early summer | **Lowest hardiness zone:** 4
Pruning: Deadhead, if desired
Propagation: Division and seed | **Dormant:** Evergreen
Native region: Central and Eastern North America

OUT OF BLOOM, this plant can easily be mistaken for a grass, as it forms a tuft of narrow, stiff leaves. But in late spring and early summer, that grass-like foliage is topped by beautiful small purple flowers, each with a yellow spot in the center. What gardeners will find for sale is usually the selection 'Lucerne', which blooms heavily and keeps it up for most of the summer. Though usually growing in moist, partially shaded conditions in the wild, this species thrives—and flowers most heavily—in full sun and is reasonably drought-tolerant.

✽ **QUICK TIP** Planted close together, blue-eyed grass makes a wonderful turflike groundcover, with flowers no actual grass can match.

Common name(s): Goldenrod
Height: 1'–4' (30–120 cm) | **Width:** 1'–2' (30–61 cm)
Bloom time: Late summer and fall
Lowest hardiness zone: 4
Pruning: Cut back in spring, as desired
Propagation: Division and seed
Dormant: Winter | **Native region:** North America

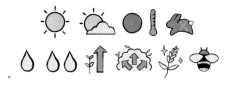

GOLDENRODS ARE THE GREAT misunderstood beauties of our native landscape. Goldenrods *don't* cause hay fever, they just get blamed for it because they flower at the same time as ragweed. Though some goldenrods are aggressive weeds, there are plenty that are wonderfully well-behaved garden plants. Consider growing *Solidago speciosa* with its huge plumes of flowers, or 'Fireworks' with an explosion of long, narrow flower clusters, or for the shade garden, *S. caesia* has graceful arching stems lined with yellow blooms. Whatever species you choose, pollinators and butterflies will thank you. Over a hundred different butterflies and moths use goldenrods as host plants, and their flowers are a key food source for pollinators heading into winter.

✽ **QUICK TIP** If you have a big area to fill, a spreading species like *S. canadensis* will take over fast, suppress weeds, and flower like crazy each fall.

Spigelia marilandica

Common name(s): Indian pink
Height: 1'–2' (30–61 cm) | Width: 1'–2' (30–61 cm)
Bloom time: Summer | Lowest hardiness zone: 5
Pruning: Deadhead to prolong blooming,
cut back in spring, if desired
Propagation: Division, seed, and cuttings
Dormant: Winter | Native region: Eastern North America

THIS IS A STUNNING native plant that is just starting to be more widely grown in gardens, and it is a perfect choice for formal gardening styles. It makes a tight globe of rich green foliage, and in the summer is covered with bright red flowers that open to a gold star at the top. Hummingbirds love them, and humans can't get enough of them either. If gardeners deadhead after the flowers fade you can get a second flush of bloom later in the summer. Though growing in shaded conditions in the wild, flowering is the heaviest in full sun.

✳ QUICK TIP Look for named selections like 'Little Redhead' or 'Ragin Cajun' to get a more compact, uniform growth habit than unnamed seedlings.

Sporobolus heterolepis

Common name(s): Prairie dropseed
Height: 2'–3' (61–91 cm) | Width: 2'–3' (61–91 cm)
Bloom time: Late summer | Lowest hardiness zone: 3
Pruning: Cut back in spring before new growth begins
Propagation: Division and seed | Dormant: Winter
Native region: Central North America

WHILE MANY OF OUR NATIVE ornamental grasses are tall, imposing, upright growers, this is a great one that stays shorter, with very fine, silky, arching foliage. It looks wonderful mixed in between other perennials, and planted close together as a groundcover, it is absolutely stunning. One of the very unusual features of this grass is that the airy clouds of flowers in the late summer are fragrant—a distinctive smell that some compare to toasted nuts or popcorn, and others find more herbal. In the winter, the whole plant shifts to a soft bronze color and will look good until spring—unless crushed by heavy snow.

✳ QUICK TIP Interplanted between taller perennials, sporobolus can fill in the ground layer and act as a living mulch to prevent weeds.

Stachys byzantina

Common name(s): Lamb's ears
Height: 6"–18" (30–46 cm) | **Width:** 1'–2' (30–61 cm)
Bloom time: Summer | **Lowest hardiness zone:** 4
Pruning: Cut back flower stems, as desired
Propagation: Division
Dormant: Evergreen or winter dormant
Native region: Europe

THE STRIKING FEATURE of this plant is the leaves, which are big and covered with silvery hairs that make them irresistibly soft to the touch. The leaves will spread to make a thick groundcover, and in early summer, send up tall flower stems with small pink blooms that are generally not attractive. Many gardeners choose to cut the flower stems off before they even bloom, and the most popular cultivars of the species have been selected for reduced flowering. Lamb's ears will grow in a range of soils and climates, but in wet soils and hot, humid summers, the foliage can get diseased and be quite unattractive. This plant looks its best in drier, cooler climates, where it can make a striking silver carpet.

❋ QUICK TIP Pulling off damaged and diseased leaves in the summer can rejuvenate a clump and make it look much better during humid weather.

Stokesia laevis

Common name(s): Stokes' aster
Height: 1'–2' (30–61 cm) | **Width:** 1'–2' (30–61 cm)
Bloom time: Summer | **Lowest hardiness zone:** 5
Pruning: Cut back in spring, as needed
Propagation: Division, seed, and root cuttings
Dormant: Winter, evergreen in mild climates
Native region: Southeastern North America

FROM A DENSE CLUMP OF LEAVES come sturdy, branching stems that end in quite large (up to 4 inches [10 cm] across) lavender or white blooms. They look a lot like an aster flower, but are much bigger and more dramatic. With a native range that stretches from North Carolina to Florida, they thrive in hot, humid weather, though they are longest lived in well-drained soils. The sturdy stems and long-lasting blooms make for great cut flowers, and the flowers keep coming for a long period over the summer. Gardeners can deadhead the faded blooms to encourage even more reblooms, or let them be to develop into attractive, spiny seedheads.

❋ QUICK TIP Stokesia are oddly rare in gardens, perhaps because they don't look their best in a pot at the nursery. But have faith—once in the ground they develop into something gorgeous.

Symphyotrichum novae-angliae

Tetraneuris acaulis
(aka *Hymenoxys acaulis*)

Common name(s): New England aster
Height: 2'–4' (61–120 cm) | **Width:** 2'–3' (61–91 cm)
Bloom time: Fall | **Lowest hardiness zone:** 3
Pruning: Pinch or cut back in early summer
to prevent flopping
Propagation: Division, cuttings, and seed
Dormant: Winter | **Native region:** Eastern North America

Common name(s): Four-nerve daisy
Height: 1' (30 cm) | **Width:** 1' (30 cm)
Bloom time: Spring, summer, and fall
Lowest hardiness zone: 4 | **Pruning:** Deadhead, if desired
Propagation: Division and seed | **Dormant:** Evergreen
Native region: Western North America

ASTERS ARE ONE OF THE STARS OF FALL, blooming heavily with purple (or white, lavender, or pink) daisy flowers as the season winds down, fueling up pollinators as they prepare to migrate or hibernate through the cold months. The wild forms of this species have incredibly showy flowers but tend to grow a bit tall and floppy in a garden setting. Cutting them back in early summer will help with this, or look for shorter, more compact selections. There are also many other wonderful species of asters to consider. Aromatic aster (*Symphyotrichum oblongifolium*) will keep blooming later into the fall than almost any other plant, and snow flurry aster (*S. ericoides* 'Snow Flurry') forms a beautiful very low groundcover.

✳ **QUICK TIP** Asters can get powdery mildew on the lower leaves, which can be unattractive, but is not very harmful.

THIS LITTLE PLANT starts flowering in the spring and just doesn't stop. It makes a low mat of foliage, and then all summer, into the fall, right up into and even past the first frost, it just pushes up an endless parade of cheerful yellow daisies. It is resolutely tough and drought-tolerant as it is native to very dry climates. In the hottest, driest weather it might slow down flowering a little, but that's all. Despite its dry origins, it adapts well to life in rainier climes provided it is given good drainage. If you want a problem-free puddle of sunshine in the garden, this is the plant for you.

✳ **QUICK TIP** *Tetraneuris* is a big genus, with a lot of other great, waterwise plants to explore. Perky Sue (*Tetraneuris scaposa*) is a great one, with lots of small flowers.

Thalictrum thalictroides
(aka *Anemonella thalictroides*)

Thymus

Common name(s): Rue anemone
Height: 6" (15 cm) | **Width:** 6" (15 cm)
Bloom time: Spring | **Lowest hardiness zone:** 4
Pruning: None needed | **Propagation:** Division and seed
Dormant: Summer, fall, and winter
Native region: Eastern North America

WALK IN THE WOODS of Eastern North America in spring and you are likely to see white clouds of flowers from this fabulous little native plant. It is a true ephemeral, coming up early in the spring, flowering, and then vanishing underground for the summer as the tree canopy leafs out. That means that they can be tucked in around your summer-growing shade perennials, and the rue anemone will give you early blooms—and food for native pollinators coming out of hibernation—before slipping gracefully away to cede the stage to your hostas and ferns.

✳ **QUICK TIP** If you can find it, snatch up the double-flowered forms of this species. 'Cameo' and 'Shoaf's Double' have tiny flowers like perfect little roses. These cultivars are slow to propagate and hard to find, but they are true garden treasures.

Common name(s): Creeping thyme, woolly thyme
Height: 2"–3" (5–7.6 cm) | **Width:** 1' (30 cm)
Bloom time: Early summer | **Lowest hardiness zone:** 4
Pruning: None needed
Propagation: Division and cuttings
Dormant: Evergreen | **Native region:** Europe

THERE ARE QUITE A FEW species of thymes that make great low, creeping groundcovers. Even the classic culinary thyme (*Thymus vulgaris*) isn't unattractive used this way, but the most popular are probably woolly thyme (*T. lanuginosus*) and creeping thyme (*T. praecox*). Both make a ground-hugging carpet in sunny, well-drained conditions. Woolly thyme has beautifully silvery leaves and rarely flowers. Red creeping thyme is all about the blooms, exploding into a sheet of lavender-pink flowers in early summer. Both species will tolerate occasional foot traffic and can even be used as a low-water lawn alternative. Just be careful walking on *T. praecox* when it is in bloom because it will be covered with pollinators.

✳ **QUICK TIP** Thyme is easy to root from cuttings, so if gardeners want to fill a big area on a budget, just buy one plant and propagate more.

Tiarella cordifolia

Common name(s): Foam flower
Height: 1' (30 cm) | **Width:** 2' (61 cm)
Bloom time: Spring | **Lowest hardiness zone:** 4
Pruning: Deadhead after flowering
Propagation: Division | **Dormant:** Semi-evergreen
Native region: Eastern North America

WHEN IN THE RIGHT SITUATION, tiarella will spread to make a carpet of attractive green leaves (marked with bronze in some selections) topped by airy clouds of small white flowers in the spring. In all but the coldest winters, the leaves stay on the plant all winter, flushing an attractive bronze color as cooler temperatures arrive. It is an absolutely beautiful native perennial for shade, but sadly not always easy to make happy. Tiarella requires the soil that is found in a healthy woodland, topped with a thick layer of slowly decomposing leaves. If you have a natural woodland, or have built healthy soils in your shade garden, it will thrive, but it is not a good choice for the degraded soils you find in newly constructed neighborhoods.

✳ **QUICK TIP** Tiarella is closely related to heucheras, and there are hybrids between the two—*Tiarella × Heucherella*—that marry some of the tiarella beauty with a little durability from heucheras.

Tradescantia
Andersoniana Group

Common name(s): Spiderwort
Height: 2'–3' (61–91 cm) | **Width:** 2'–3' (61–91 cm)
Bloom time: Summer | **Lowest hardiness zone:** 4
Pruning: Cut back in spring, as needed
Propagation: Division | **Dormant:** Winter
Native region: North America

NORTH AMERICA IS HOME to a number of different closely related species of *Tradescantia*. Those species were taken to Europe and freely hybridized. The descendants of that mixing are the spiderworts gardeners will most likely find for sale today. They have narrow, almost grasslike foliage, topped by big, three-petaled flowers that are almost always shades of purple, though there are pink and white cultivars as well. One popular cultivar, 'Sweet Kate', even has bright golden-yellow foliage. They're pretty universally vigorous and adaptable plants. Each bloom only lasts a single day, but the flowers are produced in such great numbers that the overall display is long-lasting and beautiful.

✳ **QUICK TIP** Hybrid tradescantia are sometimes listed as *Tradescantia virginiana,* but that is a quite different plant. If you can find the real thing, it is a beautiful short perennial for shade.

Tricyrtis

Trillium grandiflorum

Common name(s): Toad lily
Height: 2'–3' (61–91 cm) | **Width:** 1'–2' (30–61 cm)
Bloom time: Fall | **Lowest hardiness zone:** 4
Pruning: Cut back in spring, as needed
Propagation: Cuttings, division, and seed
Dormant: Winter | **Native region:** East Asia

Common name(s): Wakerobin, great white trillium
Height: 1' (30 cm) | **Width:** 6" (15 cm)
Bloom time: Spring | **Lowest hardiness zone:** 3
Pruning: None needed | **Propagation:** Divisions in spring when flowers fade | **Dormant:** Summer and winter
Native region: Eastern North America

LATE SUMMER AND FALL in a sunny garden can be peak blooming time, but flowers in a shade garden in the fall can be hard to come by. That is why gardeners grow toad lilies—they have attractive foliage all summer and then start flowering heavily from late summer into fall. The most common varieties for sale are *Tricyrtis hirta*, *T. formosana*, and hybrids between the two, which have white flowers covered with purple spots. But if you love this plant there are also yellows (*T. macrantha* and *T. latifolia*) and ones with variegated foliage ('Gilt Edge' and 'Autumn Glow' are the most common). Though they are generally easy to grow, rabbits do find them quite tasty.

✳ **QUICK TIP** The intricate patterns on toad lily blooms are best appreciated up close, so plant them along a path or next to a garden bench.

THE GREAT WHITE TRILLIUM is one of the most beautiful spring wildflowers of the woodlands of eastern North America. The elegant, pure-white flowers carpet the ground under deciduous trees, then go dormant and vanish for the summer, leaving space for summer-growing perennials to fill in. *Trillium grandiflorum* is the species you'll find for sale most often, but there are many other species worth growing. *T. ovatum* has similar white flowers and is native to the West Coast. Other eastern natives include *T. erectum* with dark, blood-red flowers, *T. cuneatum* with leaves beautifully patterned with silver, and *T. nivale*, the snow trillium, which blooms almost as early as a snowdrop.

✳ **QUICK TIP** Trilliums are slow to propagate, so they can be a little pricy, but they are an essential part of any native spring shade garden.

Verbena canadensis

Vernonia

Common name(s): Rose verbena
Height: 6"–1' (15–30 cm) | **Width:** 1'–2' (30–61 cm)
Bloom time: Summer | **Lowest hardiness zone:** 5
Pruning: Cut back in spring, as needed
Propagation: Division, cuttings, and seed
Dormant: Evergreen or winter dormant in cold climates
Native region: Eastern North America

VERBENA IS A FAMILIAR COMPONENT of hanging baskets and annual flower displays, but this species is a native form that is quite cold hardy and a good—if sometimes short-lived—perennial. Just like the tender verbenas grown as annuals, it spreads to make a low carpet of leaves and puts up clusters of white, pink, lavender, or purple blooms pretty much all summer long. During the summer, it will thrive in a range of different soils, but well-drained conditions are critical for it to overwinter well, particularly in colder climates. Some cultivars are more cold-tolerant than others. 'Homestead Purple' is a popular, very hardy selection.

✳ **QUICK TIP** Some botanists think this plant doesn't belong in the genus *Verbena*, so you may see it listed as *Glandularia canadensis* instead.

Common name(s): Ironweed
Height: 3'–6' (91–180 cm) | **Width:** 2'–3' (61–91 cm)
Bloom time: Late summer | **Lowest hardiness zone:** 5
Pruning: Cut back in spring, as needed
Propagation: Division, cuttings, and seed
Dormant: Winter
Native region: Eastern and Central North America

THE MOST COMMON IRONWEED is *Vernonia noveboracensis*, which is a massive perennial, reaching 6 feet (1.8 m) tall with broad, coarse leaves, and blooming in late summer with huge flat heads of rich purple flowers that will attract every butterfly in the neighborhood. It is a fantastic, beautiful plant, but only suitable for large gardens. But the genus is large, and some other species and selections are starting to be more widely available. One of the best is 'Iron Butterfly', which has very fine, almost ferny foliage, reaching only 3 feet (91 cm) tall, and topped with the same great purple flowers. If you can find it, *V. lindheimeri* var. *leucophylla* has gorgeous silver foliage.

✳ **QUICK TIP** As a rule of thumb, broad-leaved ironweeds like wet soils, while those with narrow or silver leaves do best in lean, dry conditions.

Veronica spicata

Veronicastrum virginicum

Common name(s): Spiked speedwell
Height: 2'–3' (61–91 cm) | **Width:** 2' (61 cm)
Bloom time: Summer | **Lowest hardiness zone:** 3
Pruning: Deadhead and cut back in spring, if desired
Propagation: Cuttings, division, and seed
Dormant: Winter | **Native region:** Europe and Asia

Common name(s): Culver's root
Height: 4'–7' (1.2–2.1 m) | **Width:** 2'–4' (0.6–1.2 m)
Bloom time: Summer | **Lowest hardiness zone:** 3
Pruning: Cut back in spring as needed,
deadhead if desired
Propagation: Cuttings, division, and seed
Dormant: Winter | **Native region:** Eastern North America

IN SUMMER, this plant sends up narrow spires so densely packed with thousands of tiny blooms that the effect is of one solid spike of color. There are many cultivars to choose from, with flowers in shades of blue, pink, or white, all of which make excellent cut flowers as well. After the bloom finishes, the rich green foliage keeps looking fresh and great for the rest of the summer. There are even cultivars (of the subspecies *incana*) that have silvery-grey foliage. The flower spikes turn brown and are a bit unattractive after flowering, so deadheading will keep the plants looking their best.

✳ **QUICK TIP** Several dwarf selections—only 1 foot (30 cm) tall—are on the market, so look for those if you have a small garden.

A WONDERFULLY ELEGANT PLANT, veronicastrum sends up tall stems lined with very attractive whirls of dark green leaves, and in the summer puts up many spikes of white flowers. The seedheads that follow the bloom are quite attractive, so gardeners can leave them up to enjoy over the winter, or cut the plants back after blooming to get a smaller late summer rebloom. The typical form of the species has white flowers, but the cultivar 'Fascination' has beautiful lilac blooms. This plant will grow and flower in light shade, but will probably need staking there to prevent flopping.

✳ **QUICK TIP** Like many very tall perennials, it will take a few years for a new planting of veronicastrum to settle in and reach its mature height.

Viola sororia

Common name(s): Common violet
Height: 6" (15 cm) | **Width:** 6" (15 cm)
Bloom time: Spring | **Lowest hardiness zone:** 3
Pruning: None needed | **Propagation:** Seed and division
Dormant: Winter | **Native region:** Eastern North America

THIS NATIVE PERENNIAL IS SO DURABLE, easy to grow, and adaptable that it sometimes gets labeled a weed, particularly because it is perfectly happy to grow in a regularly mowed lawn. But don't let that stop you from loving and growing this plant. Common violet stays low enough that it won't smother other plants and can form a living mulch when planted between taller perennials. The purple (rarely white or bicolored) blooms are beautiful in the spring and the heart-shaped foliage is quite attractive. Even better, violets are one of the top host plants for native butterflies and moths, supporting dozens of different species. Letting violets seed around your garden and lawn can be one of the easiest ways to boost the diversity of your local ecosystem.

✳ **QUICK TIP** The common violet is just the tip of the iceberg—over 300 species of violets are native to North America with purple, white, and yellow flowers.

Yucca filamentosa

Common name(s): Adam's needle
Height: foliage 3' (91 cm), flowers to 6' (1.8 m)
Width: 3' (91 cm) | **Bloom time:** Summer
Hardiness zone: 4
Pruning: Cut back flowering stems after blooming
Propagation: Division and root cuttings
Dormant: Evergreen
Native region: Eastern North America

THE BOLD, EVERGREEN FOLIAGE of yuccas are incredibly useful in the perennial garden to provide structure year-round, and the tough, drought-tolerant, deep-rooted plants are utterly problem-free once established. In late summer, huge spikes of white flowers shoot up over the leaves to make an impressive display. For even more color, look for variegated selections like 'Color Guard', which has bold yellow stripes down the leaves. Gardeners in Central and Western North America can also enjoy a plethora of other yucca species with a range of sizes and foliage colors.

✳ **QUICK TIP** Yuccas propagate easily from root cuttings. In fact, if gardeners try to dig out and move a yucca, it will usually resprout soon afterward from the roots. So, pick a spot and leave them there—they're hard to move!

Zephyranthes

Common name(s): Rain lily
Height: 6"–1' (15–30 cm) | **Width:** 6"–1' (15–30 cm)
Bloom time: Summer | **Lowest hardiness zone:** 7
Pruning: None needed | **Propagation:** Division and seed
Dormant: Winter or evergreen
Native region: Southern North America,
Central and South America

THIS GROUP OF LITTLE BULBS has grassy foliage and lovely six-petaled flowers (more in double-flowered cultivars) mostly in shades of white, pink, and yellow, with new breeding ever expanding that color range. They get their common name from their habit of bursting into bloom anew after each summer rainstorm. They thrive in hot, humid weather, and are fantastic choices for gardens in the Southeast. *Zephyranthes candida*, with abundant small white flowers, and *Z. minuta* (aka *Z. grandiflora*), with huge pink blooms, are great ones to start with, but more hybrids and selections are being introduced every year, each one more beautiful than the last.

✳ **QUICK TIP** Irrigation doesn't trigger rain lilies to bloom quite the same way an actual rainstorm does, so grow rain lilies in rainy climates for the best results.

Zinnia grandiflora

Common name(s): Plains zinnia
Height: 6"–8" (15–20 cm) | **Width:** 1'–2' (30–61 cm)
Bloom time: Summer | **Lowest hardiness zone:** 5
Pruning: None needed | **Propagation:** Division and seed
Dormant: Evergreen
Native region: Central North America

THE MOST FAMOUS ZINNIAS are the tall species originally native to Mexico that are popularly grown as annuals. But there are quite a few low-growing species native into the Rocky Mountains that are fantastic perennials. *Zinnia grandiflora* is one of the best, making a flat carpet of fine-textured leaves and then just blooming nonstop all summer long. The small yellow flowers are beautiful and a big hit with pollinators. The plants can spread quite rapidly, so don't put them next to small plants they can smother. Though extremely cold-tolerant, this zinnia demands dry conditions. Wet soils, especially over the winter, are lethal.

✳ **QUICK TIP** *Zinnia acerosa* is a similar looking plant but with white flowers, a less spreading growth habit, and is slightly less cold-tolerant.

Zizia aurea

Common name(s): Golden alexanders
Height: 1'–3' (30–91 cm) | **Width:** 1'–3' (30–91 cm)
Bloom time: Early summer | **Lowest hardiness zone:** 3
Pruning: Cut back in spring, if desired
Propagation: Division and seed
Dormant: Winter | **Native region:** Eastern North America

THE CARROT FAMILY, with their distinctive umbels of small flowers, are always incredible pollinator plants, and they are particularly good at feeding beneficial wasps that help control pest insects. But most of them really require full sun. *Zizia* is one of the few members of the family that thrives in shade. It can't take deep shade, but in a partial or dappled shade garden it will quickly make a healthy clump and send up clouds of pollinator-covered yellow flowers. *Zizia* is a host plant for stunningly beautiful black swallowtail butterflies, so if you see green caterpillars with black and yellow stripes nibbling this plant, leave them be.

✳ **QUICK TIP** *Zizia aptera* is a very closely related species, so similar they are hard to tell apart. Whichever gardeners can find for sale will be a great choice for your garden.

RESOURCES

USEFUL WEBSITES

Your Extension Office
Each state in the United States has an Extension office housed in a public university with the mission to support gardening and agriculture. The Extension website for your state and other states in a similar climate is a wealth of information about your local climate, soils, pests, and diseases. To find the Cooperative Extension in your state visit: https://extension.org/find-cooperative-extension-in-your-state/

Mt. Cuba Center Trial Garden
This public garden does extensive side-by-side testing of perennials to find the best performers. The information is most relevant if you live in the Mid-Atlantic region, but it is useful for nearly everyone.
Visit https://mtcubacenter.org/research/trial-garden/

Missouri Botanical Garden's Plant Finder
This is an extensive—and continually updated—database with information about nearly every perennial plant gardeners could possibly grow.
Visit https://www.missouribotanicalgarden.org/plantfinder/plantfindersearch.aspx

Plant Select
This is an organization testing and promoting great plants for the Rocky Mountain region. It is an excellent resource for gardeners in dry climates. Visit https://plantselect.org

Hardiness Zone Map
Enter your zip code to find your hardiness zone and get information on the low temperatures for your location.
Visit https://planthardiness.ars.usda.gov

Chicago Botanic Garden Plant Evaluations
This program evaluates herbaceous and woody plants in comparative trials and recommends top performers.
Visit https://www.chicagobotanic.org/collections/ornamental_plant_research/plant_evaluation

Perennial Plant Association, Perennial of the Year Program
For information about the current and previous Perennial Plants of the Year, visit https://perennialplant.org/page/PastPPOY

Pennsylvania Horticultural Society Gold Medal Program
The PHS Gold Medal Plant Program identifies outstanding trees, shrubs, vines, or perennial plants for the Mid-Atlantic region. Visit https://phsonline.org/for-gardeners/gold-medal-plants

HARDY PLANT SOCIETIES

Hardy Plant Society Mid-Atlantic Region
https://www.hardyplant.org

Wisconsin Hardy Plant Society
https://www.wisconsinhardyplantsociety.org

Hardy Plant Society of Oregon
https://www.hardyplantsociety.org

Hardy Plant Society of Washington
https://www.hardyplantsocietywa.org

JOIN THE AHS

AMERICAN HORTICULTURAL SOCIETY

TO JOIN THE AMERICAN HORTICULTURAL SOCIETY (AHS) and enjoy all the benefits membership has to offer, please visit our website ahsgardening.org/join or scan the QR code below for our membership information page.

All members receive an exciting lineup of benefits that share the joy of gardening and strengthen your skills and knowledge.

* Receive our award-winning magazine, *The American Gardener*.
* Get free admission and privileges at more than 360 public gardens and arboreta throughout North America through the Reciprocal Garden Network.

* Enjoy discounts on educational programs, garden shows, seeds, books, and more.
* Discover opportunities to explore the world's finest gardens on trips with fellow plant lovers.
* Access members-only gardening resources on our website.
* And much more.

ACKNOWLEDGMENTS

THE AHS EXTENDS GRATITUDE to its Horticultural Advisory Council members who contributed their expertise during this book's review process:

Dr. James Folsom
Dr. Mary Hockenberry Meyer
William McNamara
Claire Sawyers

The AHS staff and supporting consultants involved in the review process for this book were: Suzanne Laporte, David Ellis, Courtney Allen, Mary Yee, Susan Friedman, and Dan Adler.

The AHS expresses thanks to the book's acquiring editor, Jessica Walliser, and to the team at Cool Springs Press.

PHOTO CREDITS

Alamy: Pages 33, 34 (right), 43, 74 (left & right), 81 (top right), 87, 111 (left, right, & bottom), 112, 113, 114, 130 (bottom), 154 (left & right), 174, 184 (right), 222 (right), 234 (left), 250 (right), 257 (right)

Charlie Nardozzi: Pages 27, 45 (left), 64 (top), 81 (top left & bottom), 92, 137 (top), 140

Holly Neel: Pages 84, 108, 152

Jennifer McGuinness: Pages 14, 20, 40, 44 (top)

JLY Gardens: Pages 4, 12, 16, 17, 18 (left), 19, 25 (right), 28, 35, 37 (left, middle, & right), 41, 45 (right), 48 (left & right), 49 (left & right), 50, 51 (left & right), 53 (bottom), 54 (top & bottom), 56 (top & bottom), 57, 58, 59, 61 (top & bottom), 64 (bottom), 65 (right), 66, 68 (top & bottom), 70 (bottom), 71 (top), 72, 73, 78 (top), 79 (right), 80, 82, 83 (right), 85, 86 (top), 90, 96 (top), 99 (left), 102, 104 (left), 117, 118, 119 (left, middle, & right), 122, 128, 131, 137 (bottom), 149, 153 (left & right), 157, 159, 160, 161, 163 (top), 164, 166, 167, 170 (left), 171, 175, 176, 178, 179 (right), 180 (left), 181 (left & right), 182 (left), 183 (left), 185 (left), 186 (right), 188 (left & right), 189 (right), 190 (right), 191 (left), 192 (right), 193 (right), 194 (left), 195 (right), 197 (left & right), 198 (right), 199 (left), 200 (right), 202 (right), 203 (left & right), 205 (right), 206 (right), 207 (left), 208 (left & right), 209 (left & right), 210 (right), 212 (left), 213 (left), 214 (right), 216 (top), 217 (right), 218 (left & right), 219 (left & right), 220 (left), 221 (left & right), 222 (left), 223 (left), 224 (left), 226 (left & right), 227 (left & right), 228 (left), 230 (left), 231 (left), 232 (left & right), 234 (right), 235 (left), 237 (right), 238 (left & right), 239 (left), 240 (left & right), 241 (left & right), 242 (left & right), 243 (left & right), 244 (right), 245 (right), 247 (right), 248 (left), 249 (left), 250 (left), 251 (right), 252 (left), 253 (left), 255 (left & right), 256 (right), 257 (left), 258

Noelle Johnson: Pages 8, 23 (left & right), 44 (bottom), 83

Shutterstock: Pages 10, 18 (right), 22, 25 (left), 29, 30 (left & right), 31, 32, 34 (left), 36, 38 (left), 39, 46, 53 (top), 60, 65 (left), 69, 75, 91 (top), 96 (bottom), 97, 99 (right), 100, 103, 104 (right), 105, 106, 107, 110, 115, 116, 120, 121, 124 (left & right), 125 (left & right), 126, 129, 130 (top), 132, 133, 134, 135, 139, 142, 146, 147, 148, 151, 155, 156, 158, 162, 179 (left), 180 (right), 182 (right), 183 (right), 184 (left), 185 (right), 186 (left), 187 (left & right), 189 (left), 190 (left), 191 (right), 192 (left), 193 (left), 194 (right), 195 (left), 196 (left & right), 198 (left), 199 (right), 200 (left), 201 (left), 202 (left), 204 (left & right), 205 (left), 206 (left), 207 (right), 210 (left), 211 (left & right), 212 (right), 213 (right), 214 (left), 215 (left & right), 216 (middle & bottom), 217 (left), 220 (right), 223 (right), 224 (right), 225 (left & right), 228 (right), 229 (left & right), 230 (right), 231 (right), 233 (left & right), 235 (right), 236 (left & right), 237 (left), 239 (right), 244 (left), 245 (left), 246 (left & right), 247 (left), 248 (right), 249 (right), 251 (left), 252 (right), 253 (right), 254 (left & right), 256 (left)

Tracy Walsh Photography: Pages 9, 24, 42, 52, 62, 70 (top), 71 (bottom), 76, 78 (bottom), 79 (left), 86 (bottom), 88, 91 (bottom), 94, 144, 150, 163 (bottom)

Whitney Cranshaw, Colorado State University, Bugwood.org: Page 170 (right)

INDEX

M

macronutrients, 32–33
maidenhair fern (*Adiantum pedatum*), 180
mail-order nurseries, 100
maintenance
 caging, 154–155
 "Chelsea Chop," 152
 cutting back, 155–158
 deadheading, 150–151
 dividing as, 158–159
 garden size and, 44, 45
 large garden areas, 45
 pinching, 152–153
 preening, 154
 small garden areas, 44
 staking, 147, 154–155
 watering, 143–149
 See also fertilizing; mulching; watering; weeds
Maltese cross (*Silene chalcedonica*), 246
matrices, 79
maypop (*Passiflora incarnata*), 232
Mertensia (*Virginia bluebell*), 224
Mexican hat (*Ratibida columnifera*), 240
microclimates, 14, 18
micronutrients, 32
milkweed genus (*Asclepias*), 53
millennium ornamental onion (*Allium* 'Millenium'), 183
Mirabilis multiflora (wild four o'clock), 225
monarch butterflies, 53
Monarda didyma (scarlet beebalm), 225
monkshood (*Aconitum carmichaelii*), 179
monocarpic plants, 8
moths, 51, 52, 53, 166
mountain mint (*Pycnanthemum muticum*), 240
Muhlenbergia capillaris (muhly grass), 226
muhly grass (*Muhlenbergia capillaris*), 226
mulching
 Asian jumping worms and, 150, 168
 cold temperatures and, 18
 deep mulching, 127
 function of, 129
 ingredients, 129

 maintenance and, 129, 149–150
 planting and, 129, 135
 sheet mulching, 126–127
 soil moisture and, 23
 soil reclamation with, 39
 sourcing, 149
 See also maintenance
mullein (*Verbascum* species), 112
mum (*Chrysanthemum*), 197
mycoplasmas, 170
mycorrhizae, 32, 39

N

nativars, 55
native plants
 addition of, 55
 benefits of, 54
 definition of, 55–57
 ecosystem and, 54
 nurseries and, 55
 percentage of, 54, 61
 soil and, 39
 straight species, 55, 56
 wildlife and, 54
 wild type, 55, 56
naturalistic style, 79–80
Nepeta × *faassenii* (catmint), 226
New England aster (*Symphyotrichum novae-angliae*), 250
nitrogen (N), 32–33
nodules, 32
nurseries
 big box stores, 98
 busy times for, 96
 "clearance rack" plants, 97
 carbon footprint and, 59
 climate and, 130
 first visit to, 95–96
 form considerations and, 68
 fungicides and, 32
 growth regulators, 97
 independent garden centers, 99
 labels, 138
 mail-order nurseries, 100
 native plants and, 55
 online nurseries, 100, 101
 pesticides and, 96, 98
 plant hardiness zones and, 16
 plant health, 96–97, 170
 plant sales, 100
 plant selection, 90
 plant size and, 102, 103
 potting mixes and, 133

 quality of, 96, 99
 questions for, 18, 90, 96
 sections, 95
 selective breeding and, 56
 specialty nurseries, 99, 101
 sunlight and, 41
 viral diseases and, 170
 See also sourcing
nutrient deficiencies, 171

O

obedient plant (*Physostegia virginiana*), 235
Oenothera lindheimeri (gaura; beeblossom), 227
Oenothera macrocarpa (evening primrose), 227
online nurseries, 100, 101
opaque plastic, 126
Ophiopogon planiscapus 'Nigrescens' (black mondo grass), 228
Opuntia (prickly pear), 228
orange coneflower (*Rudbeckia fulgida*), 241
orchids, 25, 192
oregano (*Origanum*), 229
organic fertilizers, 33
organic matter
 Asian jumping worms and, 150, 168
 components of, 28
 compost as, 128
 decomposition of, 30, 32
 double digging and, 124
 mulching and, 39, 126, 127, 129
 sod stripping and, 125
 soil and, 28, 30–31, 38, 39
 tilling and, 124
organic pesticides, 50, 167
Oriental poppy (*Papaver orientale*), 112, 231
Origanum (oregano), 229
Oxalis oregana (wood sorrel), 229

P

Pachysandra procumbens (Allegheny spurge), 230
Paeonia (peony), 230
Panicum virgatum (switch grass), 231
Papaver orientale (Oriental poppy), 231
pasque flower (*Pulsatilla*), 239
Passiflora incarnata (purple passionflower; maypop), 232

primrose (*Primula*), 159, 238
propagation
    carbon footprint and, 59
    division, 105–107
    root cuttings, 112–114
    seed starts, 115–121
    stem cuttings, 108–111
Pulmonaria (lungwort), 239
Pulsatilla (pasque flower), 239
purchasing. *See* sourcing
purple cone flower (*Echinacea purpurea*), 56
purple passionflower (*Passiflora incarnata*), 232
purple poppy mallow (*Callirhoe involucrata*), 194
purple prairie clover (*Dalea purpurea*), 200
pussytoes (*Antennaria*), 185
Pycnanthemum muticum (mountain mint), 240

Q

quart pots, 103, 126

R

rabbits, 162, 164, 165
rainfall, 22, 24, 36, 37
rain lily (*Zephyranthes*), 257
raised bed gardens
    drainage and, 24, 31
    touchable plants in, 71
raking, 39
Ratibida columnifera (Mexican hat), 240
red birds in a tree (*Scrophularia macrantha*), 245
red lily beetles, 168–169
red spider lily (*Lycoris*), 224
red yucca (*Hesperaloe parviflora*), 215
repellent sprays, 164
revisions, 92
River Farm, 7
rock gardens, 80
root cuttings, 112–114
roots
    aggressive spreaders and, 175
    bare-root plants, 104
    "clearance rack" plants, 97
    leghemoglobin, 32
    mycorrhizae, 32
    nodules, 32
    pore spaces, 28, 29

pots and, 96, 112
potting soil removal, 133, 134
rooting hormones, 109
root rots, 32, 171
sandy soil and, 29
shopping and, 96, 97
"tug test," 111
water loss mitigation and, 22
rose mallow (*Hibiscus*), 217
rose verbena (*Verbena canadensis*), 254
Rudbeckia fulgida (Black-eyed Susan; orange coneflower), 241
"ruderal" species, 143
rue anemone (*Thalictrum thalictroides*; *Anemonella thalictroides*), 251
Ruellia humilis (wild petunia), 241
Russian sage (*Perovskia atriplicifolia*; *Salvia yangii*), 233

S

sage (*Salvia*), 242
salinity, 37
Salvia azurea, 53, 242
Salvia (sage), 242
Salvia yangii (Russian sage), 233
sandy soil, 29, 30, 31
Sanguinaria canadensis (bloodroot), 243
Sarracenia (pitcher plant), 243
Scabiosa columbaria (pincushion flower), 244
scarlet beebalm (*Monarda didyma*), 225
scent design, 70
Schizachyrium scoparium (little bluestem), 244
Scrophularia macrantha (red birds in a tree), 245
sea holly (*Eryngium*), 207
seasonality, design and, 72–74
sedum (*Hylotelephium spectabile*), 218
seeds
    deadheading and, 151
    weed seeds, 143
seed starting
    benefits of, 115–117
    indoor starting, 120–121
    outside starting, 117
    sprouting difficulties, 117
    step-by-step, 118–119

sustainable seed collection, 116
Sempervivum (hens-and-chicks; houseleek), 245
sensory gardens, 70–71
sentimental plants, 23, 90, 149
shade
    adaptations to, 40–41
    full shade conditions, 42
    landscapes and, 42
    mycorrhizae and, 39
    part-time shade, 171
    preference determination, 41
    shade leaves, 41
    sun leaves, 41
    temperature and, 19
    See also sunlight
shared plants, 101
Shasta daisies, 159
sheet mulching, 126–127
shopping. *See* sourcing
Siberian bugloss (*Brunnera macrophylla*), 193
signature plants, 90
Silene chalcedonica (Maltese cross), 246
Silphium (cup plant; prairie dock), 246
silty soil, 29, 30
Sisyrinchium angustifolium (blue-eyed grass), 247
size variations, 44–45
slugs, 168–169
small garden areas, 44
sneezeweed (*Helenium autumnale*), 213
snow cover, 17
snow trillium (*Trillium nivale*), 36, 55
sod stripping, 125
soil
    acidity of, 35–36
    adaptations to, 36
    aggregates, 30, 31
    alkaline soil, 36
    aluminum sulfate and, 36
    amendments, 31, 36, 39, 128
    annual disruption of, 9
    carbon sequestration, 59
    clay, 29, 30, 31
    compaction, 29, 31, 38, 124
    components of, 28–31
    compost and, 39, 128
    cutting back and, 156
    deep mulching, 127
    detritivores and, 51

tilling, 124
toad lily (*Tricyrtis*), 253
Tradescantia (spiderwort), 252
Tricyrtis (toad lily), 253
Trillium genus, 55, 170
Trillium grandiflorum (wakerobin; great white trillium), 253
troubleshooting
  aggressive spreaders, 174–175
  collapsing plants, 161
  early freezes, 174
  fencing, 162–163
  flopping, 161
  foliar diseases, 170, 171
  freezes, 174
  growing conditions and, 45
  insect pests, 166–169
  late freezes, 174
  light/shade issues, 41, 171
  mammal pests, 162–165
  mycoplasmas, 170
  nutrient deficiencies, 171
  over-fertilized plants, 34
  repellent sprays, 164
  replacement as, 160
  root rots, 32, 171
  seed sprouting, 117
  shade issues, 171
  viruses, 170
turtlehead (*Chelone*), 196

U

USDA Plant Hardiness Zones, 15, 17, 19

V

Verbena canadensis (rose verbena), 254
Vernonia (ironweed), 254
Veronica spicata (spiked speedwell), 255
Veronicastrum virginicum (Culver's root), 255
vine weevils, 168–169
Viola sororia (common violet), 256
Virginia bluebell (*Mertensia*), 224
viruses, 168, 170
voles, 165

W

wakerobin (*Trillium grandiflorum*), 253
walkways, 36, 78, 79, 85, 86
wasps, 52, 53

water
  adaptations for, 22, 24
  clay soil and, 29, 31
  conservation, 22–23, 143
  drainage, 24, 31
  dry-adapted plants, 24–25
  humidity, 25
  low-water plants, 22
  mulch and, 23
  organic matter and, 30
  perched water table, 31
  planting and, 135
  pore spaces, 28, 29
  rainfall, 22, 24, 36, 37
  raised gardens, 31
  root systems and, 22
  salinity and, 37
  sandy soil and, 29, 31
  soil drainage and, 24
  soil sogginess, 17
  xeriscaping and, 23
  See also drought; irrigation; watering
watering
  climate and, 143, 149
  depth of, 147, 148
  duration of, 147
  equipment for, 146
  hoses, 146
  new plantings, 147
  plant losses and, 149
  root rots and, 171
  spacing and, 161
  sprinklers, 146
  target of, 146
  timing of, 146
  weather monitoring, 146
  See also drought; irrigation; maintenance; water
weeds
  deadheading and, 151
  opaque plastic and, 126
  pots and, 96
  "ruderal" species, 143
  sources, 96, 143
  "weed" definition, 142
  See also maintenance
white trillium (*Trillium grandiflorum*), 36
wild buckwheat (*Eriogonum*), 206
wild four o'clock (*Mirabilis multiflora*), 225
wild ginger (*Asarum*), 188

wildlife
  beauty of, 48–49
  "charismatic species," 48
  detritivores, 51
  herbivores, 51
  hummingbirds, 48, 52, 53, 181, 209, 242
  invasive species, 58
  light pollution and, 59
  observing, 61
  pesticides and, 48, 50
  variety of, 49
  See also insects; pests; pollinators
wild petunia (*Ruellia humilis*), 241
wildscaping, 79–80
wild strawberry (*Fragaria virginiana*), 208
wild type plants, 55, 56
wintergreen (*Gaultheria procumbens*), 210
winter sowing, 117
wood sorrel (*Oxalis oregana*), 229
woolly thyme (*Thymus*), 251

X

xeriscaping, 23
xerophytes, 23

Y

yarrow (*Achillea millefolium*), 178
yellow lady's slipper (*Cypripedium parviflorum*), 36
Yucca filamentosa (Adam's needle), 256
yucca (*Yucca*), 112

Z

Zephyranthes (rain lily), 257
Zinnia grandiflora (plains zinnia), 257
Zizia aurea (golden alexanders), 258
zone system, 14–15, 16, 17–18, 19